# WILDLANDS PHILANTHROPY

*We can never have enough of Nature. We must be refreshed by the sight of inexhaustible vigor . . . the wilderness with its living and its decaying trees, the thunder cloud, and the rain which lasts three weeks and produces freshets. We need to witness our own limits transgressed, and some life pasturing freely where we never wander.*
—Henry David Thoreau

# WILDLANDS PHILANTHROPY

## *The Great American Tradition*

EARTH AWARE
*San Rafael, California*

*Essays by*

# TOM BUTLER

*Photographs by*

# ANTONIO VIZCAÍNO

# DEDICATION

*To the generous Americans—women and men, celebrated and unknown, of great and modest means—who have committed themselves to serving the community of life. For the natural areas you have bestowed upon the future, a legacy of healthy land and wild beauty, we are grateful.*

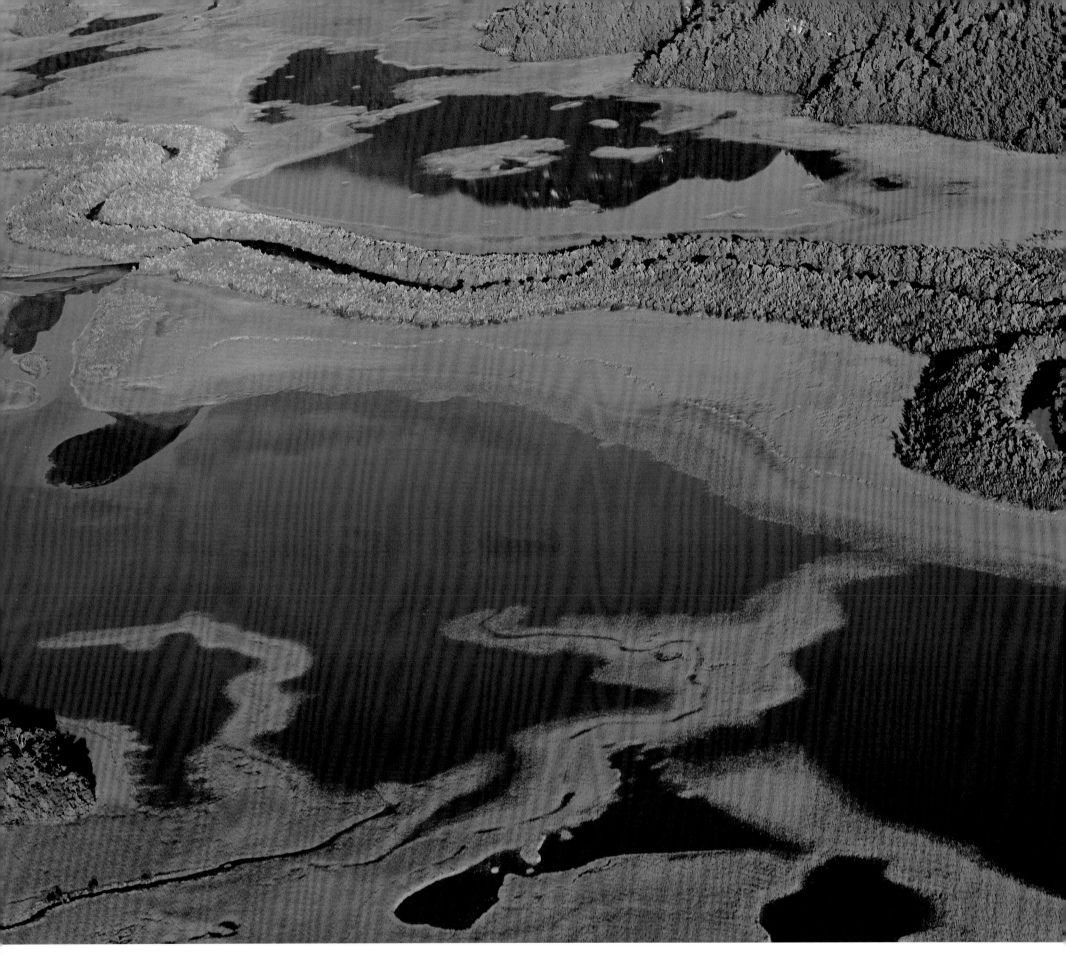

*The greatest beauty is organic wholeness, the wholeness of life and things,
the divine beauty of the universe. Love that, not man apart from that.*
—Robinson Jeffers

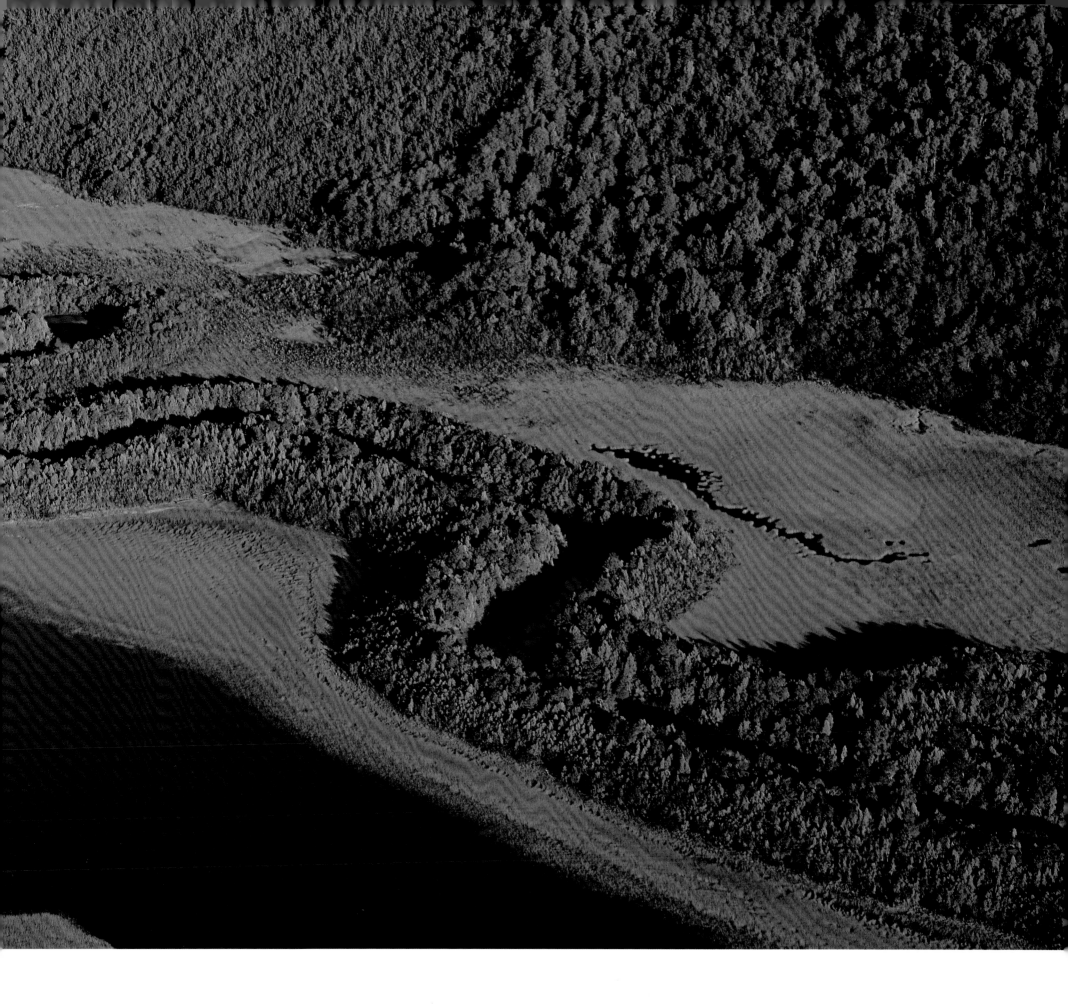

*The love of wilderness is more than a hunger for what is always beyond reach;*
*it is also an expression of loyalty to the earth . . . the only home we shall ever know,*
*the only paradise we ever need—if only we had the eyes to see.*

—Edward Abbey

*Wilderness is not—and should not be—a past and vanishing force in life. It is, as far as anyone can see into the future in our rapidly changing world, an abiding value.*
—George Marshall

# CONTENTS

# FOREWORD

## by Tom Brokaw

As a child of the Great Plains of North America I began life with the notion that the footprint of man was small and the land was vast. Just beyond the doorstep of my working-class home the prairie unfolded in great waves of tall grass or small grain, interrupted only occasionally by a small town or tiny collection of farm and ranch structures. The mighty Missouri River—that long, meandering drainage out of the mountains of Montana, through the Dakotas, and along the borders of Iowa and Nebraska—was rich with wildlife beneath its surface and along its shores. These were the images that took shape on the canvas of my formative memories.

They have stayed with me through my odyssey to bright lights and big cities, to every corner of North America, those still wild and those crowded with population and development; to rainforests, coastlines, and mountaintops on other continents; to urban majesty and city slums in every hemisphere.

So now, even though I am years and miles beyond that prairie childhood, I still constantly seek the thrill of open spaces and untamed nature. But I am also constantly in despair at the alarming erosion of America's natural heritage, the thoughtless—even reckless—invasion of land and forest, beach and swamp, desert and mountain range with roads and homes, malls, and make-believe resorts.

Nonetheless, even in my most discouraging moments, I am heartened by the quickening pace of private efforts to protect the natural glories, however large or small a space they may occupy. In the years our family has been a part of the Rocky Mountain West we have been witness to the rise of conservation easements—deed restrictions on private property that assure perpetual conservation, now routinely considered by local ranchers and out-of-state newcomers.

When my wife, Meredith, and I moved on from a corner of rural New England, we were comforted by the presence of a local land trust that was happy to receive from us a substantial tract of wetlands and old-growth trees. I miss my friends and our nest on a wooded hillside there, but I treasure the fact that no bulldozer, carpenter, or mason will disturb the wild turkeys, coyotes, bears, frogs, raccoons, and deer or land of cobble and meadow we left forever protected.

I detect among my friends a growing consciousness to treat the land as they would a piece of rare art. That is, something not just to be collected but to be conserved and shared in its original, undiminished state. The rewards go well beyond whatever tax benefits are to be realized. A protected piece of nature is a legacy of deeply satisfying proportions.

Moreover, private initiative to conserve, protect, and restore nature is a moral calling without borders. Just as citizens respond to natural catastrophes or plagues in far-off places, so should we be willing to export the imperative of private land preservation in distant nations. Nature and the foundation of life it provides are priorities without borders.

In this book you will come to know the priceless gifts of the visionaries who came before and showed the way with land-based philanthropy. We honor them by recognizing their selfless contributions and, most of all, by continuing their honorable ways.

*Something will have gone out of us as a people if we ever let the remaining wilderness be destroyed; if we permit the last virgin forests to be turned into comic books and plastic cigarette cases; if we drive the few remaining members of the wild species into zoos or to extinction; if we pollute the last clear air and dirty the last clean streams and push our paved roads through the last of the silence.*

—Wallace Stegner

# INTRODUCTION

## Generous Nature

What did I hear, walking among gants? Silence. Then the trickling waters of Redwood Creek, a little wisp of a stream that flows through Muir Woods National Monument. I heard the burbling song of a winter wren. And mixed with the sounds of nature I heard voices: A little girl chattering to her parents in Korean. An elderly Hispanic couple offering the occasional remark ("¡Que bonito!") to each other as they strolled past. Two boys, fascinated by a banana slug that oozed along a downed log, exchanging enthusiasms in Mandarin. College kids speaking German, their heads craned upward to view the trees, coast redwoods, whose kind stretch higher toward the heavens than any other creature affixed to earth.

No doubt many of the people sauntering through Muir Woods that day were, like me, visitors to San Francisco. But with our upturned faces, with hands that reached out to touch furrowed bark, we seemed less like tourists than reverent pilgrims, entering a redwood cathedral. Is that day etched also in the memory of the boys who watched the slug? Do other visitors to Muir Woods remember their time among its towering trees the same way they might, say, a visit to the Vietnam Veterans Memorial or St. Peter's Square? Perhaps they do. It is sacred space.

The trees in Muir Woods' Cathedral Grove stand today because of a charitable act a century ago. In 1905, William and Elizabeth Thatcher Kent bought the last tract of virgin redwoods in the San Francisco Bay Area to save it from logging. Two years later, a private water utility hoping to build a reservoir attempted to seize the property through eminent domain, fell the great trees, and dam Redwood Creek. Countering this threat, Kent offered the land as a gift to the American people, asking President Teddy Roosevelt to declare it a national monument. Roosevelt obliged, agreeing to Kent's request that the new monument be named for John Muir, the leading conservationist of his day and the founder of the Sierra Club.

Thus, Muir Woods was saved, like all the natural areas portrayed in this book, by private conservation funding and initiative—that is, by wildlands philanthropy—a vital yet little known tradition that has profoundly enriched the American experience.

My visit to Muir Woods came just after the September 2001 terrorist attacks. Politicians and pundits declared, as they did after each World War and the dropping of the atom bomb, that the world was fundamentally changed. Among the ancient redwoods, though, the world appeared as it ever was. Great trees lived and died on wild time. They fell, not at the whim of a corporate bottom line, but when wind, disease, or age decreed. Their massive boles then moldered on the forest floor, slowly releasing nutrients back to the soil. On these "nurse logs" young trees often sprouted. The cycles of nature continued, oblivious to human grief.

Nature goes on.

In Muir Woods I experienced the peace of wild things, which apparently was a common response to national tragedy. A Park Service employee told me that visitation at the monument dropped immediately after 9/11, then rebounded. In those unsettling days, people across North America sought out quiet places—parks and nature sanctuaries—where they might be immersed in wild beauty.

Nature heals.

Since 1864, when Abraham Lincoln signed legislation that secured Yosemite Valley's future as a park, Americans have been formally protecting examples of what John Muir called "the great fresh unblighted, unredeemed wilderness." While the initial focus was on scenic wonders such as Yosemite and Yellowstone, the rationale for land conservation has evolved beyond aesthetics and recreation to also include biological diversity and the intrinsic value of nature. Preserving our natural heritage has become a bedrock American value, transcending ideological or partisan divisions. Protected natural areas—state and federal parks, wilderness areas, wildlife refuges, private nature preserves, and other conserved lands—have come to embody our idea of America the Beautiful. The National Park System alone receives more than 250 million visits annually. Few people, however, have any idea how these places came to be preserved. Was it mere chance that the juggernaut of industrial expansion sweeping over the continent spared them?

No, it was not luck, but the intentional actions of people who worked to save wild country. Some of these visionaries, like John Muir and Aldo Leopold, helped set aside specific areas from exploitation while also laying the intellectual foundation of the American conservation movement. Countless other individuals, with names unrecorded by historians, have been the "spirited people," in the words of Wilderness Society founder Bob Marshall, "who will fight for the freedom of the wilderness." Writing in the 1930s, Marshall believed that an organized band of committed activists ("we want no stragglers") to be "the one hope of repulsing the tyrannical ambition of civilization to conquer every niche on the whole earth."

Marshall's phrase "freedom of the wilderness" is notable, for freedom—not the absence of human history—is the defining attribute of wilderness. The etymological roots of the word *wilderness* mean "will-of-the-land." Wilderness, then, is *self-willed land*, a place apart from human settlement and control where nature directs the ebb and flow of life. Howard Zahniser, the primary author of the Wilderness Act of 1964, which created our National Wilderness Preservation System, intentionally chose to use the obscure word *untrammeled* in the law's definition of wilderness: "A wilderness, in contrast with those areas where man and his works dominate the landscape, is hereby recognized as an area where the earth and its community of life are untrammeled by man, where man himself is a visitor who does not remain." A trammel is something that impedes free movement. *Untrammeled* lands are not necessarily pristine, but are free, unyoked from human dominion.

The wing of the conservation movement that sprang up to defend self-willed land shares commonalities with other social change movements but moves beyond an exclusive focus on human welfare. The movement to abolish slavery, the fight for women's suffrage, the civil rights movement—all represented great advances in extending rights to marginalized people. The wilderness movement, in asserting that wild places and creatures have a right to exist regardless of their usefulness to humans, expands the sphere of ethical concern to other members of the land community. This is a remarkable idea to emerge from a society that sees the natural world almost exclusively through the lens of economic utility.

Why this digression into history and etymology? Because none of the natural areas profiled in this book could have been saved without the philosophical and legal framework that came out of the conservation movement. Moreover, land conservation is a broadly inclusive activity. Its orientation may be to support human communities with a sustainable supply of forest and agricultural products. Or its focus may be to secure areas for ecological processes and wildlife to flourish unmolested—self-willed lands. These two realms of conservation action are essential and complementary, but our focus here is on the latter, particularly on how extraordinary Americans have used their personal resources to pass along the gift of wildness to future generations.

To be sure, private philanthropy as a mechanism to protect natural areas is a minority stream in our conservation history. The bulk of lands administered by the National Park Service, U.S. Forest Service, and other agencies came out of the preexisting federal domain. Most western national parks were designated, and legislatively separated, from this original American commons after conservationists pushed Congress to act. But on thousands of occasions when public means for conservation were unavailable, inadequate, or too slow in coming, private initiative has saved wildlife habitat.

Wildlands philanthropy is not exclusively, but is certainly overwhelmingly, an *American* phenomenon because of our cultural and constitutional dedication to private property. Buying land to exploit it is a foundation of the modern economy; buying land to protect it *from* exploitation is an adaptive conservation tool with a rich history and promising future. It is not, however, a tool that is universally applicable. In many parts of the world, including some of the most biologically diverse and wildest remaining places on Earth, the opportunity for individuals or nongovernmental organizations to purchase private land for conservation is unavailable. Where such opportunities do exist, however, some Americans have not only exported the idea of national parks, which Wallace Stegner called the best idea America ever had, but have also invested private capital to help establish new protected areas.

The cumulative effect of wildlands philanthropy by individual Americans is extraordinary, yet has gone mostly unstudied and uncelebrated. Environmental historians have focused primarily on milestones in public policy. Conservation movement heroes include champions of wildlife protection (William Hornaday), forest conservation (Theodore Roosevelt), wilderness areas (Aldo Leopold), and a nontoxic environment (Rachel Carson), but nature-oriented philanthropists, with the exception of John D. Rockefeller Jr., are little noted.

The ethnic collage of visitors I saw at Muir Woods represents but one day in the century since that national treasure was saved. Millions of people have benefited from William and Elizabeth Kent's generosity, but few remember

their names. Their gift was an early landmark in a tradition that would continue throughout the twentieth century, when some of America's most prominent families—Rockefellers, McCormicks, Mellons, and Du Ponts—used private wealth to create or expand public natural areas.

Acadia, Grand Teton, Guadalupe Mountains, Virgin Islands, and various other national parks and seashores would not exist in their current form if not for the largesse of conservation donors. The preserves maintained by the Nature Conservancy and the National Audubon Society similarly reflect private initiative. In every region of the country, one can find wildlife sanctuaries whose genesis was an individual or group of conservationists committed to their protection. Places grand and modest, well-known and obscure, are part of this great land legacy bequeathed to future generations.

In this book we have space to highlight but a few of the visionary Americans who built that legacy. Some, like Katharine Ordway, were born into wealth and chose to give it away. An heiress to the 3M fortune, Ordway found her passion for protecting natural areas late in life. Before her death in 1979, and through a foundation that subsequently dispersed her assets, Ordway gave well over $60 million to preserve remnant prairies and other outstanding habitats across the United States.

Isaac Bernheim's roots were decidedly more humble. After emigrating to America from Germany in 1867, he initially made his living as a peddler, carrying a pack basket through the countryside, before opening a liquor sales firm. His industriousness, and a growing nation's thirst for good Kentucky bourbon, eventually made Bernheim's distillery a prominent Louisville business. In the 1920s he bought thirteen thousand acres south of the city for a natural park where all would be welcome, rich and poor of every race, without distinction, and where, Bernheim wrote, "there will be in profusion all things which gladden the soul."

The landscape that gladdened Percival Baxter's soul was the Maine woods, most especially the woods and waters lorded over by the state's highest peak. As Maine governor in the 1920s, Baxter tried and failed to convince the state legislature to buy Mount Katahdin and the surrounding timberlands from the paper company that owned them. And so, after leaving politics, he bought the land himself. Through dozens of transactions over the course of thirty-two years, he assembled the largest wilderness area in New England, some two hundred thousand acres, which he donated to become Baxter State Park.

These and the other philanthropists whose stories are collected here reflect different eras, religions, geographic regions, and social strata. Persons of every socioeconomic class have helped protect America's wild nature, but parks-related giving before World War II was disproportionately the province of the rich. Some readers may quibble that the wealth amassed by Gilded Age robber barons, even if partially used for noble ends, was squeezed both from the poor and from the earth. A substantive discussion of that question would take another book. Certainly one may acknowledge the irony that in our current economic system wealth comes from converting natural capital to private capital, even while admiring the laudable decision of some individuals to return part of their riches to nature.

What common traits tend to characterize people engaged in wildlands philanthropy? Regardless of background, it seems many are attuned to wild beauty. Besides having a deep aesthetic connection to natural landscapes, they share a desire to be socially useful in a way that transcends a brief human life span. Surely this was the motivation for Percival Baxter when he wrote: "Man is born to die. His works are short lived. Buildings crumble, monuments decay, wealth vanishes, but Katahdin in all its glory forever shall remain the mountain of the people of Maine."

At the beginning of the twenty-first century, the need for wildlands philanthropy has never been greater—not to supplant, but to complement, strong public funding for conservation. As in 1928, when the dream of a Great Smoky Mountains National Park became a real possibility because John D. Rockefeller Jr. pledged $5 million to match the collected contributions of schoolchildren, individuals, businesses, and state legislatures, most large conservation projects today depend on a mix of public and private dollars. Very often the private conservation donors catalyze the effort.

Conservation-related philanthropy by foundations, corporations, and individuals is a tiny percentage of overall charitable giving, dwarfed by donations to religious, educational, medical, and cultural institutions. Relative funding levels may change in the future as societal priorities shift. Conservation biologists generally agree that human action has precipitated a global extinction spasm, a contraction in life's diversity unprecedented since the age of dinosaurs ended sixty-five million years ago. Global climate change is expected to exacerbate this ecological cataclysm. As the unraveling of nature becomes more apparent to persons outside academia and the conservation community, donors might choose to endow an endangered species or wild forest rather than a university chair or museum. Even philanthropists with a long-established charitable focus may redirect part of their giving to protect the ecological systems on which life depends, anticipating that there will be no going to the ballet on a dead planet.

Anecdotal evidence suggests that a wildlands philanthropy resurgence is underway. Examples on a grand scale include the huge investments in biodiversity conservation made by Intel cofounder Gordon Moore; the purchase and transfer to public ownership of more than six hundred thousand acres of southern California desert habitat, largely funded by an anonmous wilderness lover; the successful efforts of expatriate Americans Kristine and Douglas Tompkins to create multiple new national parks in South America; and the Yosemite-sized wildlife preserve in Tierra del Fuego donated to the Wildlife Conservation Society by the Goldman Sachs Group, an act of corporate philanthropy that also included significant personal gifts from Goldman Sachs executives.

Wildlands philanthropy is not, however, limited to successful entrepreneurs and Wall Street titans. Two related developments in the final decades of the twentieth century have effectively democratized the phenomenon. National and international conservation organizations have collectively made millions of their members into land protection funders. Of course it is one thing to write an annual membership check, and quite another to know and love a place personally, see it threatened with destruction, and commit body, soul, and wallet to saving it.

The burgeoning land trust movement offers such a means of engagement. Through local and regional land trusts, thousands of citizens are working to preserve natural areas in their own communities. The scrappy prairie dog defenders who founded the Southern Plains Land Trust, for example, represent the grassroots spirit of the land trust movement. They initially used personal loans, and strong-armed friends and family for donations, to scrape together a down payment on land that became the Fresh Tracks Nature Preserve. The cattle were removed, native plants began to recover, and the wildlife returned. Thus a handful of individuals with more moxie than money turned a tract of overgrazed ranchland into a sanctuary for burrowing owls, swift foxes, and pronghorn antelope in eastern Colorado.

Nicole Rosmarino, one of the activists who launched the effort, served for several years as the Fresh Tracks land steward. She described to me a night when she sat on the prairie in the darkness, listening to the grasses rustle, waiting for a lunar eclipse to commence. "Just as the Earth's shadow hit the moon," she recalled, "coyotes burst into song." While doing research for this book

I heard many such accounts of experiences that were deeply personal, and often fortuitous. M. C. Davis showed me around the expansive wildlife corridor he's preserved in the Florida Panhandle, pointing out the spot where he once came across more than a dozen young alligators lounging in a blackwater creek. In the Maine woods, Roxanne Quimby shared her hope that the former industrial timberlands she has purchased might someday, given time and nature's resilience, be a wild forest as beautiful as before the loggers came.

Marc Evans, a botanist who discovered the largest tract of unlogged forest left in Kentucky, recalled a day of frustration in the midst of the campaign to buy and save Blanton Forest. He was leading a hike for potential donors and inadvertently kicked up a swarm of ground-nesting wasps that stung and scattered the party. Evans went home depressed, but two young girls on the outing had a different take on the day's adventure. They later visited their grandmother and described trees with leaves ablaze in fall color. "It was like walking through a rainbow," they said, and could she help save the forest? With a $500,000 donation, that anonymous grandmother helped assure that kids will forevermore have the opportunity to experience Blanton Forest in all its buzzing, blossoming splendor.

Whenever I spoke to individuals working to protect natural areas, their stories spilled out—of interactions with wildlife, of obstacles overcome, of chance encounters that led to a major gift. The people and the land intersect in ways that enrich both, that suggest a kind of reciprocity between humans and nature that modern peoples have mostly lost.

There is no other way to say it: These stories give me hope.

To be sure, the trend of habitat loss driven by human population growth and rapacious consumption bodes ill for wilderness and wildlife. But if one looks across the broad sweep of American conservation history, it is impressive—miraculous even—to see how much has been accomplished by a relatively small number of people who simply loved the land, and were willing to back up affection with action.

It may sometimes seem a distant dream to achieve a society where every species, whether wildflower or warbler or wolf, is accorded space enough to thrive. If that day does come, I believe it will be from the accumulated actions of individuals whose lives reflect the land ethic articulated by Aldo Leopold, that "a thing is right when it tends to support the integrity, stability, and beauty of the biotic community. It is wrong when it tends otherwise."

Measured by this standard, William and Elizabeth Kent's gift of a primeval redwood grove to the American people could not be more right. Standing among silent giants in Muir Woods National Monument, I was grateful for the Kents' generous nature. If you've never been to Muir Woods, or to Acadia National Park in Maine, or to Beidler Forest Sanctuary in South Carolina, you may enter them through Antonio Vizcaino's photographs in this book. But someday soon, go visit in person. Take the kids, and look for banana slugs among the redwoods. Watch the sunrise from Acadia's Cadillac Mountain. Dip your toes into the dark waters of Beidler's Four Holes Swamp (check first for gators). Let your children get really, really muddy.

If you find the experience meaningful, consider what actions you could take, large or small, to help create a wilder, more beautiful America. Is there a place—a forest, grassland, or marsh—where wild creatures are today at home, but with no protections from the bulldozers of tomorrow? Do you know a piece of abused land that might be healed if someone were to buy it, and offer it kindly care? What could you do to pass along the gift of wildness?

# AMERICAN PHILANTHROPISTS

*And the Places They Saved*

# MUIR WOODS NATIONAL MONUMENT

William Kent's Progressive Vision

*John Muir (1838–1914)*
*and William Kent (1864–1928)*

Imagine, for a moment, the word beautiful spoken in German and Japanese, Portuguese and Korean, and a half-dozen other languages as well, mixed with the rustle of trickling waters and a winter wren's ebullient song. That, or something akin to it, is the sound of Cathedral Grove on a typical day. The language of beauty may vary, but the response to it seems universal—at least in Muir Woods National Monument. Across the bay from San Francisco in Marin County, California, the monument attracts pilgrims from around the world who converse in hushed tones, faces craned upward to the light slipping down through the forest canopy. The towering redwoods stand mute unless a breeze ripples their branches, their scale dwarfing all other life around them. For people unaccustomed to the immensity of redwoods, they seem otherworldly.

It is right that we should gaze upon them with reverence, for coast redwoods have achieved a kind of immortality; their kind has grown on Earth for 250 million years, and some individual redwoods alive today were saplings long before a famous Jewish prophet was born in Bethlehem. Through twenty centuries and more they have welcomed the cool, moist weather of the northern California coast. No other living thing on Earth reaches greater heights. Along with their shorter but more massive cousins, the giant sequoias of the Sierra, coast redwoods are the titans of the arboreal world, with many individuals exceeding 350 feet tall. (The tallest tree in Muir Woods is a relatively diminutive 258-footer, an individual comparable in height to a twenty-six-story office tower.)

But as ecologist Reed Noss has written, "A redwood forest is more than just big trees. From the bewildering variety of life and past life (e.g., woody debris) on the forest floor to the intricate community of fungi, lichens, liverworts, vascular plants . . . earthworms, millipedes, mollusks, insects, and salamanders tens of meters up in the redwood canopies, the redwood forest is a complex ecosystem." Preserving that complexity was not the first priority for European-American settlers to the redwood region, a narrow band of suitable habitat roughly thirty miles wide that stretches five hundred miles along the Pacific coast from the southern tip of Oregon down to Monterey County, California. Summer fog rolling off the ocean and winter rains grew towering trees that produced straight-grained, easily workable, rot-resistant—and therefore highly valuable—timber. While much of the region now supports second- and third-growth redwoods, less than 5 percent of the structurally complex, old-growth redwood forest survives, making it an endangered ecosystem.

At just 554 acres, Muir Woods National Monument is a relict and reminder of that original, unlogged forest. This small natural area has a big job, beyond even its role as sanctuary for the last ancient redwoods of the San Francisco Bay Area, which initially were spared from logging because the site was difficult to access. More than seven hundred thousand people visit the monument each year. They walk the trail along Redwood Creek enjoying the great trees and occasional splashes of color, a Pacific trillium perhaps, or Oregon oxalis, on the forest floor. In a virgin redwood grove only diffuse light typically reaches the ground, but where a tree fall has opened a gap in the canopy, some visitors stand in a warm shaft of sunlight listening to a park ranger explain life and death among the redwoods. They hear how these thousand-year-old trees are mere youngsters

*My dear Mr. Roosevelt: I thank you from the bottom of my heart for your message of appreciation, and hope and believe it will strengthen me to go on in an attempt to save more of the precious and vanishing glories of nature.*

—William Kent

for their kind, how the species reproduces from seeds and root sprouts, how a redwood's bark is exceptionally thick and fire-resistant.

Besides being a preeminent institution for interpreting the redwood ecosystem, Muir Woods is also a useful port of entry into conservation history, for its creation included several key actors, among them naturalist John Muir, President Theodore Roosevelt, and William Kent, a forward-thinking California congressman who would later help create the National Park Service.

Born in Chicago in 1864 to an affluent, politically active family, William Kent moved to Marin County as a boy. Typical of his social class, Kent was educated in private schools, and attended Yale University before starting a business career in Chicago. Like Teddy Roosevelt, Kent was an avid sportsman, owned a ranch in the West, and became a political reformer. While on the city council and as president of the Municipal Voters' League of Chicago around the turn of the century, he opposed corruption and advocated for city parks. Returning to Marin County, Kent established himself as a prominent civic force and was elected to Congress, where he served three terms, from 1911 to 1917. During his first campaign he ran as a Republican; during both reelection cycles he ran as a progressive Independent.

In 1905 William Kent and his wife, feminist Elizabeth Thatcher Kent, purchased 611 acres of wild forest on Mount Tamalpais, in Marin County. Kent wanted to preserve the stand of unlogged redwoods, but also had considerable business interests in the area. After the great San Francisco fire of 1906, a private utility offered to buy part of the land with the intent of damming Redwood Creek to create a water reservoir. When Kent refused to sell, the North Coast Water Company started eminent domain proceedings.

Capitalizing on the postfire political climate, in which new infrastructure was considered a pressing social need, the developer sought to profit from the virgin grove's timber value as well as to create a local water monopoly. Kent saw the attempt to seize his property as both a threat to the land and bad legal precedent, and politically outmaneuvered his adversary. Knowing that under the 1906 Antiquities Act the president could designate national monuments around "objects of historic or scientific interest," Kent decided to save the forestland along Redwood Creek by giving it away. On the day after Christmas in 1907, he mailed a deed for 295 acres, including the area coveted by the private utility, to the secretary of the interior, and asked that President Roosevelt declare it Muir Woods National Monument in honor of the famous writer and wilderness champion. A few weeks later, Teddy Roosevelt did so. The reservoir scheme was foiled. The redwoods were saved.

President Roosevelt sent a letter thanking Kent "most heartily," and suggested that "all Americans who prize the undamaged and especially those who realize the literally unique value of the groves of giant trees, must feel that you have conferred a great and lasting benefit upon the whole country." He also expressed admiration for John Muir, with whom Roosevelt had gone camping in Yosemite a few years previous, but offered that perhaps the new national monument should be named for Kent, as he was the land's donor. In his reply, Kent demurred, saying, "So many millions of better people have died forgotten, that to stencil one's own name on a benefaction, seems to carry with it an implication of mandate immortality as being something purchasable."

"By George! you are right," the president responded. "It is enough to do the deed and not to desire, as you say, to 'stencil one's own name on the benefaction.'" In corresponding with Muir

about the new protected area, Kent wrote, "I know the dreams we have will come true and that men will learn to love nature. All I fear is that it may be too late." Muir replied with effusive thanks: "This is the best tree-lover's monument that could possibly be found in all the forests of the world. . . . Saving these woods from the axe and saw, from money-changers and water-changers and giving them to our country and the world is in many ways the most notable service to God and man I've heard of since my forest wanderings began . . . . Immortal Sequoia life to you."

Muir and Kent's mutual admiration would suffer a few years later when they found themselves on opposite sides of the conservation movement's defining early battle—the fight over damming the Tuolumne River within Yosemite National Park to create the Hetch Hetchy Reservoir as a water source for San Francisco. On this proposed water impoundment, Congressman Kent was a key booster, along with the chief of the U.S. Forest Service, Gifford Pinchot. John Muir, who extolled Yosemite's glories to a national audience through his writings, was bitterly opposed. The rhetoric was heated: "These temple destroyers, devotees of raging commercialism, seem to have a perfect contempt for Nature," Muir railed, "and instead of lifting their eyes to the God of the mountains, lift them to the Almighty Dollar." Kent, in turn, characterized Muir as "a man entirely without social sense. With him, it is me and God and the rock where God put it, and that is the end of the story."

The battle over Hetch Hetchy raged for years, and cleaved the nascent movement into camps: utilitarian conservationists, such as Pinchot, who stressed the "wise use" of natural resources, and preservationists, personified by Muir, who extolled the aesthetic and intrinsic value of wild nature, regardless of utility to humans. Hetch Hetchy was the last great campaign of Muir's conservation career, and life. When Congress gave final approval in December 1913 allowing the dam builders to proceed, Muir was beaten. His health declined, and by Christmas 1914 the great wilderness advocate was dead.

Even as the conservation community fractured over Hetch Hetchy and other issues, the various societal impulses toward nature protection and social progress seemed to find some accommodation in the person of William Kent. After the fight was won to desecrate Muir's sacred Yosemite temple, Kent helped pass legislation creating the National Park Service. (Until that act's passage in 1916, the roughly thirty national parks and monuments that been designated had no single agency to administer them.) Ironically, supporters of the park service bill plotted strategy in Kent's Washington, D.C., home just a few years after Hetch Hetchy supporters had gathered there to chart their campaign to despoil a wild canyon in Yosemite National Park.

Kent's preservationist side was later ascendant when he made an additional donation to Muir Woods in 1921, and when he advocated for the whole of Mount Tamalpais to become a national park. That effort foundered, but Kent and others succeeded in protecting the area as Mount Tamalpais State Park, spurred in part by another gift of land from the Kent family.

Today, Muir Woods National Monument and adjacent state lands on Mount Tamalpais form a roughly seven-thousand-acre wild sanctuary in the heart of a cosmopolitan urban setting. For the millions of past visitors and millions of future visitors to this redwood cathedral, it is a cross-cultural exporter of wild beauty. Of that legacy, even John Muir would be proud.

# CAMEL'S HUMP STATE PARK
## A Tale of Two Mountains

*Joseph Battell (1839–1915)*

Four centuries ago, while exploring the lake that now bears his name, Samuel de Champlain and his party spied a prominent peak to the east. They called it "Lion Couchant," seeing the formof a resting or crouching lion in its two-humped aspect. Ira Allen, one of Vermont's famed Green Mountain Boys during the American Revolution, later marked it "Camel's Rump" on a 1798 map. Perhaps that was a typo, or possibly later cartographers thought the appellation too coarse, but by 1830, Vermont maps called the mountain Camel's Hump, and the name stuck.

It stands just 4,083 feet above sea level, but Camel's Hump looms large in the hearts of Vermonters. It's as central to the state's identity as maple syrup and a stoic response to inclement weather. The Vermont quarter released by the U.S. Mint depicts the mountain's leonine profile behind a hardy Vermonter collecting maple sap.

With its facsimile on a shiny new coin, millions of Americans now have Camel's Hump rattling around in their pockets. It's probably best that they don't come visit, for the hiking trails on the mountain are already among the state's most popular. In bad weather one might have the summit to oneself, but a crisp fall weekend may see hundreds of hikers climbing the Hump. They'll begin in woods of maple, birch, and beech before ascending into a conifer forest of spruce and fir, which shrinks into krummholz just below the rocky, open summit. Krummholz, German for "crooked wood," is a zone of gnarled vegetation where the trees hunker down, surviving fierce weather and poor growing conditions by staying knee high.

On a clear day, the view is sublime: undulating green mountains extend north and south, to the west are Lake Champlain and the Adirondacks, far to the east lies the granite hulk of New Hampshire's Mount Washington. It's hard to imagine this promontory of grayish-green schist submerged under mile-thick ice, but it once was, and just an eyeblink ago in geological time. Advancing glaciers smoothed the north aspect of Camel's Hump and plucked material from its southern edge, forming a nearly vertical precipice and the mountain's distinctive profile. The present-day ecology is also a relict of glacial history. The ice may have melted thirteen thousand years ago, but some of the mountain's residents still hanker for the Pleistocene. An Alpine Meadow natural community, rare for this latitude, with plants such as Alpine bilberry and Labrador tea, sits atop the mountain, essentially a little piece of Canadian tundra in Vermont.

As notable as what one sees here—rock, sky, forest—is what one doesn't see. No chairlifts. No warming huts or ski trails. Camel's Hump is the state's only peak higher than four thousand feet without a ski resort marring the natural splendor. It is in stark contrast to Mount Ellen, eighteen miles south along the spine of the Green Mountains. The former is forever preserved for wildlife and people, surrounded by nearly twenty-four thousand acres of state forestland. The latter is developed for industrial recreation. The sprawling Sugarbush ski resort covers Mount Ellen and two other peaks of the multisummit Lincoln Ridge.

The irony is that conservationist Joseph Battell once owned Camel's Hump and Mount Ellen— and went to his grave in 1915 believing that he had protected the original, wild character of both.

Joseph Battell was born into a prominent Vermont family in 1839. His maternal grandfather was a U.S. senator, his father and uncle were civic leaders, his brother-in-law served as governor. Battell had a scholarly mind, although he never finished formal education. Taken ill, "from overstudy" according to one account, he dropped out of Middlebury College to travel in Europe. After returning home, he began assembling a large tract of forestland in Ripton, Vermont, where he operated the Bread Loaf Inn.

Battell had strong, often unconventional opinions on all manner of topics, which he expressed in the state legislature, as a newspaper publisher, and through prolific writings. His books included a quirky tome that sought to illuminate the properties of light and sound, debunk evolution, and critique other modern scientific theories through the form of dialogues between a girl and a pine tree. Battell was also a leading promoter of the Morgan breed, and his horses received first-place honors at the 1904 St. Louis World's Fair, besting President Teddy Roosevelt's Morgan, which took only second place in its class.

In an 1891 speech, Battell exhorted his fellow state legislators to protect Vermont's forests from "timber butchers, lumber merchants, and firebugs." One of his goals, largely met in his lifetime, was to secure all lands within view of the Bread Loaf Inn, so that the mountain scenery he cherished would not be scarred by logging. He continued buying forested properties for decades, eventually owning about thirty-five thousand acres, which likely made his private landholdings the largest in the state when he died in 1915.

Battell directed the bulk of his estate to Middlebury College, including more than thirty thousand acres of forestland. In his will he described the "extensive destruction of the original forests of our country," and "the benefits that will accrue to . . . the citizens of the State of Vermont . . . from the preservation of a considerable tract of mountain forest in its virgin and primeval state." Along with a cash gift to endow their stewardship, Battell conveyed his wild lands surrounding the Bread Loaf Inn to be held "in trust as a park for the benefit of . . . Middlebury College and the students thereof."

"It shall be the duty of said trustees to preserve as far as reasonably may be the forests of said park," Battell wrote, "and neither to cut nor permit to be cut thereon any trees whatsoever except such as are dead or down and such as it may be necessary to cut in making or repairing needful roads; it being a principal object of this devise to preserve intact said wild lands . . . as a specimen of the original Vermont forest."

Battell also willed four thousand acres along Lincoln Ridge, including Mount Ellen, to the federal government to become a national park. At the time, however, there was no single federal agency responsible for managing the several national parks that Congress had designated in the West; the legislation creating the National Park Service would not be passed until the following year. Congress declined Battell's gift, deeming it "inexpedient to accept . . . and to establish a national park" in Vermont, and so those lands became part of the residual estate and also went to Middlebury College.

Battell's bequest of land, cash, and buildings was valued at more than $300,000 (equivalent to $6 million in today's dollars). The college accepted the gift and formed a committee to interpret and implement Battell's directions. That committee faced the dilemma of weighing competing goods—honoring the wishes of a donor while maximizing benefit to the institution. Much discussion ensued, centering on the college's responsibility as perpetual trustee of a new forest preserve versus the need to capture value from the estate. After an initial reading of the will in 1915, one committee member wrote to Middlebury College president John Thomas, "The wild lands are not meant to be revenue producing." But in correspondence to Thomas the following year, the same college trustee offered a detailed parsing of the will and recommended that the Battell lands be managed in two categories, "park" lands that would not be logged, and "forest" lands that would, distinctions that do not appear in Battell's will.

A 1925 "Report of Committee on Battell Forest to the Board of Trustees" confirms that an interpretation bifurcating Battell "park" and "forest" lands had been adopted. The committee's 1933 report showed a $42,225 surplus from logging revenues from the previous eight years but states that "the Forest still presents a serious financial problem for its fullest protection and development. At the same time, there is urgent need for new dormitories. . . . Girls and boys should be favored over trees." Thereafter the college began selling the former Battell holdings, both "park" and "forest" lands, to the federal government. Land sales between the 1930s and 1950s transferred some thirty-three thousand acres to the Green Mountain National Forest, with the college retaining only two thousand acres of the former Battell lands.

Today, the mountains Joseph Battell admired from the porch of his inn are mostly public land. Much of the acreage is protected as Battell intended, as part of the congressionally designated Breadloaf and Joseph Battell Wilderness areas. But large areas of the national forest formerly owned by Battell have been degraded by clearcutting, road building—and, in the case of Lincoln Ridge, ski resort development—since coming under Forest Service management. Perhaps the most flagrant act contravening Battell's wishes, however, was that Middlebury College even developed its own ski area, the Snow Bowl, on lands it had mapped as part of the Battell "park."

With the benefit of hindsight, it's easy to understand the challenge, both philosophical and administrative, that Battell's gift posed to the college, which at the time was a small, financially strapped institution. A progressive thinker, Battell had asked the school to serve as perpetual guardian of a wilderness park at a time when few people understood the ecological and cultural benefits of wild forests. The Battell lands committee, reflecting the larger society, viewed the forest through the lens of economic utility. Today Middlebury is one of the nation's best colleges, with an outstanding environmental studies department. One can only speculate how the students might have benefited from a natural classroom in which to study forests "in their original and primeval condition" had the former Battell lands been retained by the college and remained unlogged, as Battell intended. One can only imagine Mount Ellen as it might have been, wild and undefiled, centerpiece of a national park in the Green Mountains, if Congress had accepted Battell's bequest.

Joseph Battell's story is both an inspirational and a cautionary tale. It is not easy to ensure that one's wishes be properly interpreted after death. It is better to conduct one's philanthropy while alive, as Battell did in 1911 when he assured that the summit of Camel's Hump would be preserved in all its wild glory: "I, Joseph Battell . . . in consideration of the love I bear my native State, do . . . convey and confirm to the STATE OF VERMONT for A STATE PARK a mountain called CAMELS HUMP," he wrote. The gift of roughly one thousand acres, including the mountain's rocky peak, was gratefully accepted, and became the nucleus around which the present natural area was formed. Every person who looks out from its heights is a witness to Joseph Battell's conservation ethic living on in the unsullied summit and the intact forest cloaking Vermont's favorite mountain.

# ACADIA NATIONAL PARK
## A Consecrated Altruism

*George Bucknam Dorr*
*(1853–1944)*

How long does it take for waves to soften square-edged chunks of granite into round cobbles? Only the sea knows, and it has plenty of time. Witness the polishing action of salty spray, rising and falling tides, innumerable iterations of rushing water smoothing stone, plucking the tiniest of particles to deposit them wherever the currents choose. Over the eons, the world is transformed.

Compared with ocean time, a human life span is trivial—our allotted three-score years and ten seem hardly enough to make a mark on Earth—but our stories, songs, and history books are filled with people who do precisely that. Sometimes we name mountains after them. A person sitting in the predawn dark at the height of land in Maine's Acadia National Park, waiting for first daylight to strike America, will see those rays soar over the ocean and across the summit of Dorr Mountain before striking Cadillac Mountain's pink granite. Of the many souls who wake early to catch that sight, it's safe to assume that most simply enjoy the view—the gradual appearance of the Schoodic Peninsula jutting into the Atlantic as the lightening sky allows discernment between water and land. Few will be thinking of George B. Dorr, "the father of Acadia," but the unspoiled country about them is largely the legacy of his life's work to preserve Maine's Mount Desert Island.

Millions of people visit Acadia each year—to ramble its forest paths and watch thunderous waves crash into its shoreline. Students come to learn about coastal ecology and the various natural communities in a park that begins at sea level and tops out at 1,532 feet, the highest point on the North Atlantic seaboard. Birders flock here to spy seabirds and warblers, and others of the more than 335 bird species identified as residents or passing visitors. Families soak in the sights and sounds of nature.

The island's long history as a destination for vacationers began in the 1840s, when painters of the Hudson River School, including Thomas Cole and Frederic Edwin Church, popularized the region with their canvases. Their unintended marketing of the island's natural attributes stimulated a wave of tourism—the era of "rusticators," when city folk came to enjoy the scenery and fresh air. Originally—and aptly, some would say—incorporated as "Eden," the once-remote fishing village of Bar Harbor had by 1880 become a cosmopolitan destination offering accommodations at thirty hotels. That hotel era passed relatively quickly as Bar Harbor became the Newport of the north; many of America's elite families institutionalized their seaside idylls by building waterfront mansions, referred to as "cottages." The cottagers, with surnames such as Rockefeller, Astor, and Pulitzer, enjoyed a whirl of social activity in the summer season.

George Bucknam Dorr, son of Charles Hazen Dorr and Mary Gray Ward of Boston, moved in these social circles. Heir to a textile fortune, Dorr was a scholarly man whose sagacity and political astuteness made him a force for conservation. Dorr's long struggle to create a national park on Mount Desert Island began in 1901, when he received a letter from fellow cottager Charles W. Eliot, the pioneering educator and president of Harvard University, Dorr's alma mater. Eliot's son, a landscape architect, had helped found the nation's first nonprofit land conservancy, the Massachusetts Trustees of Public Reservations, to develop and hold park lands in that state. The elder Eliot proposed a similar organization in Maine that would protect land on Mount Desert Island. Dorr rounded up several friends, including his neighbor George Vanderbilt, to attend Eliot's inaugural meeting of the group. Dorr became vice president and

*It is an opportunity of singular interest, so to develop and preserve the wild charm and beauty of this unique spot on our Atlantic coast that future generations may rejoice in it yet more than we.*

—George Bucknam Dorr

executive officer of the Hancock County Trustees of Public Reservations, which subsequently secured its corporate charter.

The organization accepted a few land donations but was largely inactive during its early years; then, in 1908, using his own and another trustee's money, Dorr arranged to purchase the summit of Cadillac Mountain. Thereafter he worked vigorously, soliciting gifts of land and money, identifying and taking options on exceptional natural areas, and in many cases using his own funds to purchase key tracts. (In the land transactions records of the trustees, twenty-nine properties list Dorr as the grantor.)

By 1913 the group held five thousand acres on the island in perpetual trust for the public. In January of that year, Dorr was at home in Boston when word reached him that opponents had proposed legislation in the Maine statehouse to annul the Hancock Trustees' corporate charter. Dorr immediately took the train to Augusta and helped friendly legislators to defeat the bill, but the near-death experience for the nonprofit organization prompted a tactical shift. He realized "on how unstable a basis our Reservations rested" and decided that "the only course to follow to make safe what we had secured would be to get the Federal Government to accept our lands for a National Park." George Dorr was soon making regular trips to Washington, D.C., employing his many influential friends, and enlisting new ones, to help make his dream a reality.

One moment in a long life: It is 1916, a warm summer day in Bar Harbor, with enough breeze stirring the ocean to keep sailors happy and onshore partygoers comfortable. Men in linen jackets and straw hats mingle with women in long dresses as Charles Eliot calls to order a celebratory meeting. Using the 1906 Antiquities Act, President Woodrow Wilson has recently signed a declaration accepting the lands assembled by the Hancock Trustees to become Sieur de Monts National Monument. "The labors of years have been brought to a cheerful and hopeful consummation," Eliot says. "One of the greatest satisfactions," he continues, ". . . is that good work done for the public lasts, endures through generations; and the little bit of work that any individual of the passing generation is enabled to do gains through association with such collective activities an immortality of its own." A second speaker rises to credit the "successful accomplishment" of the new national monument to the "farsightedness and public spirit" of Charles Eliot and "the energy, the persistence, the unfailing tact, the consecrated altruism of George B. Dorr."

Then Dorr addresses the group. Rather than revel in the present victory, due in such large measure to his own tireless advocacy, Dorr notes that "what we have achieved is a beginning only. . . . We need more land, much more, that we may . . . make the Park what it should be, a sanctuary and protecting home for the whole region's plant and animal life, and for the birds that ask its hospitality upon their long migrations. Make it this, and naturalists will seek it from the whole world over, and from it other men will learn to cherish similarly wild life in other places."

Dorr became superintendent of the new Sieur de Monts National Monument at a salary of $1 per year and immediately began lobbying for a federal appropriation to support monument operations, expansion, and an upgrade to national park status. All were achieved. In 1919 Dorr successfully shepherded through Congress legislation to rename the monument Lafayette

National Park, having found Sieur de Monts "difficult of pronunciation for Americans not versed in French." Lafayette became just the second national park in the East, and the first created from donated lands. (Mackinac Island in Lake Huron was briefly designated a national park in the late 1800s, before being given to Michigan to manage as a state park.)

Ever looking to increase Lafayette National Park's holdings, Dorr seized an opportunity a few years later to secure a large tract on the Schoodic Peninsula, across Frenchman Bay from Mount Desert Island. The potential donors, however, were Anglophiles and disdained the notion of a gift to a park named for the French statesman and Revolutionary War general. Dorr worked with congressional allies to alter the park's purchase boundaries to include the peninsula and to formalize another name change. The land was given, and in 1929 Lafayette became Acadia National Park. This ideal name would stick, conveying both the contemporary understanding of "Acadia" as the North Atlantic coast region settled by the French, and its historical derivation from Arcadia, the "rustic paradise" of Greek mythology.

Through its various nominal and organizational incarnations, the conservation effort on Mount Desert Island benefited from the generosity of many private donors and the indefatigable nature of George B. Dorr, who remained Acadia National Park's superintendent until his death. Only one figure rivals Dorr's contributions to land preservation on the island—John D. Rockefeller Jr., at the time the nation's leading philanthropist. Rockefeller was central to Acadia's growth and development. Among other properties, he assembled several tracts along the island's southeastern shore, from Sand Beach to Otter Point, and donated them to the Park Service. An avid horseman, Rockefeller also funded construction of roughly fifty miles of carriage roads for equestrian and pedestrian use, and much of today's Park Loop Road. Working closely with Dorr, over a period of decades Rockefeller purchased and preserved 10,700 acres, nearly a quarter of Acadia National Park's current land base of 47,000 acres. A giant in the conservation movement, Rockefeller was during the same period helping to support park creation across America.

Allies like Rockefeller and Eliot were invaluable, but George Dorr's greatest asset was his own supreme devotion to a particular place. A lifelong bachelor, Dorr was, in a fashion, married to the wild forests, rocky shores, and glacial lakes of Mount Desert Island—a landscape that sustained him even as he became increasingly blind. He exhausted his energy and family fortune to see it protected.

Regardless of the season, when Dorr was in residence at Oldfarm, his home in Bar Harbor, he would take a daily plunge into the frigid Atlantic waters. Possibly it was that morning ritual and years of rambling about the island that kept him robust into old age. At seventy-two and shod in light moccasins, he ascended Mount Katahdin, Maine's highest peak, reportedly leaving younger men in his wake. Dorr lived in Bar Harbor until his death at ninety-one and, in one of his final acts, donated his beloved Oldfarm property to the Park Service.

George B. Dorr's altruistic spirit is now consecrated for all time in the rocky summit of Dorr Mountain and the surrounding wildlands of Acadia National Park. "Whatever changes come," he once wrote, "the Park as a possession of the people will be as permanent as man's need for recreation and enjoyment of great coastal scenery."

# BERNHEIM ARBORETUM AND RESEARCH FOREST
## A Patriot's Dream

*Isaac Wolfe Bernheim
(1848–1945)*

Americans love a rags-to-riches story. We are deeply familiar with that narrative—it is the foundation of our mythic sense of national history and identity. We even have a linguistic shorthand for it. Simply say "American Dream," and you need not articulate the particulars, whether immigrants disembarking at Ellis Island who will make good in a welcoming land or college dropouts tinkering with lines of computer code in the basement, ready to surf a digital wave into the billionaire's club formerly reserved for captains of industry. It's a world of opportunity. Work hard and you can get ahead.

When Isaac Bernheim got off the boat from Germany in 1867, he probably didn't buy one of Horatio Alger's ubiquitous dime novels about spunky teenage boys making a success of themselves through honest labor. He was just eighteen years old, and had a mere four American dollars in his pocket. If he had found a copy of Alger's *Paul the Peddler; or the Fortunes of a Young Street Merchant* dropped on Battery Street, he might have turned to the book's final page to see the hero declare: "I am not rich yet . . . but I mean to be some time if I can accomplish it by industry and attention to business." Bernheim was about to live the story.

Isaac Wolfe Bernheim was born in the small village of Schmieheim in the Black Forest region at a time when German Jews were compelled to live in certain communities, were drafted into the military but could not rise above a certain rank, were taxed but could not vote. The product of a society that institutionalized prejudice, even as a child Isaac knew and revered Thomas Jefferson's writings on liberty. Bernheim's father, a prosperous merchant, died when young Isaac was seven, and the family's fortunes declined despite his mother's remarriage. The boy's formal education ended at age thirteen, when he began three years as an unpaid intern to a shop owner in Freiburg, before landing his first job. Enticed by stories of America, and with promise of employment at an uncle's factory in New York City, Bernheim booked passage across the Atlantic, joining a great wave of European immigration.

Alas, New York was undergoing a post–Civil War recession, and his uncle could offer no work, but he did help the youngster get equipped with some trifles to sell, and Isaac set off to earn his keep as an itinerant peddler. There were hardships—winter was cold, and after he'd earned enough to buy a horse, it took ill and died—but Bernheim later looked back on those first days in America fondly. "The new avocation afforded me many opportunities to familiarize myself with the language and customs of the people and with the country itself as perhaps no other pursuit could," he wrote. "It developed me physically, and what was worth still more to me, it gave me a spirit of independence and self-reliance which stood me in good stead afterward. . . . I trudged along the peaceful Pennsylvania highways dreaming of future triumphs."

Triumph he did. Bernheim soon ended up in Paducah, Kentucky, where some of his relatives had settled. There he began a successful career. He married the lovely Amanda Uri, and brought his brother Bernard from Germany to work with him. Within a few years, Bernheim Brothers would expand from liquor wholesaling into distilling, outgrow sleepy Paducah, and move its operations to Louisville. America was growing, and Americans had a growing thirst for good Kentucky bourbon.

In subsequent decades Bernheim became a leading businessman of the region. An outspoken proponent of Reform Judaism, he was apparently too progressive even for fellow reformers, who shouted him down during his speech to the 1928 conference of the World Union for Progressive Judaism in Berlin when he endorsed certain liberal reforms and offered a fierce critique of political Zionism.

As a philanthropist, Bernheim funded a library building at Cincinnati's Hebrew Union College, a recreation center for the Louisville Young Men's Hebrew Association (similar to the YMCA), and a new wing on a Louisville hospital. On a visit to Washington, D.C., he noted with embarrassment that the Capitol Building's National Statuary Hall had no Kentuckians among the honored. Bernheim funded a vote among the state's schoolchildren on who should be included there and then commissioned busts of politician Henry Clay and Ephraim McDowell, a pioneering Kentucky surgeon, to be installed in the hall. He also commissioned public sculptures of Abraham Lincoln and Thomas Jefferson; Jefferson's was erected in front of Louisville's old courthouse building, where it still stands. In dedicating the monument to his hero, Bernheim remarked, "The principles of the Declaration of Independence are as old as the Bible itself, but Jefferson—the humane Jefferson—gave them force and effect."

Beyond these charitable activities, Bernheim imagined a more lasting contribution, a legacy written on the land that would express his deep patriotism and gratitude toward his adopted country. In his 1929 book, *Closing Chapters of a Busy Life*, he wrote of this dream, describing how it "ripened into maturity . . . in never to be forgotten walks and talks with my wife" in the quiet woods of their country estate. That dream was deferred, but not abandoned, when Amanda died in 1922. "At last," Bernheim later wrote, "the physical materialization of my dream was brought about in the incorporation of the Isaac W. Bernheim Foundation, and the acquisition of more than thirteen thousand acres of wild 'Kentucky Knob' land situated within twenty-five miles of the city of Louisville—an estate exceeding twenty square miles admirably suited for my purpose."

The purpose was a preserve and arboretum, a "sanctuary for birds that fly and fowl that find their home on the water," he wrote. "I visualize a natural park where there will be in profusion all things which gladden the soul and please the sight of man." Bernheim also imagined the park containing a natural history museum modeled on Denver's, which he much admired, and offered his gift as a "a center of friendly intercourse for the people of Kentucky . . . a place to further their love of the beautiful in nature and in art . . . and as a means of strengthening their love and devotion to their state and country." The park would be free and open to everyone—an unusual sentiment in the segregated American South of 1929. Bernheim insisted that "no distinction will be shown between rich and poor, white or colored. Every respectable man, woman and child will be made welcome, and all will be treated with an equal consideration."

Bernheim Arboretum and Research Forest, overseen by a board and endowed by a trust fund that Bernheim set up, opened to the public in 1950, five years after his death. Workers had built an infrastructure of hiking trails and roads, and a landscape design firm had created an arboretum and horticultural plantings near the park entrance. In the intervening half century, the forest has received millions of visitors and its mission has evolved. The picnickers and perambulators Bernheim expected still visit his park, natural and artistic beauty is still fostered here, but environmental education programs also teach broader ecological principles and interpret the local landscape, the Kentucky Knobs country. Too small to be deemed mountains, the so-called "knobs" are steep-sided hills that form a semicircular ring of rough topography in Kentucky's Outer Bluegrass region.

Bernheim Forest's current size is approximately fourteen thousand acres, of which twelve thousand acres comprise a natural area and research forest, the site of ongoing studies. Natural communities have been inventoried, and with partners the staff has implemented an ambitious stream restoration project that is offering valuable lessons about how to improve water quality and fish habitat where original stream channels were diverted.

Relatively flat, arable land was scarce in the Knobs country, and pioneers often straightened or moved naturally meandering stream channels to make more room for crops in the bottom of a hollow. Massive clearing of the forest was also common; much of the wood was consumed by charcoal kilns. Through habitat loss and direct persecution, every native species of large mammal was eliminated from Kentucky by 1850 except white-tailed deer, which barely survived. Today deer are overabundant in many areas, black bears and bobcats are making a comeback in the wilder strongholds of the state, and elk have been reintroduced successfully.

Despite the increasing wildness in some parts of Kentucky—and specifically at Bernheim Forest, as formerly cutover lands mature into a diverse, structurally complex forest—it may be a long while before wolves and cougars again wander through the region. In the 1920s, when Isaac Bernheim purchased his thirteen thousand acres from the United States Trust Company, the roads in the area were poor and Louisville seemed distant. Today, it's a short commute, and on a clear day, one can see the downtown skyline from the fire tower at Bernheim. The city's proximity means a ready audience for programs but poses a growing threat to the forest's ecological integrity. The landscape is becoming increasingly fragmented, auguring a future, absent concerted action now, that would leave Bernheim an isolated island of wildness in a sea of exurban sprawl.

Bernheim Forest's dynamic staff and board seem well poised to meet this challenge, carrying Isaac Bernheim's dream into a new century, and using this natural enclave and educational resource to export a larger conservation vision in their community. If they succeed—if a coalition of partner organizations, businesses, local landowners, and governments can protect wildlife corridors from Bernheim Forest to other conservation lands—in coming decades the forest will be the core of a regional green infrastructure, a future that Isaac Bernheim, an American patriot, would surely endorse.

# BAXTER STATE PARK
## No Man's Garden

*Percival Proctor Baxter
(1876–1969)*

Dawn. The air is thick with the smell of balsam. Mist rises from a forest-clad pond. Through the ether comes the wail of a loon, an ancient sound that has haunted the Great North Woods far longer than people have been present to hear it. The scene is a wilderness archetype, but here in northern Maine's Baxter State Park, it is simply the way the world has been and will be. One might be tempted to describe this wild country of moose and spruce as changeless, but the adjective would be inapt. The land is ever changing, full of possibility, because its community of life is not circumscribed by human will.

As the mist dissipates, a presence appears, looming over the forest wilderness. Katahdin, its name derived from the Penobscot Indian terms for "greatest" and "mountain," is surely that. The loons, whose lineage stretches back some sixty million years, are relative newcomers compared to the venerable mountain. Hikers ascending Katahdin scramble over granite a half-billion years old that was once a giant pluton, or plug, of molten rock formed deep underground. Through subsequent mountain-building events, that igneous rock was variously thrust up and worn away. The granite pluton, far harder than surrounding material, survived the endless progression of years while softer stone eroded. Through deep time and multiple glaciations, the mountain has stood—scraped and submerged at times by ice, but always reemerging into the sunshine, a cloak of green softening its rocky margins.

Standing far above the surrounding country, the mile-high mountain helps create its own weather, which is typically unpredictable. A lenticular cloud often hovers over the multisummit ridgeline. Even when the sky is clear below, Katahdin is frequently enshrouded in the "plumes of Pamola," supposedly the breath of Katahdin's fierce resident spirit. While the mountain was central to Penobscot cultural mythology, the local people apparently were content to leave its summit to Pamola.

The first known ascent was in 1804 by Charles Turner, who described the "immense labor" it required; his and most subsequent early parties that reached the top did so in miserable conditions. Henry David Thoreau's 1846 Katahdin climb was similarly arduous. He reached the expansive tablelands on the ridgeline but did not proceed to any of the summits. In *The Maine Woods*, he recounts being buffeted by winds and weather, caught "deep within the hostile ranks of clouds," calling the scenery "vast, Titanic, and such as man never inhabits."

Thoreau's singular sensibility—his attunement to wildness—and skillful observation of natural phenomena combined in *The Maine Woods* to produce an early classic of wilderness literature. Long before forest ecologists would formally describe the divergent properties of primeval versus logged forests, Thoreau was commenting poetically on the former—"It is all mossy and *moosey*. . . . The trees are a *standing* night, and every fir and spruce which you fell is a plume plucked from night's raven wing"—and describing how the latter "has lost its wild, damp, and shaggy look, the countless fallen and decaying trees are gone, and consequently that thick coat of moss which lived on them is gone too." In the wilderness around Katahdin, Thoreau reveled in the landscape's "primeval, untamed, and forever untameable Nature." Unlike the trammeled woodlots of Concord, this was "that Earth of which we have heard, made out of Chaos and Old Night. Here was no man's garden."

Percival Proctor Baxter, for whom Mount Katahdin's highest summit is named, first saw the great mountain on a fishing trip with his father in 1903. "Percy" Baxter had been born

*Man is born to die. His works are short lived. Buildings crumble, monuments decay, wealth vanishes, but Katahdin in all its glory forever shall remain the mountain of the people of Maine.*

—Percival Proctor Baxter

into a wealthy and influential family in 1876; his father, James, was a successful businessman and longtime Republican mayor of Portland, Maine. While a student at Bowdoin College, Percy and fellow supporters of William McKinley took the train to Bath, where populist Democratic presidential candidate William Jennings Bryan was to speak. Fearing the young Republicans would cause a disruption, local police stopped them and arrested Baxter. He sued for false arrest and later won a penny in damages.

Following Harvard Law School and foreign travel with his father, Baxter began a life in business and politics. He served several terms in the state legislature, eventually becoming state senate president. Then, in 1921, the governor died, elevating Baxter to the office. (Those free-thinking Mainers don't bother with a lieutenant governor.) He was forty-four years old, Maine's youngest governor ever, and won reelection in 1922.

Both personally and professionally, Baxter was an iconoclast, a staunch fiscal conservative with a progressive streak. He appointed Catholics, Jews, and women to some government posts. He never married, and continued living with his father in the family residence. He opposed vivisection and once withheld a contribution to Bowdoin, his alma mater, because the biology students there dissected animals. While governor, and commuting regularly to Augusta, he received special dispensation from the railroad to bring his beloved Irish setters into the passenger compartment, and even had the capitol flags flown at half-mast when his favorite dog died. An uproar ensued. Baxter vigorously defended his action, claiming that his pets "constitute my immediate family," and suggested that if the controversy had helped stimulate people to think about "their responsibilities toward . . . animals," then part of his purpose had been served.

Despite being called a traitor to his class, Baxter clashed with the state's dominant corporations on two defining issues: development of public power resources (he believed electricity generated by damming Maine rivers should not be exported but used to benefit local citizens), and creating a public wilderness park around Mount Katahdin. His stance put him at odds with the powerful Great Northern Paper Company and other large timberland owners, which generally opposed taking land out of production forestry.

Baxter had climbed Katahdin in 1920 while serving in the state senate, and it had made a lasting impression on him. He called it "the greatest monument of Nature that exists east of the Mississippi River. This mountain raises its head aloft unafraid of the passing storm and is typical of the rugged character of the people of Maine." He was wholly committed to seeing it in public ownership. "Shall any great timberland or paper-making corporation, or group of such corporations, themselves the owners of millions of acres of Maine forests," he challenged, "say to the People of this state, 'You shall not have Mount Katahdin, either as a memorial of your past or as heritage for your future'?"

Baxter even offered to donate his salary as governor for two years if the state legislature would appropriate an initial $10,000 toward buying Katahdin, but opponents blocked every attempt to pass park-related legislation. During the same era, some Maine conservationists proposed a Katahdin-area national park but their idea similarly foundered. After leaving public office, Baxter remained dedicated to his cause but for a few years conducted little public advocacy. His strategy had evolved. Where a publicly funded park initiative had failed, Baxter determined to use private capital—his own. Maine's greatest mountain, once in the public domain, had been given over to private interests. He would buy it back.

In 1930 Percival Baxter purchased partial interest in nearly six thousand acres of the Maine woods, including Mount Katahdin. Before the other partial owner, a park foe, could be bought out by persuasion or eminent domain, Baxter tried to donate his holdings to the state. The governor at the time, however, was nervous about accepting the gift, fearing controversy and legal complications. Baxter wrote him, "I know that this is a generous act, prompted by genuine public spirit. If there be those who criticize it, I shall not be broken hearted. Let us go through with it and take the consequences." They did. The lands in question were subsequently legally divided, the park foe accepted other property and compensation, and Baxter ended up with clear title to the Katahdin tract. The legislature formally accepted it, creating Baxter State Park in 1933.

The story might have ended there, but for Baxter it was only a beginning. For the next three decades, parcel by parcel, he bought land around the mountain and donated it to the people of Maine. His assembled gifts, the last one coming in 1963, totaled more than two hundred thousand acres, making Baxter State Park the largest wilderness area in New England. "A map showing the different acquisitions . . . over the years," Baxter recalled, "would remind you of your grandmother's patchwork quilt, which finally in some mysterious way came out of the confusion into one large piece."

Throughout his life, Baxter remained personally engaged in the park's management. Having been impressed with the progressive forestry practices he'd seen in Scandinavia and Germany, he set aside a portion of the park's land, about twenty-nine thousand acres, as a scientific forestry management area where research, experimental logging, and hunting would be allowed. The vast bulk of the park, however, would remain a wilderness area, with strict protections against timber harvesting, development, hunting, and even floatplane use. Baxter's initial gift came with restrictions "that the land so conveyed shall be forever used for public park and recreational purposes . . . shall forever be left in its natural wild state . . . shall be forever kept as a sanctuary for wild beasts and birds . . . and that no roads or ways for motor vehicles shall hereafter ever be constructed . . . thereon." Subsequent deeds included similar language. And in a final act of generosity, Baxter left nearly $7 million to endow the park, ensuring perpetual stewardship of the land for future generations.

During the era in which Percival Baxter made his first down payments on wilderness recovery in the Maine Woods, there were numerous other examples of private action to establish state and national parks and private nature preserves. But most of those initiatives were collective efforts. Baxter's example of an individual's buying and sometimes swapping blocks of timberland to consolidate a single large ownership for wild nature was unprecedented in its scale.

The resurgence of the forest around Katahdin during the last seventy-five years is Baxter's living legacy. The wolves and caribou present in the region when Thoreau tramped through are gone, but the country is otherwise remarkably intact. The land displays that damp and shaggy look Thoreau admired, and loon song floats over sparkling waters, perhaps one day to be rejoined by a chorus of wolves. Thanks to Percival Baxter, there is a place in the northwoods to welcome them home, a park that, as he directed, "must remain the wild stormswept, untouched-by-man region it now is . . . where nature rules and where the creatures of the forest hold undisputed dominion."

# HAWK MOUNTAIN SANCTUARY

## Killing Ground No More

*Rosalie Barrow Edge*
*(1877–1962)*

Who can know the mind of a broad-winged hawk, soaring along Pennsylvania's Kittatinny Ridge, gently buoyed by thermal updrafts? Gathered in great flocks called kettles—hundreds or even thousands of birds moving in concert—the broadwings honor an ancient compulsion to migrate. Their annual journey between summertime breeding habitat in eastern North America and wintering grounds in Central and South America is doubtless prompted by culture and custom (and genes), but could it also be that they enjoy the trip? Sailing south in mid-September over a forest shedding its green uniformity for a riot of fall colors, might the hawks be, well, having fun?

Professional wildlife biologists of every discipline, including ornithologists, are trained to collect data with dispassionate objectivity. Ascribing human attributes to wild creatures, anthropomorphizing them, is strictly taboo. But for a simple lover of things wild and free, it's difficult not to wonder about such questions while atop the North Lookout at Hawk Mountain Sanctuary in Berks County, especially on an autumn day when the hawks are on the move. During the three-month fall migration, expert hawk counters are here, tallying not just broadwings, but bald and golden eagles, Cooper's and sharp-shinned hawks, red-tailed and red-shouldered hawks, merlins and peregrine falcons, and other birds of prey as they pass over the mountain. Scores of amateur birders are present, too, attracted to the world's first and foremost sanctuary established to protect raptors, the lions and tigers of the avian world.

For more than seventy years, the sanctuary has attracted bird enthusiasts, from local schoolkids to the ornithological elite. Some eighty thousand visitors flock to Hawk Mountain each year, many during the migration season with the hope of witnessing one of nature's recurrent miracles. Rachel Carson, whose book *Silent Spring* helped launch the modern environmental movement, visited the lookout in 1945 and wrote: "They came by like brown leaves drifitng on the wind. Sometimes a lone bird rode the air currents; sometimes several at a time, sweeping upward until they were only specks against the clouds or dropping down again toward the valley floor below us; sometimes a great burst of them milling and tossing, like the flurry of leaves when a sudden gust of wind shakes loose a new batch from the forest trees."

Carson's hawk-watching experience, while described with exceptional lyricism, is one shared by generations of bird lovers, thanks to Hawk Mountain Sanctuary's founder, Rosalie Edge. Edge's name is far less known today than Carson's, but she was likely the most effective wildlife advocate of her time, and the first woman to significantly influence the course of conservation in America.

Born into the polite society of New York City, there was little about her background to foretell her future campaigns for wilderness and wildlife. She married a wealthy British engineer, raised a family, traveled widely, enjoyed birdwatching, and was active in the fight for women's suffrage. In 1929 she was a fifty-two-year-old lady of independent means, separated from her husband. The right to vote had been won, and Rosalie Edge was ready for a new challenge. A skilled organizer with a gift for political repartee, she turned her talents to saving nature.

Edge founded the Emergency Conservation Committee in 1930 and headed the group until her death in 1962. Foreshadowing the rise of grassroots radical environmentalism a half century later, Edge took strong positions and was as happy to highlight the failures of mainstream conservationists and government regulators as to criticize industry. Working out of a tiny office

*When we who have a feeling for birds observe a mighty eagle, or the perfection of a tiny warbler, we see, not the inspiration of God filtered through human agency, but the very handiwork.*
—Rosalie Barrow Edge

and never taking a salary, she kept the organization lean and uncompromising. She knew how to make news, and rallied conservationists about various wildlife issues through a series of pamphlets. Edge and conservation colleagues wrote them, and she distributed more than a million copies over the years, with titles like "The Audubon Steel-Trapping Sanctuary," "It's Alive!—Kill It!" and "The United States Bureau of Destruction and Extermination," the latter an exposé of the U.S. Bureau of Biological Survey's predator-killing program.

Disproportionately influential relative to its size (the Emergency Conservation Committee essentially was Edge, two close associates, and a mailing list), the group waged battles to reform the Audubon Association, create Olympic and Kings Canyon national parks, and add a valuable grove of sugar pines coveted by loggers to Yosemite National Park, among other issues. Edge's aggressive rhetoric and strategic savvy were a novelty in a time when virtually all government officials, and prominent conservationists, were men. J. N. "Ding" Darling, head of the Biological Survey, the agency that later became the U.S. Fish and Wildlife Service, once said of Edge, "I know instinctively when she arrives in town as I can feel the swish of her sword and hear her battle cry." She was described, even by her friends, as "militant," "belligerent," and "the only honest, unselfish, indomitable hellcat in the history of conservation." While embroiled in a lawsuit against the Audubon Association, which she ultimately won, the opposing lawyer called Edge "a common scold." She enjoyed the tepid insult and repeated it often. "Fancy how I trembled," she recalled.

Into the deepest recesses of human history, people have been fascinated by birds of prey. Their keen eyesight, majestic flight, and hunting prowess make raptors natural totems. Falconry was once the hobby of nobles. Despite Ben Franklin's opinion that it was a bird of bad character, the bald eagle became our national symbol. In advertising, military iconography, even sports, the symbolic potency of raptors continues in our culture. On Sunday afternoons in autumn, couch-bound football fans will be rooting for their "eagles" and "falcons" to crush the other team. Would the burly front linemen feel so tough if they were playing for the Philadelphia Vireos or Atlanta Chickadees?

Cultural attitudes toward predacious birds have been far from universally favorable, however. Hostility toward wild predators that roam the earth and soar the skies has had a darkly rich history in America and has resulted in the dramatic population declines of many species. Bounties abetted the wholesale killing. An 1885 Pennsylvania law put a bounty of fifty cents per head on birds of prey; before the so-called Scalp Act was rescinded two years later, some 180,000 hawk scalps were turned in, leading to increased rodent populations and an unexpected drain on state coffers. Other state bounties on raptors were enacted in later decades, including a $5-per-bird incentive to kill goshawks in the 1920s. That species was rare in Pennsylvania, few hunters could identify raptors on the wing, and thus the reward served as an inducement to kill all hawks. An unholy alignment of profit motive, "sporting" interest, and pervasive cultural myths about birds of prey combined to create a toxic milieu for migrating raptors along the Kittatinny Ridge. Near Drehersville, at a place locals called Hawk Mountain, shooters blasted away at the passing birds, the roar of their gunfire described by one conservationist as "almost continuous," resembling a "Fourth of July celebration on a vast scale."

In the early 1930s, this carnage came to the attention of an avid young birder named Richard Pough. Dick Pough would go on to be a great force for conservation during the next half century.

He wrote popular birding guides for the National Audubon Society, founded the Open Space Institute, and lost his curator's job at the American Museum of Natural History when he publicly opposed the controversial Echo Park Dam project in Dinosaur National Monument. He cofounded the Nature Conservancy, served as its first president, and through tireless matchmaking between philanthropists and conservation groups helped save many natural areas across North America.

Then managing a Philadelphia camera shop, Pough visited Hawk Mountain one Sunday in October of 1932 and witnessed the massacre. The following weekend, he returned with his brother Harold and some birding colleagues. They collected hundreds of carcasses below the gunners' perch, grouped them by species, and took shocking photos of the dead hawks. Pough began publicizing the hawks' plight among birding organizations and, while giving a talk about Hawk Mountain in New York City in 1933, met Rosalie Edge. The following June, he arranged to rendezvous at the mountain with Edge, her son Peter, and a local realtor. The party scrambled through the woods and up to the lookout. "The laurel was in bloom, and the view was overwhelming," Peter Edge recalled decades later. "My mother arranged to lease the two-square-mile area for a year at a cost of $500, with an option to purchase the whole for $3,500, about $2.50 an acre."

Before that year's fall migration, Rosalie Edge recruited a young couple to act as wardens of the mountain. Maurice Broun, a self-trained ornithologist, had the kind of courage the job required. At great personal danger, he and his wife, Irma, faced down and turned back the gunners. Within a few years, Edge raised the funds to acquire the property, founded a nonprofit to oversee it, and transferred title; she served as president of the Hawk Mountain Sanctuary Association for the rest of her life. Maurice Broun would serve as curator of the new sanctuary for more than three decades, establishing it as an internationally known center for raptor conservation.

At more than 2,600 acres, and abutting other conserved lands, Hawk Mountain Sanctuary today forms the nucleus of one of the largest blocks of protected forest in southeastern Pennsylvania. Miles of hiking trails allow a visitor to experience the sanctuary's natural pleasures, but with wildlife protection the preeminent objective, nearly half the property is closed to public use. From marbled salamanders to bobcats, smoky shrews to black bears, an array of wild creatures flourishes where dead and dying hawks once littered the forest floor. Now the smell of life is ubiquitous—hay-scented fern and flowering dogwood, and the good, rich aroma of last year's leaves becoming soil. A recent inventory of the preserve recorded nearly 300 plant species and 292 species of fungi, some 35 kinds of reptiles and amphibians, and 37 mammal species. And *birds*, of course; more than 250 *avian* species are residents of, or pass by, Hawk Mountain. These are merely statistics, though, the faintest way to describe a wild forest. Sauntering through the mature oak and maple woods, looking out upon the rolling topography and down to the Schuylkill River, one begins a different kind of tally—of reasons to give thanks for this wonderful place.

Rosalie Edge, Dick Pough, Maurice and Irma Broun, and the other pioneering conservationists responsible for Hawk Mountain's transformation from killing ground to sanctuary are honored in the continuing legacy of conservation here. The echo of gunfire from the lookout is now a distant memory, replaced by birdsong, rustling leaves, and the not quite perceptible sound of wind rushing over feathers—of hawks in flight.

# GREAT SMOKY MOUNTAINS NATIONAL PARK

## The People's Park

*John D. Rockefeller Jr.*
*(1874–1960)*

In 1926, a girl from Knoxville named Grace Wright pledged five cents to help purchase private lands for a new national park along the Tennessee–North Carolina border. Two years later, John D. Rockefeller Jr. would pledge $5 million to the fundraising drive. While her name is lost to history and his contributions to American conservation are rightfully celebrated, both individuals were caught up in the excitement of the early parks movement. During the 1920s the National Park Service was a hotbed of activity as conservationists petitioned the young agency on behalf of their favorite natural areas. Civic leaders from around the country were busy garnering political support for the scenic lands they favored, a phenomenon that reflected both pride of place and a desire to seize market share in the nascent leisure travel industry. Henry Ford's Model T had made automobile-based tourism a possibility for working people, whetting the wanderlust of millions of Americans.

Anne Davis of Knoxville, Tennessee, is credited with launching one such park campaign in 1923, when after a summer trip to the West with her husband, Willis, she asked, "Why can't we have a national park in the Great Smokies?" The Davises, who were socially prominent, began proselytizing for their idea. Anne Davis was later elected to the Tennessee state legislature, where she helped pass legislation authorizing state funding for the first major land acquisition toward a future park, seventy-eight thousand acres from the Little River Lumber Company. By the following year, Willis Davis had recruited a local pharmacist, Colonel David Chapman, who soon became a leading figure in the park effort, and other area businessmen to form the Great Smoky Mountains Conservation Association.

Several individuals from across the mountains in North Carolina also became prominent park supporters, including state senator Mark Squires and the famous outdoor writer Horace Kephart. Kephart was a Pennsylvania-born librarian and frontier history buff who became so enthralled with the adventurous life that he retreated—leaving both family and profession—to the Smokies in 1903. He lived there among the mountain people for the rest of his life, drinking (and recovering from drinking), tramping the backcountry, and writing popular books, including *Our Southern Highlanders*. Kephart thought a national park could best counter the rapacious logging then denuding the Smoky Mountains.

"One or two large lumber companies own practically all the virgin forest that I have been featuring as one of the chief attractions of this majestic region," he wrote. "They aim to destroy it: to cut down those gigantic trees and cut them into so many board feet of lumber, leaving a desert of stumps and briers in their place." Through his writings Kephart promoted the Smokies, highlighted the threat that large timberland owners posed to the Southern Appalachians' last virgin forests, and helped counter park opponents, mostly in the timber industry, who favored creating a national forest in which commercial logging would continue.

After much lobbying by conservationists, Congress passed legislation in 1925 authorizing the secretary of the interior to study the boundaries for three new parks—the Smokies on the Tennessee–North Carolina border, Shenandoah in Virginia's Blue Ridge Mountains, and Mammoth Cave in Kentucky—and to accept land, or money for the purchase of land, within them. The act did not officially authorize the parks—that would come later—or provide any federal funds for land acquisition, but it settled the question of where the first national parks in the Southern

Appalachians would be established. Thus began a flurry of fundraising activity in Tennessee and North Carolina for the Smokies site. The two state legislatures made appropriations, the municipal governments of Asheville and Knoxville, which anticipated becoming gateway communities to the future park, made timely financial contributions, and private fundraising began in earnest.

This was the context in which Grace Wright and her Central High School classmates offered their pocket change for the park in 1926. Some 4,500 schoolchildren from four East Tennessee counties made gifts totaling $1,391.72, an inconsequential sum relative to the estimated $10-million cost for the park lands, but the kids' enthusiasm gave a big psychological boost to the funding drive in Tennessee, which soon exceeded its statewide goal. It was a high point, but several obstacles loomed. Park foes, led by large timberland owners, bitterly fought the park idea. Buying more than 6,600 separate tracts of private land and assembling them into a contiguous conservation area posed a gargantuan logistical and legal challenge. Sustaining fundraising momentum proved difficult.

A low point came in 1928, when contributions to the park initiative waned. The situation seemed dire, and the national park service's assistant director, Arno Cammerer, was tapped to solicit John D. Rockefeller Jr.'s support for the Smokies. Cammerer had a friendly relationship with Rockefeller, who was already deeply engaged in parks-related philanthropy, having made notable contributions to Grand Teton and Acadia national parks, among others. With Colonel Chapman's assistance, Cammerer made a successful pitch, and Rockefeller pledged $5 million, on a matching basis, from a family philanthropy set up by his father. When the gift was announced publicly on March 6, 1928, bells pealed throughout Knoxville as the news spread.

Many years of work were required to assemble a vast public natural area from formerly private land. These labors were recognized when twenty-five thousand people gathered in September 1940 at Newfound Gap in the heart of Great Smoky Mountains National Park to celebrate its birth. Perhaps Grace Wright and some of the other schoolchildren who contributed their pocket change to the park were among them. The governors of Tennessee and North Carolina were there, and National Park Service officials, and the "mother" of the park idea, Anne Davis. John D. Rockefeller Jr., without whom the Smokies preservation movement would surely have foundered, sent his regrets, but the president himself, Franklin D. Roosevelt, came to formally dedicate the park.

That so many worked so hard for a national park in the Smokies—and even during the Great Depression gave of their own dollars to advance the project—is a historical wonder. Just as the steep-sided, sheltered valleys of the Southern Appalachians, "coves" in the local vernacular, are a biological wonder. From their deep, rich soils springs a frenzy of life. In the remote coves of Great Smoky Mountains National Park, where the logger's ax never rang, tracts of primeval forest survive that are living relics of the presettlement landscape. The trees here may not rival the West's sequoias for size, but they are giants of their kind. The tallest recorded tree in the East, a statuesque white pine along the Smokies' Caldwell Fork Trail, measured 207 feet high before Hurricane Opal lopped off its top 21 feet in 1995. A yellow buckeye in the Gabes Creek area is more than 19 feet in circumference. For people who have never seen an old-growth forest, little of which survives in the East, these places seem almost magical, a bit like stumbling into

Tolkien's Middle Earth. The park's arboreal diversity is also notable; a savvy dendrologist might identify some 130 tree species within this five-hundred-thousand-acre protected area, nearly as many as grow in all of Europe.

The trees watch over a profusion of life nearly unmatched in North America. More than four thousand plant species, two hundred species of birds, and sixty mammal species have been identified in the park. Innumerable reptiles and amphibians, gastropods, and insects also call these mountains home. The present-day diversity is partly due to the region's glacial history. Twenty thousand years ago, during the most recent ice age, the Laurentide ice sheet covering much of eastern North America didn't quite reach the Southern Appalachians, which became a sanctuary and mixing ground for all manner of species. For a time, plants from north and south were thrust together like kids at recess sent into the gym when a thunderstorm kicks up. After the storm, they disperse again to their favorite spots on the playground. In the case of the Smokies, the more northerly plants that had fled south during the ice age ascended the mountains, looking for a cooler spot to settle when things warmed up. Thus a hiker on the Appalachian Trail today will find on Mount LeConte and some of the park's other high mountains a forest of spruce and fir, a natural community they will see again a thousand miles later in northern New England, if their legs hold out.

While the park's ecology makes it a mecca for scientific research, it's safe to assume that few visitors, with the exception of an occasional arachnologist, come to see or study the handsome spruce-fir moss spider, a miniscule tarantula that lives only in the park. (The species now teeters on the edge of extinction because air pollution and exotic insects are killing the spruce-fir forest, damaging the spider's mossy hunting grounds.) Rather, the nearly ten million people who enjoy Great Smoky Mountains National Park every year—ironically, mostly in cars—are drawn by its wild grandeur, by the sight of something so different from most Americans' sprawling suburban experience. Here in the midst of a long-settled landscape, a big, wild, beautiful place still exists.

For better or worse, the Smokies are highly accessible, within six hundred miles of half the American population, and gorgeous. (Notwithstanding Gatlinburg, Tennessee, that quintessence of commercialism and eyesore on the park's northern boundary.) The park embodies the paradox facing the National Park Service: how to save extraordinary places both *for* and *from* people. This is the conflict codified in the 1916 legislation that created the National Park Service, and which enjoined it to manage the public lands under its purview to "conserve the scenery and the natural and historic objects and the wildlife therein and to provide for the enjoyment of the same in such manner and by such means as will leave them unimpaired for the enjoyment of future generations." It's a tall order, made all the more difficult by the relative paucity of public funding and respect accorded our national park system, an incongruous neglect, given the parks' tremendous popularity with the American people.

Despite the air pollution and other negative effects of human activity, Great Smoky Mountains National Park remains wildly attractive. The folds and twists of the landscape, the sparkling waters, even the smell—a rich, earthy odor—suggest life afroth with possibility. Each season offers its own pleasures, but on an early summer's day, with the mists still hanging in the valleys and birdsong echoing in the forest canopy, there may be no better place to experience what Horace Kephart called "a real forest, a real wildwood, a real unimproved work of God."

# GRAND TETON NATIONAL PARK
## The Longest Battle

*John D. Rockefeller Jr.*
*(1874–1960)*

*Horace Albright*
*(1890–1987)*

In the beginning, of course, there is *the land*. And then, when people attuned to its beauty and ecology seek to formalize the land's protection, there comes *the fight*. From Alaska's Kenai Fjords to Washington's Olympic Mountains to the Everglades of Florida, a similar story has enfolded. Conservationists propose a national park. Anticonservationists oppose the idea. A battle ensues. When the area in question contains exploitable resources—that is, where there's money to be made—the conflict is likely to be fierce.

So it is ironic that probably the most sustained and rancorous such fight in American history was over country with little marketable timber or minerals. The treasure is the scenery. For decades, partisans clashed over whether Wyoming's Teton Mountains and the valley of Jackson Hole at their base would become a national park. The opposing camps held competing ideologies about private property versus public ownership, local control versus federal management, development versus aesthetic appreciation. When the strife concluded and Grand Teton National Park was established, the preservationists had won a victory for every American and those yet unborn.

For pilgrims to Jackson Hole today, the long-ago dispute is little remembered. What matters is the view. The remarkably flat valley extends north between mountain ranges, the Snake River meandering through its grassy bottomlands. With no foothills to clutter the scene, the Tetons loom to the west. Their jagged summits, rising to more than thirteen thousand feet and dotted with snowfields, are reflected in a series of glacial lakes on the valley floor.

This is the landscape that captivated founding National Park Service director Stephen Mather and his protégé Horace Albright when they first viewed it in 1916. "I had never beheld such scenery," Albright later wrote. "I knew the Sierra Nevada and had climbed Mount Whitney, but here before us were the Alps of America. Mather and I were both flabbergasted, and we agreed that this whole magnificent area ought to be added to Yellowstone National Park." Albright, who later succeeded Mather as director of the Park Service, committed himself to seeing the Tetons preserved.

The notion of expanding Yellowstone south to include the Tetons was first broached in the 1890s, but no action was taken. At the time, only a few dozen settlers occupied the valley named for David Jackson, a mountain man who overwintered there in 1829. The climate was harsh, and the land marginal for agriculture. Its outstanding potential was as a park and wildlife habitat, particularly as winter range for elk. But as more settlers came to the valley, different visions for its future became inevitable. Some cattlemen and business owners stridently opposed federal involvement that might limit livestock grazing or other development.

During the late teens and early 1920s, while serving as the superintendent of Yellowstone, Horace Albright promoted a Park Service solution to the problem of increased development in Jackson Hole. At the time, a group of conservation-minded area residents, largely composed of dude ranchers, were also struggling with how to secure the valley's future, and in 1923 they invited Albright to meet with them at the cabin of local conservationist Maud Noble. The group did not uniformly support national park designation but sought to preserve the valley's frontier ethos, and believed that a recreation area of some sort, in public ownership, was desirable. The gathered conservationists also discussed the need to recruit a conservation buyer, a wealthy individual who would purchase private lands in the valley for future transfer to the Park Service.

Initial efforts to find a philanthropist went nowhere, but eventually the right individual emerged. John D. Rockefeller Jr., son of the Standard Oil tycoon, was already known for park-related giving, having been a key contributor to Acadia (then named Lafayette) National Park in Maine and other natural areas. Rockefeller had first visited Yellowstone as a boy with his family in 1886. In 1924 he brought three of his own sons to see the West. Albright helped arrange accommodations for the party in Yellowstone and directed them south to Jackson Hole for a day, but like other superintendents of national parks on the family's tour, he was under orders not to solicit Mr. Rockefeller.

Two years later, the Rockefeller family again visited Wyoming on summer holiday, and this time no gag order was imposed. Albright escorted Rockefeller and his wife, Abby, through Jackson Hole to see the encroaching development marring its beauty—a tacky dance hall, a burned-out gas station, and an overhead power line that the Forest Service had run on the west side of the road despite Albright's request that it be built to the east, where it would do less damage to the mountain view. Mrs. Rockefeller asked what could be done. At an especially panoramic overlook, as they watched moose feeding and the sun setting behind the mountains, Albright outlined his dream for the area: the Teton Mountains and valley below them as part of the national park system.

Albright soon received a letter from Rockefeller asking him to prepare maps and cost estimates for purchasing private lands in Jackson Hole. That winter, Albright went to New York with the materials; he suggested that roughly fourteen thousand acres at the foot of the mountains might be got for $397,000. Rockefeller was displeased, saying that he had wanted an estimate of the costs involved for an ideal project, not just the lands west of the river. Albright's initial surprise turned to euphoria, and he ordered revised maps and cost estimates prepared.

Rockefeller thereafter committed to the plan, with the direction that his involvement remain anonymous so as not to inflate land values. He endorsed Albright's suggestion that a front company be set up and local agents empowered to begin buying private properties—from willing sellers, at fair prices—in the valley. He entrusted the enterprise to subordinates, and expected it to be quickly completed. Fortunately, Rockefeller and Albright were tenacious park supporters, for more than two decades of continuous struggle lay ahead before the drama would conclude.

During the 1920s, two government agencies, the extraction-minded U.S. Forest Service and the preservation-minded National Park Service, were often at odds over who would manage scenic lands in the public domain. Sometimes overtly and sometimes discreetly, the Forest Service opposed the park campaign for the Tetons, which would transfer national forest land currently under its management to the Park Service. Even as Rockefeller money, channeled through the Snake River Land Company, was securing private properties in the valley, park advocates won a partial victory in 1929, when Congress designated the original Grand Teton National Park.

It was, however, as one historian later characterized it, "a stingy, skimpy, niggardly little park" that achieved only half the conservationists' objective. Those are perhaps overly harsh words for a natural area that covered nearly one hundred thousand acres and encompassed the glorious Teton Range, but the point is valid. The mountains' rugged nature already largely protected them from exploitation, and the new park's boundaries would not prevent sprawling development in the valley below, including near the lakes. The battle for more complete protection continued, with park opponents blocking expansion into the valley for the following fourteen years.

By 1942 the fight had been variously boiling or simmering for decades, with the sentiment of popular opinion in Jackson Hole shifting back and forth over time. John D. Rockefeller Jr. had spent $1 million to purchase thirty-two thousand acres in the valley. He'd spent half as much again paying taxes and upkeep while waiting more than a decade for the government to accept the land as a gift. Park opponents had long vilified him as an arrogant eastern millionaire conspiring with federal bureaucrats to boot hardworking sons of the frontier from their land.

Even patient men have their limits. Rockefeller wrote Interior Secretary Harold Ickes in November 1942, expressing the reluctant conclusion that he "should make permanent disposition of this property before another year has passed." In a subsequent letter to Franklin Roosevelt, Rockefeller informed the president of his intentions regarding Jackson Hole. "Because it is so uniquely beautiful an area," he wrote, "you will understand with what deep regret I am at length abandoning the effort to make it a place of permanent enjoyment for all the people, to which I have devoted myself so assiduously during these many years."

Rockefeller's threat spurred the administration to action. Using powers granted to the president under the 1906 Antiquities Act, in March 1943 Roosevelt designated Jackson Hole National Monument, encompassing both mountain and valley lands.

A furor erupted. The governor of Wyoming vowed to "utilize all police authority at my disposal to exit from the proposed Jackson Hole National Monument any federal official who attempts to assume authority." The state's congressional delegation essentially blocked the National Park Service from receiving appropriations to operate the new monument for three years. The Forest Service reluctantly transferred 130,000 acres under its jurisdiction, but in an act of spite, the ranger station at Jackson Lake was gutted. However, the boldest attempts at legislative rollback—to abolish the monument and even repeal the Antiquities Act—failed.

As time passed, opposition dissipated. Prosperity tended to heal old wounds, and within a few years even some strident park opponents admitted they had been wrong. In 1949, the Rockefeller lands were formally deeded to the government, and the following year Wyoming senator Joseph O'Mahoney introduced a bill in Congress to upgrade the monument to national park status. President Harry Truman signed the law establishing the present 310,000-acre Grand Teton National Park in September 1950.

When one stands in the Snake River with fly rod in hand, or sits near its banks on a warm summer's day, the eye naturally rises to the wall of chiseled granite looming above the valley. In the high country, a solitary wolverine traverses talus slopes on its daily rambles. Grizzly and black bears look for lunch. Higher still, climbers seek the mountain summits. Far below them, bison, pronghorn, and elk forage on the sagebrush flats. Horace Albright, John D. Rockefeller Jr., and countless other visitors have come under the spell of this landscape. Can anyone today imagine a better use for the Teton country than as a national park?

In hindsight it is surprising that a remote, sparsely settled Wyoming valley—at least one with no gold—could have triggered a conflict so contentious, one that engaged not just area residents but government agencies, national conservation groups, America's preeminent philanthropist, and politicians ranging from local officials to the president of the United States. Perhaps that is a testament to just how enchanting the land is, how we mortal men and women are held in thrall when gazing upon those craggy peaks, which even still are rising into the western sky.

1956

# VIRGIN ISLANDS NATIONAL PARK
## Paradise Found

*Laurance S. Rockefeller*
*(1910–2004)*

Any given day in February, people wake up in places like Buffalo and Minneapolis, look out their windows, and begin thinking about a Caribbean holiday. They liberate their cars fromsnowbanks. Driving to work, if the roads aren't white-knuckle icy, they may again escape into a reverie in which snow becomes white sand beaches and howling wind is merely the rustle of palm fronds in a gentle ocean breeze. Whether they know it or not, the poor frozen souls are dreaming of Virgin Islands National Park.

The fact that paradise is an actual place, in a U.S. territory (no passport required!) and easily accessible from the East's major cities, is both wonderful and problematic. Modest in size but immodestly lovely, Virgin Islands National Park on the Caribbean island of St. John is like heaven but far easier to get to. Therein lies its curse. The National Park Service's task of accommodating visitors while preserving the integrity of such a small and biologically rich place is an ongoing challenge.

The park covers roughly 7,000 acres on St. John and about 5,600 acres of ocean bottom adjacent to the island. During one recent year it attracted 770,000 visitors. Gargantuan cruise ships steam into port at nearby St. Thomas, and many of the disembarking passengers catch the ferry to St. John, swelling the island's tiny population. All of this is to say that being a tropical heaven in an age when travel is easy and affordable is not all fun in the sun. That there exists a Virgin Islands National Park at all—to dream about, to visit, and to protect from ourselves— is itself a small miracle. Unlike neighboring St. Thomas and St. Croix, most of St. John is relatively wild, and permanently protected from development because of the park. Ubiquitous commercialism on other Caribbean islands gives a good idea of what St. John's fate would have been had not Laurance S. Rockefeller quietly purchased private land on the sleepy island in the early 1950s and later donated it to the American people.

Laurance Rockefeller was born to a life of privilege, wealth, and responsibility. His family nameplate, among the nation's most prominent, conferred on him and his siblings certain opportunities for influence, but also daunting standards for achievement. He was grandson to John D. Rockefeller, the Standard Oil tycoon, and the son of John D. Rockefeller Jr., a pious gentleman of Victorian manner who spent a lifetime engaged in systematic charitable giving to conservation, historic preservation, and educational causes. Laurance and his siblings were steeped in the family philanthropic tradition and encouraged to be socially useful. While his brothers Nelson and Winthrop would shine in politics, Laurance took, as his biographer Robin Winks has written, a "quieter path" in life, a path that led to places of great natural beauty saved for all Americans, for all time.

A 1924 photo depicts John D. Rockefeller Jr. with three of his five sons, Laurance, Nelson, and John D. III, while visiting national parks in the West. Bedecked in proper riding attire, the four Rockefellers stand in front of a horse, pine boughs in the background. A teenage Nelson, the future governor and vice president, displays the open posture and smile of a natural politician. Laurance, then fourteen, is unsmiling, his eyes in shadow from a cap pulled low; he stands slightly behind his brothers, with his father's hand resting on his shoulder. One might read overly much into such a picture, what it portends about the decades ahead, but there is the suggestion that Laurance would be the reserved Rockefeller, and the one anointed to continue the family conservation legacy.

*I profoundly feel that the art of living is the art of giving. You're fulfilled in the moment of giving, of doing something beyond yourself. That's the moment of truth.*
—Laurance S. Rockefeller

That summer adventure, one of three western vacations Laurance took with his father and various siblings during boyhood, introduced him to the wonders of Mesa Verde, Yellowstone, and Glacier national parks. It was a formative trip for Laurance and auspicious for the American conservation movement, for it marked the first meeting between John D. Rockefeller Jr. and future National Park Service director Horace Albright, who was then Yellowstone's superintendent. Rockefeller and Albright's lifelong collaboration advanced numerous conservation projects, and Albright later became a mentor to Laurance. The trip also was the Rockefellers' first exposure to the Tetons, a landscape that father and son would work the rest of their lives to preserve.

Prior to the 1924 trip, Laurance had done yardwork to earn money for a camera. He became the party's documentary photographer, an avocation that continued into adulthood and sharpened his eye for landscapes. Unlike many men of his time and social class who came to love wild country through hunting or fishing, Laurance's developing conservation ethic was influenced by his childhood experiences in nature and by the less extractive outdoor recreation he pursued as a young man—horsemanship, sailing, and photography. His studies in moral philosophy at Princeton deepened his thinking about the relationship between people and land.

While less often in the public eye than his brothers, Laurance became known in adulthood as a pioneering venture capitalist, for developing vacation hotels in beautiful settings, and for medical- and nature-related philanthropy. Rockefeller funded conservation initiatives through various foundations and inculcated a passion for land protection in his own children. He was, by any standard, an influential and effective advocate for preserving America's natural heritage, although not immune from criticism, for he generally steered a middle course between the favored policy positions of industry and environmentalists.

Beginning in the 1940s, he and his wife, Mary French Rockefeller, began exploring the Caribbean islands in their boat *Dauntless*. When they visited St. John in 1952, they found the sparsely populated island enchanting. Rockefeller began buying property with a dual intent. In Caneel Bay he developed a resort hotel amid the ruins of a former sugar plantation, a relict of the island's colonial history as part of the Dutch West Indies. (The United States had purchased St. Thomas, St. Croix, and St. John from Denmark for $25 million during World War I to preclude a German submarine base in the region, and to help secure the newly opened Panama Canal.) Laurance also amassed roughly five thousand acres on St. John, which became the initial land base of a new Virgin Islands National Park. He used the nonprofit entity created by his father to purchase private lands for addition to Grand Teton National Park in similar fashion here, to buy and hold lands on St. John for eventual transfer to the National Park Service.

An internal park service document from the 1930s had proposed a national park or monument be created on St. John, some conservationists supported the idea, but little progress occurred until Laurance Rockefeller entered the scene. In recognizing a good conservation opportunity and turning it into reality, it might be said that Laurance had fully become his father's son. With Laurance and Mary Rockefeller present, Virgin Islands National Park was dedicated in 1956, on the same day that the Caneel Bay resort opened for business.

After the Virgin Islands success, Rockefeller helped expand Redwood National Park in California and Haleakala National Park in Hawaii, and donated his home and land in Vermont to become Marsh-Billings-Rockefeller National Historical Park. He supported extensive land conservation in New York's Hudson River valley, chaired a presidential commission on outdoor recreation, and served on dozens of organization boards and committees. His proposal for a national park in the Adirondacks was unsuccessful, and possibly a deft political ploy, but it helped generate political support during his brother's governorship for a new regulatory agency that would better protect the Adirondack State Park.

In the 1990s, a half century after his father purchased and donated private lands in the Jackson Hole valley and donated them for addition to Grand Teton National Park, an elderly Laurance Rockefeller requested a meeting with then–interior secretary Bruce Babbitt. "He walked into my office," Babbitt recalls, "pulled out a sheaf of papers from an old leather satchel, and asked me to read a particular paragraph." Babbitt, who had a deep affection for the national park system he oversaw, was being lobbied by commercial interests to allow a proposed runway expansion at Jackson Hole Airport that would have further compromised the park. Laurance Rockefeller pointed to the reversion clause in the document that accompanied the original gift; it stipulated that if the government ever wanted to give away park land donated by the Rockefeller family for commercial development, the entire gift could be rescinded. Babbitt was delighted. "Well, that settled that," he says.

The first humans to reach St. John came in dugout canoes paddled from South America. Today people cruise by on gaudy floating casinos. In between came a rich history, much of it ugly for people and for nature, the darkest times being the plantation era when slaves toiled in the sun, clearing the native vegetation to make room for sugar cane. Despite that land use history and the island's small area, it and the nearby ocean offer remarkable diversity—from moist tropical forests where West Indian locust, sandbox, and hog plum trees grow, to drier forests characterized by acacia, black mampoo, and the most excellently named gumbo-limbo trees. Ram Head, a dry, windy peninsula on the island's southern shoreline, supports no trees at all, only desertlike scrub, including cacti and century plants. Offshore are coral reefs where the bizarrely beautiful staghorn, brain, elkhorn, and other corals provide refuge to a multitude of colorful fish.

If the massive ships anchored in Cruz Bay symbolize the external threats to Virgin Islands National Park, perhaps its coral reefs best represent what is at risk. Coral reefs are global hotspots of biological diversity, and many Caribbean reefs, like others around the world, are dying. A relatively narrow range of conditions—clear waters, warm temperatures, and an absence of pollution—is crucial to sustain the reef-building colonial animals. Recent evidence suggests that diseases brought in on Saharan Desert dust particles blown across the Atlantic are partly to blame for coral declines in the Caribbean. It's yet another example of ecology's central insight: everything is connected.

Walking along the beach at Cinnamon Bay, one is reminded of these connections, for the sandy white material between one's toes is primarily composed of minute particles of polished coral, produced both by wave action and by the digestive systems of parrotfish. The fish eat algae off coral formations, grind the coral into powder, and then expel it. A visitor snorkeling among the coral reefs may understand intellectually that Laurance Rockefeller's gift to the National Park System has ecological value of global import, but the experiential value of Virgin Islands National Park is equally priceless. So too, is the park's value as psychic balm, for somewhere, perhaps in Buffalo or Minneapolis, someone is comforted by the notion that paradise is out there, a wild green island in a warm blue sea.

# MCCORMICK WILDERNESS
## Rewilding White Deer Lake

*Gordon McCormick*
*(1895–1967)*

Two scenes, separated by time:

*A summer afternoon in 1910, deep in the woods of Michigan's Upper Peninsula.* Two woolen-clad gentlemen emerge from the forest into a lakefront clearing where sits a compound of rustic buildings. The hikers carry canvas knapsacks and wear lace-up boots. One, in the fashion of the day, sports a bow tie. Passing the kitchen building, from whence the aroma of dinner preparation emanates, they descend to the lake and stride onto a small muscle-powered ferry, attached via lines to a flywheel on shore and another on an island some sixty yards out. Pulling on the rope, they quickly cross over. On the island each man retires to his half of the imposing two-story log structure with a massive stone chimney. Once freshened up and in dinner jackets, they join their guests on the raft's return trip to the mainland for a sumptuous meal. Although they might refer to it as the "rough camp," Cyrus McCormick and Cyrus Bentley's White Deer Lake wilderness retreat is an oasis of woodsy opulence where they enjoy solitude and socializing. Through the years, a staff of up to two dozen—cooks, gardeners, butlers, carpenters, even a resident architect for a time—keeps the remote camp running, providing every possible comfort for guests, who include friends, family members, and some of the era's leading business tycoons.

*A summer afternoon ninety-five years later.* A lone hiker enters the same clearing and looks across to the island, which, in the soft light and drizzle resembles a Thomas Cole painting. She is kept dry by a high-tech waterproof jacket and carries a nylon backpack filled with camping gear. From the trailhead, she has walked several miles along a footpath that was once the access road to the McCormick camp. Where the buildings stood, the remnants of a few foundations are visible, cracked stone and concrete giving way to ferns and trees. No structures remain. The island is a dark silhouette against a gray horizon. The slate paths that once connected cabins are now covered in moss carpeting. The soft rustle of wind in conifer branches still drifts in the air but no longer blends with music from Cyrus Bentley's Victrola. This day it merely serves as background to a hermit thrush, whose flutelike song echoes through the forest. There will be no French wine poured into crystal this evening, no gay laughter mixing with birdsong and lapping waters. As the hiker sets off down the trail to find a campsite here in the McCormick Wilderness Area, a cow moose, unseen, leads her calf into the lake shallows to feed.

There can be something melancholy about a place like this, where natural processes are gradually erasing signs of human history on the landscape. It can make a person feel small and our works ephemeral. Conversely, it is also a helpful check on the arrogance of humanism, a reminder that our species' perceived hegemony over the Earth is, at least in the long run, illusory. Many recovering wilderness areas of the eastern United States are hopeful examples of nature reclaiming dominion over a particular place, of human actions and natural processes working together to rewild the landscape. This is true of the McCormick Wilderness—nearly seventeen thousand acres of northern Michigan woodlands that weathered an onslaught of logging in the 1800s, received meticulous tending by the McCormick family during much of the twentieth century, was given to the American people in 1967, and now enjoys permanent protection as part of the National Wilderness Preservation System.

Cyrus Hall McCormick II was the eldest son of the man who invented the first mass-produced mechanical reaper, an innovation that changed the world. When his father died in 1884, McCormick, then in his twenties, assumed the presidency of the McCormick Company.

*A wilderness, in contrast with those areas where man and his works dominate the landscape, is hereby recognized as an area where the earth and its community of life are untrammeled by man, where man himself is a visitor who does not remain.*

—The Wilderness Act of 1964

In the following decades he became one of the nation's foremost industrialists. In 1902, financier J. P. Morgan helped orchestrate a merger among five prominent farm equipment manufacturers. The McCormick Company, the Deering Company, and other former competitors combined to form the International Harvester Company, with Cyrus McCormick as president. A young Chicago attorney, Cyrus Bentley, handled much of the associated legal work. McCormick and Bentley became friends and hiking partners.

Just as affluent men from eastern cities escaped to the Adirondacks and Maine to hunt and fish, it was common for Midwesterners of Bentley and McCormick's social class to establish game clubs in northern Michigan and Wisconsin. The two gentlemen became members of the exclusive Huron Mountain Club on Lake Superior but also formed a partnership and in 1904 began purchasing property twenty-five miles south for their own wilderness retreat. Through the decades and many transactions, the landholdings around their White Deer Lake camp expanded, and under Cyrus Bentley's direction, a trail between the two private enclaves was flagged and maintained.

Bentley was punctilious, which manifested itself not only in the strict accounting demands he placed on White Deer Lake's staff (detailed daily reports on each worker, expenses tracked to the penny), but in the exacting standard he insisted upon for hiking trails. Woodland paths were to be smoothed, wet spots filled in, and cleared to a width where a hiker with open umbrella would not be annoyed by tree branches. Perhaps the qualities one seeks in a corporate attorney are not precisely the same one wants in a camping companion. In any case, McCormick and Bentley spent less time together as the years passed, having an informal arrangement wherein each partner enjoyed full run of White Deer Lake during alternate summer months. The partnership was dissolved in 1927, and Bentley's personal items, including a grand piano, were shipped back to Chicago. Around this time, Cyrus McCormick banned deer hunting on the property, and thereafter the expansive woodlands were a sanctuary for his family, their guests, the camp staff, and the wild creatures of the northwoods.

Kathleen Tonkin Cooley, daughter of White Deer Lake's longtime superintendent, remembers Cyrus McCormick II as an unpretentious "kindly gentleman" whom his son Gordon called "Popsy." When Cyrus died in 1936, Kathleen's father, Ted Tonkin, wrote in his journal that "his kindness and understanding was unsurpassed, and this beautiful place will always be a reminder of his love for the finer and nobler things of life."

Gordon McCormick, who had grown up tramping the woods of the White Deer Lake property, inherited both the land and his father's appreciation for wild forests. Gordon was a Princeton-trained architect who, because of his family wealth, never needed to hold a job. In the years prior to World War II, Gordon had workmen expanding and improving the camp—renovating the main cabin, constructing a new boathouse, even building an architecturally elegant $50,000 woodshed. He also continued buying land, more than doubling the estate's acreage during his lifetime.

Gordon McCormick was a large man with a large personality who relished fine food and drink. While Prohibition did not prevent intoxicating libations from being available at White Deer Lake (Cyrus Bentley's personal liquor cabinet was raided by thieves in 1927), when the ban ended, Gordon reacted positively: "As Repeal is really here it might be well for the Camp Account to include enough stimulant for emergencies—these emergencies coming no oftener than Cocktail Hour every afternoon!" Gordon's generous spirit was often directed at the workers who tended White Deer Lake, including the Tonkins. When Kathleen Tonkin went off to business college

in Chicago, she found that McCormick had established a bank account in her name to help with education expenses.

Gordon didn't marry until late in life, had no children, and as he aged began thinking about what would become of White Deer Lake. Like his father, Gordon wanted the land to remain as untouched as possible. Kathleen Tonkin's brother Cecil, by then grown up and a professional forester, suggested that Gordon visit the U.S. Forest Service research laboratory in Wisconsin, which he did, and was apparently impressed by its forest research program. After considering various possibilities, Gordon decided that upon his death, the land would be given to the Forest Service. As a tribute to his father, it would become the Cyrus H. McCormick Experimental Forest.

Gordon McCormick died in 1967, and as he intended, the land came into public ownership as part of Michigan's Ottawa National Forest. The area was open for recreation and research, but unlike most acreage administered by the Forest Service, was off-limits to commercial logging. The buildings began to decay, were vandalized, and then were dismantled in the early 1980s, setting the stage for the former McCormick family retreat's becoming a wilderness area in 1987.

It's been said that only God and Congress can create a wilderness. Any pious person will certainly ascribe greater powers to the former, but the entity also deserves its due. Under the Wilderness Act of 1964, Congress may designate as "wilderness areas" tracts of generally wild, roadless country on federal public land managed by the Forest Service, National Park Service, Fish and Wildlife Service, or Bureau of Land Management. Wilderness designation permanently preserves these areas for wildlife habitat and quiet recreation, and precludes future development, logging, and motorized uses. More than seven hundred separate units currently make up the National Wilderness Preservation System, in total giving some 107 million acres of federal public land this highest level of legal protection.

The primary author of the Wilderness Act, Howard Zahniser, was a Pennsylvania native. As an easterner, and particularly from his experience in New York's Adirondack Park, where the forests had been recovering since the 1800s, he understood that wilderness could grow as well as shrink. In defining wilderness areas as places "where the earth and its community of life are untrammeled by man," Zahniser consciously used language applicable to untouched western lands and eastern landscapes in the process of rewilding. Untrammeled lands are not necessarily pristine, but are free to follow their own course, not bent and shaped to fit human desires. Consistent with the etymological roots of the word *wilderness*, they are self-willed lands.

With dozens of lakes, streams, and muskegs, the headwaters of four rivers, and robust wildlife populations, the McCormick tract is a fitting addition to the wilderness system. For nearly a century, its twenty-seven square miles of rugged forest have rarely seen a logger's ax. Old-growth pines watch over the lakes. The hiking trail that Cyrus Bentley cut from White Deer Lake to the Huron Mountain Club is long since abandoned, impassable save to moose and intrepid bushwhackers. Because of Gordon McCormick's gift, here is a place open to all Americans ready to experience the values that wilderness offers: solitude, primitive recreation, and spiritual renewal. Beyond these human values, though, the McCormick Wilderness offers a more fundamental gift to our fellow members in the land community—for loons and lichen, wolves and warblers, and innumerable other wild creatures—it is, simply, *home*.

# APPLETON-WHITTELL RESEARCH RANCH
## A World of Good Grass

*Ariel Appleton (1918–2004)*

The story of how the West was won, or lost, depending on one's perspective, has long been a mainstay of popular entertainment, but the superficially heroic depictions in film and fiction generally leave out a central character—the land. Sure, rugged mountains and rolling grasslands are there behind John Wayne, but only as back-drop to human conflict and resolution. The bigger drama is the one that produced the scenery. It played out over millions of years as geological processes raised and leveled mountains, seas formed and drained, glaciers advanced and retreated. Always, always, nature adapted, filling the landscape with plants and animals fitted to the terrain. On a typical day twenty thousand years ago, for instance, a visitor to the North American West would have seen sun and sky stretching over a cast of dire wolves, saber-toothed tigers, mastodons, ground sloths, and other large mammals whose diversity and abundance rivaled Africa's Serengeti.

Alive only in the mind's eye of a few paleoecologists, that Wild West is even more lost to us than the latter-day one of thundering bison herds and rivers thick with salmon. We have mammoth bones and Anasazi potsherds to help us enter its history, but our popular conception of the West usually focuses not on extinct creatures or cultures, but on that mythical embodiment of American manhood, the cowboy. From Buffalo Bill Cody's Wild West Show to the Marlboro Man, marketers have employed the cowboy persona to sell their wares, and no cultural icon is more deeply entwined with our national identity.

There could hardly be a more archetypal cowboy landscape than the Sonoita Plain (sometimes called the Sonoita Valley), a high-elevation grassland dotted with trees in southeastern Arizona, twenty miles north of the Mexican border. Think of the classic 1948 movie *Red River*, with John Wayne and Montgomery Clift. A wagon train of pioneers heading for California appears in the film's opening frame, the flat grasslands stretching away, rimmed by mountains. That's the Sonoita Plain, where much of the film was shot. The Hollywood depiction used the valley as a stand-in for Texas, but the scene communicates a valuable lesson about the region's land use history: livestock grazing is a recent influence here. "It's good land, good grass for beef," says John Wayne early in the movie, as he leaves the group with his bull and cow to go start a great herd, which he does after stealing land from its Mexican owner.

From the die-off of the Pleistocene's large mammals around thirteen thousand years ago (likely due to killing by human beings, newly arrived on the continent) until Spanish explorer Francisco Coronado's 1540 expedition introduced cattle and horses, the Sonoita Plain had been grazed by deer, pronghorn, and small mammals but was generally without big herds of grazing animals. The war against Mexico in the 1840s and against Native American nations in subsequent decades opened the area to Anglo settlement; by the 1880s cattle ranching became the dominant industry in the valley. A multiyear drought the following decade killed off most of the livestock. Thousands of starving cows ate everything in sight, with dire consequences for the valley's native plants and wildlife.

Even with the constraints that climate imposes on this arid land, ranching has remained the predominant land use on the Sonoita Plain just as it has in most of the American West, where livestock grazing occurs on an estimated five hundred million acres of public and private land. The cow is, of course, an introduced domestic animal whose wild progenitor, the aurochs, evolved in moist European woodlands. Cattle are prone to staying near water, defecating, destroying streamside vegetation, and causing erosion. Their introduction and pervasive presence in North America was essentially a vast, uncontrolled experiment. Practically no place was spared from the influence of livestock grazing, and very few large areas currently exclude domestic animals.

So it is an anomaly that in the heart of the Sonoita Plain, there is an expansive block of land where no cattle roam, and haven't for decades. No horses, sheep, or goats, either. And even as local ranches have begun growing less beef and more ranchettes, this land has remained wild—regained wildness, even—reversing the usual trajectory of land health in our time. The 7,800-acre Appleton-Whittell Research Ranch, which perhaps should be called an "unranch," is home to javelina and badgers, bunchgrass lizards and Mojave rattlesnakes, grasshopper sparrows and prairie falcons, and many other creatures that flourish amid its waving grass. That grass, including some nineteen perennial species with evocative names like Arizona cottontop, Texas beardgrass, wolftail, and tanglehead, forms the foundation of the research ranch's natural communities. From diminutive sod-grasses to big sacaton—a bunchgrass that may grow as high as an elephant's eye (*Oklahoma* was also filmed nearby)—it is a world of good grass. Some creatures eat it. Some eat the creatures that eat it. Some hide in it, trying not to be eaten. And none of it is being transformed into beefsteak.

Beefsteak is, however, what Francis Henry Appleton III (Frank) and Ariel Appleton had aimed to produce when they came to Arizona, initially to a farm outside Tucson, and then in the late 1950s to the Sonoita Plain, where they consolidated two smaller properties. For the next decade their ranch was managed to produce high-quality Hereford breeding stock. The couple—she of a prominent Santa Barbara family and relative of Gifford Pinchot, Teddy Roosevelt's primary conservation advisor; he a Harvard grad and navy pilot in World War II—was socially progressive. Ariel served as first president of the Tucson chapter of Planned Parenthood. When President John F. Kennedy launched the Peace Corps, the Appletons signed on as directors of the first delegation of volunteers to Costa Rica. They served there from 1962 to 1964, and when President Kennedy visited the country, he reminded Frank that they'd sat across the room from each other at grammar school in Massachusetts.

After returning home to Arizona, the Appletons' concern deepened about the perils of exceeding Earth's carrying capacity. "More and more we have come to realize that there is a great gap in understanding what is helpful and what is harmful to land," Ariel explained to a reporter. One year in the mid-1960s, their agricultural operations netted just $1,200. The experience suggested that environmentally sensitive ranching on the Sonoita Plain could not be done profitably. They made a bold choice. The cows would go. In 1969, with the approval of their children, who were about to lose a good bit of their inheritance, the Appletons established a nonprofit foundation, began transferring the ranch property to it, and made a $100,000 initial gift to launch its operations.

Forevermore the land was to grow things wild and free, including human knowledge. The ranch would be a wildlife sanctuary and field station where scientists could study a grassland ecosystem absent livestock grazing, a place to watch how the land reacts once unshackled from human control. "Understanding how the Research Ranch functions should help us understand the effects of all sorts of land use," Ariel wrote. "We cannot understand the consequences of our efforts to manage this land until we know how it manages itself."

In 1980, the research ranch's long-term stewardship was assured when the National Audubon Society added the property to its sanctuary system, and a $1 million gift from the Whittell Trust endowed its future operations. Several decades of data have now been collected on the land's ecological recovery. Much of the research was overseen by ecologists Carl and Jane Bock, and the findings are described in their book *The View from Bald Hill*. While that elegant work of scientific reportage is nuanced, a central conclusion emerges: with the removal of livestock, the diversity of life on the ranch has flourished.

Deeply connected to the land, Ariel was divorced from Frank in the 1970s but stayed on the ranch at least seasonally until health concerns compelled a permanent return to California near the end of her life. Despite having no formal training as a scientist, she became an expert on the Bolson tortoise, an endangered species of desert reptile that once ranged into the American Southwest but whose only wild population now persists, barely, in Mexico. She published articles in the *Proceedings of the Desert Tortoise Council*, built incubators, and pioneered a successful captive breeding program for the species at the research ranch. "She had a sixth sense about animals," recalls Jane Bock, who became close friends with Ariel over the years. "My mother would have been a medicine woman in another culture," says Bryce Appleton, the oldest of Frank and Ariel's four children. A dozen years older than her only sibling, Ariel had grown up with a menagerie in the semiwilds of Hope Ranch in Santa Barbara. "Her friends were animals," Bryce says. "She was truly a child of nature and instilled that in all of us."

Ariel Appleton's ultimate goal—that "with responsible attitudes of stewardship, most certainly without the arrogance of dominion, we may yet find a way to live in brotherhood with all the forms of life that earth sustains"—still seems a distant mountain to reach, with many rivers and canyons to negotiate in the intervening miles. About the research ranch she once wrote, "Research, conservation, and education were our initial purposes. . . . It was originally intended that this land serve as an ecological control area." These nearer landmarks have been achieved, possibly more fully than she and Frank ever imagined. The research ranch's most direct benefit to wildlife is as refuge, a sanctuary from a society hell-bent on destroying natural habitat, but for people engaged in the larger conversation about preserving the American West's biological diversity, the ranch's value as a reference site without livestock is inestimable. The ongoing research conducted here helps inform that conversation, which, particularly when focused on public lands livestock grazing, is often more like a brawl. Negotiating a peace treaty between conservationists and livestock producers is not ostensibly part of the research ranch's mission, but its work perhaps offers a scientific and nonpartisan way to help turn that confrontational rhetoric back toward constructive conversation, one that begins with an understanding of land health.

Ironically, when Frank and Ariel Appleton made the remarkable decision to give their land back to nature, they were acting as contrarians in the best mythic tradition of the West. In a time and place where any land not put to "productive" (read: profit-making) use was thought to be wasted, they left the safe wagon train of popular convention and, like John Wayne, set off alone into uncharted territory. Choosing to grow wild creatures and wild thinking instead of beef surely displayed inner fortitude and an independent streak—typical, one might even say, of the cowboy way.

1969

# FRANCIS BEIDLER FOREST SANCTUARY
## The Swamp Primeval

*Norman Brunswig*

Light filters through the forest canopy, strikes dark water, and conjures an illusion: the canoe seems to float between massive cypress trees and their inverted reflection. The air is "close"—a genteel southern euphemism for damned hot and sticky. But what would one expect? It's springtime in a swamp. More specifically, in South Carolina's Four Holes Swamp, a glorious sixty-mile-long forested wetland that drains ever so slowly toward the Edisto River on its way to the Atlantic.

The tea-colored water isn't muddy, just stained from the organic material and tannins leached from tree bark. Four Holes Swamp is typical of the "blackwater" stream systems that once meandered over vast reaches of the southeastern United States' coastal plain. It's atypical in that at least some of the original forest here has survived. Francis Beidler Forest, a sanctuary administered by the National Audubon Society, now protects twenty-three square miles of the swamp. The heart of the preserve is roughly 1,700 acres of virgin baldcypress and tupelo gum, the largest pristine example of that forest type left in the world.

Beidler Forest is a kind of time-travel portal, offering a glimpse of the landscape that greeted European settlers in the New World. When botanist William Bartram explored the region in the 1770s, he waxed eloquent about a venerable cypress. "We are struck with a kind of awe," he wrote, "at beholding the stateliness of the trunk, lifting its cumbrous top towards the skies, and casting a wide shade upon the ground, as a dark intervening cloud, which, for a time, precludes the rays of the sun. The delicacy of its colour, and texture of its leaves, exceed every thing in vegetation." The "streamers of long moss that hang from the lofty limbs and float in the winds" added "to the magnificence of their appearance." Bartram also noted the distinctive flaring buttresses of the cypress trees, and the odd "knees" of their root mass, which poke above the water like conical wooden stalagmites.

Unfortunately, Bartram's enthusiasm for the continent's natural diversity, even as manifest in wet and boggy regions, was uncommon for the time. American attitudes toward wetlands were generally negative. Swamps were to be avoided, drained, logged off, and occasionally hidden in—as South Carolina's legendary "Swamp Fox," General Francis Marion, did between leading guerrilla attacks on the British during the Revolutionary War. Few nature lovers took to the swamps, but plenty of lumbermen did. Several species common to bottomland forests offered rot-resistant lumber, but the heartwood of mature cypress was especially useful. Marketing by the Southern Cypress Manufacturers Association helped the industry boom in the late nineteenth century, and by 1913 more than a billion board feet of timber had been milled from cypress logs floated out of places like Four Holes Swamp.

One of the largest timberland owners in the South Carolina Low Country was Chicago businessman Francis Beidler, whose Santee River Cypress Company began buying up property in the late 1800s. By 1905 the company had expansive landholdings, but accessing much of the area was difficult. After a decade or so, most logging was suspended. Beidler was a committed conservationist who'd visited Yellowstone shortly after it was designated the world's first national park. He was keenly interested in the scientific forestry principles then being advanced in Europe, and being promoted in the United States by Gifford Pinchot, first chief of the Forest Service. Beidler apparently made a decision not to log the primeval forest in Four

*Dick Pough and the Goodhill Foundation grant catalyzed the second big spurt of growth that put this place on the map, and inspired me to go further. It just changed the way I thought about our capacity to build the preserve.*

—Norman Brunswig

Holes Swamp. The ancient tupelo gum (also called "swamp tupelo") and baldcypress trees remained standing.

After Beidler's death in 1924, his heirs controlled the land. However, during the Great Depression of the 1930s, several state politicians, including a young Strom Thurmond, successfully lobbied the Roosevelt administration to support a hydroelectric project north of Four Holes Swamp to link and impound the Congaree, Santee, and Cooper rivers, creating two giant reservoirs now known as Lakes Marion and Moultrie. The largest landowner in the Santee and Congaree swamps was the Beidler family, and when the government sought to seize the land through eminent domain, Beidler's son, Francis Beidler II, opposed the condemnation. "He fought this thing hammer and tongs—and lost," says Norman Brunswig, executive director of Audubon South Carolina. "So sixty thousand acres of his land, much of it virgin forest, was flooded, the trees cut down, chained to the bottom to keep them from floating into the turbines, burned up in piles. It was horrific. Beidler was so heartbroken and angry from that experience that he put his remaining South Carolina holdings in the hands of a lumber company for maintenance, went back to Chicago, and never came back to the state."

For several decades, the Beidler family turned its attention to other business, and little was done with its timberlands. In the 1960s, however, renewed logging on the Beidler property attracted the attention of local conservationists and the National Audubon Society, which had successfully established the Corkscrew Swamp Sanctuary in Florida the previous decade. That initiative saved the South's other best example of unlogged cypress forest and a vital rookery for wading birds, thanks to the Lee Tidewater Cypress Company, John D. Rockefeller Jr., Theodore Edison (youngest son of the inventor), and bird lovers from around the country.

To establish Francis Beidler Forest in 1969, the Audubon Society launched a similar campaign and, in cooperation with the Nature Conservancy, raised roughly $1.5 million to purchase 3,415 acres in Four Holes Swamp from the Beidler family. Some funding for the sanctuary came from an improbable source—the bequest of a flamboyant California millionaire with a penchant for fast cars, beautiful women, and exotic animals.

George Whittell Jr. was born into one of San Francisco's most affluent families in the 1880s. Rebellious as a youth, at various times he ran off and joined the circus, eloped with a showgirl (a marriage his parents had annulled), married a movie actress, and drove an ambulance for the Italian army before America entered World War I. Later, after settling into high society, he became a notorious playboy, bought forty thousand acres at Lake Tahoe, built a chateau there, commissioned the sleekest speedboat on that or any other lake, and kept a pet lion as his constant companion. Like his poker buddy Howard Hughes, Whittell became a recluse in his older years. When he died in 1969, he left $50 million, mostly to animal welfare and conservation groups. The National Audubon Society used its share of the windfall from the Whittell Trust to expand and support its system of nature sanctuaries across the United States, including Francis Beidler Forest.

Deep in the swamp, the world is hushed. An alligator lolls in the water. A yellow-crowned night-heron roosts in the trees, waiting for cover of darkness to forage. Life appears to move slowly, but these periods of tranquility are sometimes interrupted by natural disturbances, a hurricane or flood that reshapes the landscape temporarily, before the regular tempo of seasonal change in the swamp resumes.

Similarly, the institutional life of Francis Beidler Forest includes the long, slow process of winning hearts and minds for nature, punctuated by periodic pulses of growth in reaction to threats or opportunities. The preserve has expanded to nearly fifteen thousand acres as of 2005, and Audubon scientists have mapped a comprehensive design for assuring the Four Holes Swamp's ecological integrity through strategic additions to the sanctuary and conservation easements in the larger watershed. (Conservation easements are voluntary deed restrictions on private property, negotiated by a landowner and qualifying agency, that restrict certain land uses and thereby ensure perpetual conservation.)

"At a couple of critical times, we made quantum leaps," says Norm Brunswig, who was hired on as sanctuary manager fresh out of grad school in 1973 and has overseen Beidler Forest's growth ever since. "We almost doubled in size in the mid-1980s with a major campaign to fill in conservation gaps in the floodplain," he says. Dick Pough, a former Audubon staffer and cofounder of the Nature Conservancy, helped secure a $750,000 matching grant for Beidler Forest from the Goodhill Foundation, the charitable trust established to disperse the assets of the late 3M Company heiress Katharine Ordway. Norm Brunswig got so revved up meeting the match that he shot right past the original fundraising target. With $2 million to spend, he brokered a deal to purchase a large tract of the swamp owned by a timber company and established an internal fund for future land acquisition.

A second pulse of growth occurred in 1997, when a local cement manufacturer sought a permit to expand its operations. State regulators allowed the project to proceed but required mitigation; the company purchased and donated 4,000 acres to the sanctuary. In 2005, another 1,600 acres were acquired, helping bridge the gap between Beidler Forest's two main blocks of protected habitat.

Many people and institutions have supported this work, but Norm Brunswig's central role in the expanding conservation success at Four Holes Swamp is clear. Like most skillful fundraisers, though, he tends to deflect the credit to others, suggesting that it's "way easier to get money to buy land than to help manage it." On the latter point, Francis Beidler III and his family have been generous supporters since the sanctuary's birth. "The Beidlers' ongoing role in making the effort successful can't be overstated," says Brunswig.

The vibrant educational programs, ongoing research and monitoring, and engagement with local people have made Francis Beidler Forest a valuable community asset. That value is visible most directly in the innumerable creatures who call it home, and in the multitudes of visitors who stroll the boardwalk through the swamp, learning about its ecology. Less visible is the continually expanding database that contains more than twenty-five years of information on the swamp's hydrology, water quality, and wildlife.

At Beidler Forest one can gaze upon cypress trees that emerged from the muck more than a thousand years ago. These quiet sentinels standing over dark water are the wild legacy of an eclectic stream of conservationists, including a nineteenth-century timber baron who spared the trees, an eccentric playboy whose bequest helped buy the land, a conservation matchmaker who secured a crucial grant, and local activists who fought a proposed stock car racetrack near the preserve. Add to these assets a sanctuary manager with vision, a knack for fundraising, and a powerful commitment to place, and the stars aligned to save the swamp primeval.

1971

# KONZA PRAIRIE BIOLOGICAL STATION

Katharine Ordway's Tallgrass Preserve

*Katharine Ordway (1899–1979)*

Wind. Sky. Grass. An ocean of grass. The oft-used metaphor for the American prairie is a fitting one. A perpetual breeze causes ripples in grass like waves on water. And like the marine realm, much prairie life is inscrutable, taking place beneath the surface. For European settlers, the great grassland sea was a mighty expanse to cross, often on the way to somewhere else, somewhere with a milder climate and more trees. As one western traveler wrote in 1860, the prairies "are like the ocean in more than one particular but in none more than this: the utter impossibility of producing any just impression of them by description."

The eastern third of this prairie ocean was the tallgrass region, stretching in a north-south band from Manitoba to central Texas with one protrusion, a "prairie peninsula" extending east across Iowa and Illinois. With moderate rainfall, rich soils, and long summer days, the grass grew up to ten feet high. Here was a land in constant motion, with wolves stalking elk and deer, Swainson's hawks hunting rabbits, bison shuffling through the grass.

Under a sky that arcs across the world to touch distant horizons, the native plants, animals, and people had adapted to the prairie's rhythm. Like the Inuit of the Far North, whose languages contained many terms for snow, the Kansa and Iowa (pronounced "Ioway") tribes of the prairie had languages inspired by place. The Iowa word *wahánré*, for example, meant, "to walk under and through brush or tallgrass while pushing it aside."

Whereas the mixed- and shortgrass prairies of the more arid lands farther west were likely to be described by European immigrants as a barren wasteland, the tallgrass bespoke productivity. Coming into the country in the late summer of a year with good rainfall, the newcomers could hardly have viewed the scene as anything but an unexploited Eden, a land ripe for "improvement" once inconvenient indigenous people and wildlife were eliminated. As indeed they were. Frontier expansion proceeded apace, driven by population growth, government policy, and a climate of boosterism ("Nature is uncommonly helpful to the settler here"). Beyond these proximate causes of the tallgrass prairie's ultimate demise, though, was an idea—the powerful cultural myth of Manifest Destiny.

Men came. Their iron plows, forged of elements torn from the earth, began to score its surface. In short order the region's distinctive association of perennial grasses and wildflowers, which had flourished under the sun for thousands of years, was put asunder. Acre by acre, homestead by homestead, the land was converted to agriculture. Biologists estimate that the scattered remnants of unplowed tallgrass prairie now total only 2 to 4 percent of its original extent, making it among the most endangered ecosystems in North America. Even the surviving scraps generally have been subjected to negative influences, including overgrazing by cattle and disruption of natural wildfire cycles, the latter as crucial to the prairie's life as sunshine and rain.

One of the few places with significant remaining tallgrass is the Flint Hills of eastern Kansas. The rock underlying the ocean of grass here owes its existence to an ancient inland sea, whose 250-million-year-old sediments became the shale and limestone substrate of the area's rolling topography. Where steep-sided hills and rocky ground made the plowman's job impossible, some original prairie survived. Ranchers worked it and conservationists mostly overlooked it, their eyes turned west toward mountain vistas and old-growth forests.

By the 1950s, however, some scientists began advocating for prairie preserves where the elemental forces that shaped the land—fire, grazing, soil, and climate—might be studied.

Lloyd C. Hulbert, a professor at Kansas State University, led the search for a site where the university could establish a research station. Hulbert's dream was finally realized in 1971, when an anonymous donor agreed to fund the Nature Conservacy's purchase of roughly nine hundred acres of tallgrass prairie a few miles south of Manhattan, Kansas, to become the Konza Prairie Research Natural Area. A few years later, a gift from the same individual, subsequently revealed as Katharine Ordway, allowed the conservacy to purchase an adjacent property, and Konza grew by another 7,220 acres, making it the nation's most expansive preserve of tallgrass prairie.

Some people discover their life's purpose early, some late, some perhaps not at all. Katharine Ordway, an intelligent woman with a taste for travel, fine art, and natural beauty, falls into the middle category. Born in 1899 in St. Paul, Minnesota, she was sixty-seven years old when she made her first major gift to the Nature Conservancy, to create the Lucius Pond Ordway/ Devil's Den Preserve in southern Connecticut, named for her father. The gift and new preserve pleased her, and over several years, she invested roughly $1.5 million to expand Devil's Den to 1,400 acres and hire a sanctuary manager. Thereafter her conservation interest blossomed.

During the final thirteen years of her life, until her death in 1979, Ordway contributed $12 million toward saving natural areas, and informed the directors of her foundation that after her death its assets should "be used in acquiring land . . . for conservation purposes." Katharine Ordway's total giving to conservation projects while alive and through her Goodhill Foundation posthumously totaled at least $64 million, making her one of the most generous wildlands philanthropists of the twentieth century. Some conservationists have suggested that her giving, in total effect, rivals that of John D. Rockefeller Jr., a far richer and more famous individual. By comparison, Katharine Ordway remains relatively unknown, despite her extraordinary contributions to preserving America's natural heritage.

Like Rockefeller, Ordway was the child of a successful industrialist, and she also apparently found pleasure in giving away inherited wealth. In 1905 her father, Lucius Ordway, was recruited to invest in a nearly bankrupt business called Minnesota Mining & Manufacturing; the cash infusion allowed the 3M Company to survive and grow into the industrial powerhouse of Scotch tape and Post-it notes fame.

Katharine Ordway was the fourth of five children, a timid only daughter who studied botany and art in college and got most of the way through Yale Medical School before rethinking a career in medicine. She became increasingly immersed in conservation issues in the 1950s through a monthly roundtable at the American Museum of Natural History organized by Richard Pough, an adroit matchmaker between conservation causes and funders. A hero in the fight to save Hawk Mountain in Pennsylvania, he had worked for the National Audubon Society, written popular birding guides, and cofounded the Nature Conservancy in 1951. Pough, the conservancy's first president, introduced Katharine Ordway to the organization.

After her Devil's Den experience, Ordway funded Nature Conservancy purchases of prairie remnants in Minnesota and Missouri, but she had something larger in mind than these small natural areas. Katharine Ordway knew and loved prairie plants, and imagined an expanse without the sights and sounds of people, where blue grama grass reached to the sky. A place like Konza Prairie. By underwriting its protection, helping buy 2,200 acres of tallgrass for a second sanctuary in the Flint Hills south of Konza, and protecting a 7,800-acre mixed-grass prairie preserve in South Dakota (named for her cousin Samuel Ordway), she was quietly, through the Nature Conservancy, creating the first system of prairie preserves in the United States.

Following her death, Dick Pough and the other trustees of the Goodhill Foundation honored Ordway's wish that the foundation not be perpetual, and gave themselves five years to disperse its assets. They met that goal, helping fund the fifty-four-thousand-acre Niobrara Valley Preserve in Nebraska, the twenty-three-thousand-acre Sycan Marsh Preserve in Oregon, the nine-thousand-acre Ordway/Swisher Preserve in Florida, and many other natural areas. Through major challenge grant gifts, they helped the Nature Conservancy to raise money from other sources and to create a land acquisition fund. In sum, more than seventy natural areas across North America were protected at least partly through Katharine Ordway's generosity.

Beyond these specific wild places saved for posterity, however, Ordway's philanthropy had another significant effect. Her relationship with the Nature Conservancy helped that organization mature. Now the world's largest and best-known conservation nonprofit, in 1966 the conservancy had a small staff and budget. A period of explosive organizational growth began when the conservancy started forging relationships with major donors like Katharine Ordway, particularly during the presidency of Patrick Noonan in the 1970s. Then the *wunderkind* of the land conservation movement, Noonan negotiated the original Konza land purchase, worked with Ordway on numerous projects, and was close to her personally. When she died in 1979, he helped scatter her ashes along Ordway's favorite woodland path.

The wind seems constant at Konza Prairie. In a rare still moment the rustle of the waving grasses quiets and one hears the prairie soundtrack—meadowlarks and sparrows singing, the soft hoot of a greater prairie chicken, a grunting bison in the distance, all backed by an insect chorus. Now renamed the Konza Prairie Biological Station, the area is a site for long-term ecological research funded by the National Science Foundation. The destruction of the tallgrass prairie was incremental, and so also is the way researchers here are gradually replacing our ignorance of prairie ecology with knowledge. Will they unlock all of the land's mysteries? No. To think so would be hubris, and the best biologists are often the most humble in the face of nature's complexity.

The protected area at Konza Prairie, more than thirteen square miles, is generally open only to researchers, but a public nature trail through part of the preserve and ongoing educational programs invite community participation in the life of the prairie. The research agenda focuses on understanding that life—how fire and grazing affect plant diversity, how the tallgrass ecosystem reacts to disturbance and maintains its health. With her scholarly nature, it's a fair guess that Katharine Ordway would have been interested in such questions. She once made plain to her associates that her "primary charitable interest is the preservation of open land," with an emphasis on "keeping the land wild and not developing [it] for the amusement or entertainment of people." At Konza Prairie, and at dozens of other natural areas large and small around America, that goal has been fulfilled, and her wild legacy lives on. The great fortune she inherited came from converting the earth's natural capital into products for the marketplace. It was not her choice to be born into wealth, but when a passion for the prairie sank deep roots in her, she chose to reinvest in the land.

# GUADALUPE MOUNTAINS NATIONAL PARK
## Lonely as a Dream

*Wallace Pratt (1885–1981)*

The only thing constant about nature is change. The Guadalupe Mountains of western Texas and southern New Mexico have seen plenty. Sometimes that change comes fast, as when a flash flood sculpts the land. Sometimes change is slow, as attested by the very nature of these mountains, the weathered remains of the Capitan barrier reef, formed in a great inland sea a quarter billion years ago.

The area's cultural history is similarly dynamic. Two national parks, Carlsbad Caverns and Guadalupe Mountains, today attract tourists and nature lovers to the region. Before them came ranchers and oil prospectors, before them pioneers and the nation's first transcontinental mail route, before that a sustained and bloody campaign to displace the Mescalero Apache people from their native land. And before the Apache, earlier peoples, about whom little is known, lived here for a dozen centuries, hunting game with stone tools. Referring to the even more arid salt flats and forbidding country to the west and south, historian Hal Rothman has suggested that the Guadalupe Mountains have always been a dividing line between "a place where people could make a living, albeit a hardscrabble one, and where such endeavor was simply impossible."

The region's human history, though, seems inconsequentially brief compared to the drama that unfolded across deep time as these limestone mountains were created, submerged, and finally exposed. This is a place whose story is older than most people can imagine. It takes a special kind of person to read the landscape, to look at rock and fathom the interminable series of minute actions that accrete into geological events. Geologists and visionaries can do this, can gaze upon the Guadalupe Mountains and see the waves lapping on the shores of an ancient sea.

Guadalupe Mountains National Park, modestly sized by Texas standards at eighty-six thousand acres, is a land of extremes. It's dry—awfully dry—except for when it's wet. On those occasions, water streams down the canyons, and the salt flats in the low country may become ephemeral lakes. It's hot—terribly hot—except for when it's freezing cold, usually after the sun goes down, on more than one hundred days per year. It's windy—ferociously windy in the late winter and spring—except for when it's dead calm, often just after sunrise, when first light strikes the wall of rugged mountains that rises from creosote bush–covered scrublands. And it's prickly—a hiker might say extremely prickly—for it seems that most of the one-thousand-plus species of plants identified in the park have sharp edges or spines of some kind. With roughly fifty species of cacti alone, including the delightfully named prickly pears, hedgehogs, and pincushions, the park should appeal to cactus lovers. Surveying the country from atop Guadalupe Peak, the highest point in Texas, inveterate desert rat Edward Abbey proclaimed, "This is a harsh dry bitter place, lonely as a dream. But I like it."

Of the many outsized things about this landscape is its immoderate beauty. Certainly Wallace Pratt thought so. A petroleum geologist, Pratt's scientific approach to finding oil allowed the company he worked for to more than double its output in the three years following 1920. Born on the ides of March in 1885, Pratt was a personable, small man who once referred to himself as a "never-prepossessing one-hundred-fifteen-pound Kansas Yankee." It was appropriate that

*It was—and is—the most beautiful spot in Texas.*
—Wallace Pratt

he worked for Houston-based Humble Oil and Refining, for humble he was. Pratt's innovations fundamentally changed the oil industry. Even after he'd become a legendary figure in his field, he downplayed his success: "I was lucky," he said. "The time just happened to be ripe for someone with my bag of tricks to come down the pike."

While looking for oil in West Texas in the 1920s, Pratt was enticed by an acquaintance to take a weekend trip to what was described as the prettiest spot in the state. "He took us to McKittrick Canyon," Pratt later recalled, "and I decided that it was the most beautiful spot I had ever seen." A rare perennial stream flowing off the eastern slope of the Guadalupe Mountains had carved the canyon, which teemed with life. The typical Chihuahuan Desert scrub gave way to a streamside zone of lush vegetation where Texas madrone trees, velvet ashes, and bigtooth maples flourished. Pratt was smitten and joined with partners to buy land there. When the stock market crashed later in the decade, he bought them out, and in 1930 commissioned a vacation house of local stone built in the canyon. Pratt referred to it as the Stone Cabin. "People call this 'Pratt's hunting lodge,'" he said, "but I never hunted on this ranch and didn't let anybody else hunt on it either."

Wallace Pratt was not the only one devoted to the desert oasis. J. C. Hunter, a prominent local oilman and county judge also began buying lands in and around McKittrick Canyon in the 1920s. The Guadalupe Mountain Ranch he assembled, and which his son J. C. Hunter Jr. continued to expand after his death, grew to seventy thousand acres. Judge Hunter became a leading advocate for making McKittrick Canyon and environs a park, and managed his property with that future in mind.

Our idea of national parks today is as wildlife sanctuaries and places to interpret natural and cultural history, but many early park campaigns were tied to economic development and the "good roads" movement, which was at its apex in the 1920s. Parks were as likely to be promoted by local chambers of commerce as by conservation groups. Henry Ford's Model T made cars affordable to millions of Americans, and automobile-based tourism was exploding in popularity.

Across the border in New Mexico, Carlsbad Cave National Monument had been designated in 1923 (national park designation came seven years later), and El Paso businessmen hoped to similarly attract tourist dollars. Many supported J. C. Hunter's idea for McKittrick Canyon, and economic boosters in El Paso and Carlsbad linked the park effort to their campaign for a new road between the communities. The booster groups organized an automobile tour between the towns, and Hunter hosted a picnic in McKittrick Canyon on a summer day in 1928 that drew five hundred people, including the governors of Texas and New Mexico. A highway between El Paso and Carlsbad was finished in 1929, but despite the work of park advocates over many years, McKittrick Canyon remained unprotected. J. C. Hunter's dream for the Guadalupe Mountains, however, did not die with him.

Wallace Pratt, by then an executive at Standard Oil of New Jersey, moved with his wife, Iris, back home to Texas in 1945. They had once been trapped at the stone cabin in McKittrick Canyon by a flood and realized that a year-round dwelling on their property would be better situated in the mountain uplands outside the canyon. The long stone house Pratt commissioned there was similar in profile to an oil tanker. Called *Ship on the Desert*, the home offered panoramic views of the surrounding desert and mountains. In semiretirement there, Pratt stayed active lecturing, writing, and promoting geology education. And he kept the park idea alive.

While Pratt's first attraction to the region may have been aesthetic, over time he became an ardent conservationist dedicated to preserving the land's biological and geological attributes.

"We are still desperately ignorant about the earth, our only habitat, our home, and the home of all life as we know it," he once told an interviewer. Perhaps better than anyone, he recognized the Guadalupe Mountains as a place where geologists from around the world would come to study the premier example of a fossilized reef. The area needed permanent protection, and Pratt devoted himself to that end. In the late 1950s, he offered his land in McKittrick Canyon to become a new national park. The government accepted, and in three transactions from 1959 to 1961, the Pratt family donated 5,632 acres to the National Park Service.

Despite this generous act, establishing a park that fully protected the canyon and surrounding mountains was not easy. National parks traditionally had been designated out of existing federal lands, or, when parks were created from private property, the land had been given to the government (as at Acadia). Pratt sought but failed to find a philanthropist willing to buy the Hunter ranch from J. C. Hunter Jr. and then donate it to the park service. This left park advocates the difficult task of securing a federal appropriation to purchase the land. Many practical hurdles intervened—finding the money, getting the state of Texas and several private owners to give up mineral rights under the land, gaining congressional authorization, and developing a management plan for the new park. All were overcome. The park was authorized in 1966 and formally designated in 1972. J. C. Hunter's dream was realized, and Wallace Pratt's achievements would include more than a knack for finding oil; his legacy would be written in rock, in a canyon forever available for study and enjoyment.

Creating Guadalupe Mountains National Park took decades but, as park campaigns go, was not especially contentious. Many supporters were locally prominent, influential citizens. The vestiges of economic boosterism characterizing the park idea's originators, however, soon clashed with the growing wilderness movement over how the park would be developed. In the 1950s and 1960s, the National Park System's management philosophy emphasized visitor accommodations and access. Included in the proposed plan for Guadalupe was a mechanized tramway that would haul visitors up Pine Springs Canyon into the high country. Although a local congressman favored the tramway, the Sierra Club and other groups actively fought it, it was unaffordable, and a survey showed that most visitors opposed it. The Park Service quietly let the idea die. Guadalupe Mountains National Park would be managed to protect the land's natural character, and over half of the park was formally dedicated a wilderness area by Congress in 1978.

Strolling in McKittrick Canyon in late autumn, visitors are treated to colorful fall foliage, an unexpected sight in the Chihuahuan Desert, made even more delightful when accompanied by the descending trill of a canyon wren. The trail ahead will be long and sometimes steep, but some miles hence, hikers will ascend onto McKittrick Ridge and through a pass over the mountains. Tomorrow they might explore the high-elevation conifer forests where mule deer, black bears, and mountain lions roam, and then climb to the summit of Guadalupe Peak to take in the view from the top of Texas: Wallace Pratt's gift to posterity, a home for cactus, coyotes, and rattlesnakes amid rocks that once were living creatures at the end of a sea.

1973

# SEVILLETA NATIONAL WILDLIFE REFUGE
## In Rhythm with Nature

*Elizabeth-Ann Campbell Knapp*
*(1914–1990)*

This isn't merely big-sky country, it's huge. The sky is everywhere, stretching over desert and mountains. Looking west across Sevilleta National Wildlife Refuge from high in central New Mexico's Los Piños Mountains, it's apparent that a monsoon season thunderstorm is kicking up. This morning's wispy white streaks over the Ladrone Mountains have grown into a miles-high pillow of cumulonimbus clouds—those big, puffy ones of children's drawings—now turned dark and menacing. The thunderhead rises over Ladron Peak and comes sweeping across the broad valley between mountain ranges. Its shadow traces a perpendicular line over the Rio Grande River and across the McKenzie Flats. Occasional lightning arcs through the sky.

With thunder rumbling across the desert, it's not difficult to imagine this scene millions of years ago, when Black Butte, the eroded cinder cone on the flats below, was an active volcano spewing acrid smoke. Today, however, the fireworks come from above the earth. One can smell moisture now, and the pungent aroma of piñon-juniper woodlands as a sheet of rain strikes the high country. Small rivulets of water gather into streams rushing down the gullies. To the north and south, the desert remains lit by sunshine, but here the sky goes dark, and a deluge ensues. Then the storm passes. The heat returns, and rock again bakes in the sunshine. The golden yellow bunchgrasses, so long waiting for moisture, will be green tomorrow.

Afternoon thundershowers are a welcome late-summer phenomenon on the Sevilleta National Wildlife Refuge, often contributing more than half of the area's ten inches of annual precipitation. At 230,000 acres, Sevilleta is one of the largest wildlife refuges south of Alaska, and among the wildest, because it has been generally closed to the public since its creation in 1973. The refuge is home to a biological field station operated by the University of New Mexico and is a long-term ecological research site funded by the National Science Foundation. Scientists here study a wide range of topics, from the rodent-transmitted hantavirus to global climate change. A meeting place for several major life zones, or biomes, the refuge is a nexus for research on how those communities—Chihuahuan desert, Great Plains grassland, Great Basin shrub-steppe, and piñon-juniper woodland—transition into one another and change over time due to various factors, including weather patterns. All manner of information about today's ephemeral storm was recorded by meteorological instruments scattered around the refuge.

Sevilleta, though, is not just a place where ecologists collect data. It is nearly 360 square miles of wildlife habitat where bands of pronghorn and mule deer run free, where golden eagles soar on thermals and bears roam the mountains. To a person unaccustomed to the scale and style of the desert, the land may at first seem overwhelmingly vast and empty, but a closer look begins to reveal its riches. More than 350 bird species use the refuge, and over 1,200 species of plants have been identified. From lizards to mountain lions, the land is filled with creatures whose homes will never be developed into ranchettes for retirees. The rarest of sounds, the howl of a Mexican gray wolf, can even be heard at Sevilleta. As part of the Fish and Wildlife Service's recovery program for that endangered species, wolves are acclimated in large enclosures at the refuge before their release into the wild in the Apache and Gila national forests.

The refuge is, in short, a remarkable place—and the result of a remarkable gift to the American people. In donating Sevilleta to become a national wildlife refuge, the family of General Thomas D. Campbell, the property's onetime owner, made what is probably the single largest gift of private land to the public in U.S. history.

Human beings, present in the Rio Grande Valley for several thousand years, are relative newcomers to the scene. The pronghorns have been here far longer. Often colloquially called antelope (true antelope live in Africa), the species' scientific name, *Antilocapra americana*, reflects its American heritage. The fastest animal in the Western Hemisphere, the pronghorn is a New World native whose ancestry stretches back millions of years. Which explains why a pronghorn can, if so moved, run at sustained speeds of thirty to forty miles per hour, and in short bursts reach seventy miles per hour. None of this ungulate's current predators, save perhaps men in pickup trucks, remotely approaches its speed. Pronghorn fleetness is an evolutionary anachronism. They are running from the ghosts of predators past—the dire wolves, giant short-faced bears, American lions, and cheetahs with which they once shared western North America.

Those large carnivores were long gone in the 1500s when the Spanish got to the area now known as New Mexico, where they found indigenous peoples well organized in pueblos and an economy based on growing corn, beans, squash, and cotton. The bloody Pueblo Revolt of 1680 drove the domineering Spanish out for a few years, but they later reasserted claim, and European settlement began anew. In 1819, the Sevilleta de la Joya land grant, made under the authority of Spain's King Charles IV, gave sixty-seven petitioners legal title to 220,000 acres stretching from Ladrón Peak to the ridgeline of Los Piños Mountains. After most of California, Arizona, and New Mexico became part of the United States following the Mexican-American War of 1846–1848, American courts confirmed the land grantees' property rights. But the Sevilleta community failed to pay property taxes on its communally held lands, and in the 1920s, the land was sold for back taxes. Socorro County bought it, and auctioned the property in 1936. Thomas Campbell was the winning bidder, and for nearly thirty years thereafter his company operated a cattle ranch at Sevilleta.

Born on the North Dakota prairie in 1882, Tom Campbell grew into an ambitious, strikingly handsome man. He was already managing his family's four-thousand-acre wheat farm as a teenager, and after earning engineering degrees became a leading promoter of mechanized farming. During World War I he secured funding from J. P. Morgan's investment bank to lease some ninety-five thousand acres of tribal land in Montana. A drought caused most of his wheat crop to fail, and his deal with Morgan collapsed, but Campbell ultimately succeeded in applying the logic of industrialism to growing grain.

Through the Campbell Farming Corporation, launched in 1922, he was soon the world's largest wheat grower, sometimes called the "Henry Ford of agriculture." By the 1940s he had added five hundred thousand acres in New Mexico to the company's landholdings. In 1964, two years before Campbell's death, the Sevilleta lands were transferred to a family foundation he'd established, and the ranching operations there ended.

Elizabeth-Ann Campbell Knapp, Tom Campbell's daughter and head of the Campbell Family Foundation, later recalled how family members "were faced with the decision of exploiting and developing" or choosing a "more visionary and lasting use of a vast tract of land." Knapp was intent that the original land grant stay intact and be permanently preserved as a natural area, and in the late 1960s she began seeking a conservation organization or public agency to manage the Sevilleta lands.

"No one was interested at first," recalls William C. Ashe, a career Fish and Wildlife Service professional who at the time directed the agency's Division of Realty for the Southwest Region. "It would have been a helluva thing to manage for most organizations, and it was in a very degraded condition." But like Knapp, Ashe saw extraordinary potential in the Sevilleta landscape. "Conservation is a long-term business," he says. Ashe recommended to Elizabeth-Ann Knapp a coordinated top-down and bottom-up strategy: She should go to Washington, D.C., and lobby officials in the Interior Department. He would build support for Sevilleta regionally within the Fish and Wildlife Service. It worked, and they got the green light to add the land to the federal refuge system.

Ashe worked closely with Patrick Noonan, then-president of the Nature Conservancy and a legendary conservation dealmaker, to arrange a complex transaction whereby the Campbell Family Foundation would convey the property, worth an estimated $10 million, to the conservancy. The conservancy, supported by the Mary Flagler Cary Charitable Trust, would reimburse the foundation $500,000 for surveying and other legal costs incurred with the land donation. Then the conservancy would reconvey title to the Interior Department. Noonan and Ashe crafted deed language that strictly protected the area's "integrity and natural character . . . by creating a wildlife refuge managed as nearly as possible in its natural state" and included a clause that stipulated the land would revert to the Nature Conservancy if the terms were breached. This language helped insulate future refuge managers from political pressure to allow cattle grazing or other extractive uses on the land. After months of intensive work, this agreement was struck in December 1973.

Elizabeth-Ann Campbell Knapp took great satisfaction from the conservation legacy the family had launched at Sevilleta. "I think she was extremely proud of it," says Phoebe Knapp Warren, a Montana artist who succeeded her mother as head of the Campbell Family Foundation. Elizabeth-Ann Campbell Knapp was an architect who lived primarily in Princeton but shuttled between New Jersey, Montana, and New Mexico while running the Campbell Farming Corporation for seventeen years following Tom Campbell's death. She retained a deep fondness for the Sevilleta landscape from spending time there with her father, and until her death in 1990 she remained watchful that management at the new refuge reflected its donor's intent. "My mother was even bothered if a road was too gussied up," says Phoebe Warren.

There is no doubt today that the forward-thinking vision Elizabeth-Ann Campbell Knapp, William Ashe, and Pat Noonan shared for Sevilleta was correct. Time and nature's recuperative powers have launched a resurgence of wildness at Sevilleta. "I was there twenty-five years after the acquisition, and the change was remarkable," says Ashe. "It still has a way to go, but if it continues, it will be one of the real gems in the National Wildlife Refuge System." Every day at Sevilleta, natural processes play out their ancient rhythms. Scientists, as unobtrusively as possible, strive to understand them. Most of the time, though, no human eye watches the action unfold, as life on the refuge proceeds at nature's pace: a black-tailed rattlesnake, perfectly still, waits for an unlucky desert cottontail to become its breakfast, while pronghorns race across the grassland faster even than a passing thundercloud.

1976

# TOM YAWKEY WILDLIFE CENTER
## An Ark for Rare and Common Creatures

*Thomas Austin Yawkey*
*(1903–1976)*

Ask the average person to name an endangered species. Grizzly bear or bald eagle is the likely reply. Perhaps someone will say spotted owl or snail darter, the tiny fish that became a cause célèbre in the 1970s, when it delayed construction of Tennessee's Tellico Dam. It's a safe guess, though, that few people could name more than a handful of the nearly 1,300 endangered species currently on the federal list.

Somewhere between endangered species obscurity and celebrity is the red-cockaded woodpecker. Relatively nondescript with mottled black and white markings, slightly smaller and more svelte than a robin, the bird doesn't quite live up to its name. Only males display any color whatsoever, and their two small red markings on the head are rarely visible. Red-cockaded woodpeckers are not flashy. But the bird is a flagship for conservation because its fate is so closely tied to that of the larger ecosystem in which it lives, the longleaf pine forest. Once the dominant forest type across the entire coastal plain of the southeastern United States, longleaf pine forests covered more than ninety million acres before European settlement of the Americas. Now that forest is 99 percent gone—and the mature pines that red-cockadeds require for nesting cavities are scarce indeed.

The red-cockaded woodpecker's relatively unusual social structure (for birds) and cooperative behavior were well suited to those halcyon pre-Columbian days but today are maladaptive. Unlike most bird species, in which the primary form of social organization is the breeding pair, red-cockadeds generally live in an extended family group. When there was a continuous forest with plenty of large, old pines, a low reproductive rate was adequate to keep the red-cockaded's niche filled. There was little pressure for juveniles to leave the group quickly or to disperse far from the tree where they were hatched. They could wait around for a year or two and assist with housekeeping, take on the role of avian au pair, helping mom and dad raise this year's clutch. Sooner or later, because of natural mortality, chances were good that an existing cavity nest would become available in either their own or adjacent territory. A young male's reproductive prospects might be maximized by sticking close to home rather than setting off to find an unoccupied territory, an available female, and a tree in which to excavate a cavity.

For a male red-cockaded woodpecker hoping to get lucky, the bachelor pad is everything—and the standards for that penthouse suite are quite exacting. First, it needs to look out over an open, parklike stand of pines with a grassy understory, the kind of habitat that was maintained through prehistory by regular lightning-set wildfires. Without frequent burning, the forest fills in with a shrubby understory, and red-cockaded woodpeckers abandon the site. Second, red-cockadeds are apparently the only woodpecker species worldwide that excavates nests exclusively in live trees, with a very strong preference for longleaf pine, although loblolly or slash pines may sometimes be used. Nest building represents a tremendous energetic output; digging a cavity is tough work and can take months or even years to complete. It is easier in old-growth pines, where an endemic fungus has begun to soften the heartwood. After the excavation is complete, the bird pecks the bark around the opening so that pine resin oozes out, forming sticky accretions that are an effective deterrent to predators, particularly tree-climbing snakes with a taste for woodpecker eggs and nestlings.

These natural traits—dependence on mature longleaf pines for nesting, low reproductive capacity, and disinclination to disperse long distances—represent a triple whammy of bad luck for red-cockaded woodpeckers in the present, highly fragmented landscape. Some ornithologists estimate the red-cockaded population has declined 99 percent since European settlement of North America. The U.S. Fish and Wildlife Service, the agency responsible for helping endangered species recover, suggests that the bird occupies something less than 3 percent of its original range. Those are grim figures. After the species was listed in the 1970s, population levels continued to decline for years, precipitously in some cases. But even if its preferred habitat is in short supply, at least there is no shortage of concern for the red-cockaded woodpecker. Tremendous effort has gone toward saving the species—by understanding its ecology, monitoring population trends, altering forest management practices, and encouraging recovery through various techniques.

At the twenty-thousand-acre Tom Yawkey Wildlife Center, biologists are monitoring red-cockaded woodpeckers and actively helping to maintain the habitat they require. A complex of three islands on the South Carolina coast, the Yawkey Center is home to small numbers of red-cockaded woodpeckers, piping plovers, and other endangered species, and serves as a seasonal stopover for vast numbers of common waterfowl. The sanctuary was given to the people and wildlife of South Carolina in 1976 by Tom Yawkey, longtime owner of the Boston Red Sox. Yawkey was a man who loved birds, baseball, and the array of wild creatures he shared this land with for most of his life.

For as long as boys have rambled about in forests, they have learned to appreciate wild creatures by observing, stalking, and, sometimes, killing them. Tom Yawkey's formative experiences as a sportsman began in the 1910s at his uncle William Yawkey's South Island rural estate, once a slave-era rice plantation. For a kid from Detroit, the woods, ponds, and beaches of the Carolina lowcountry must have been heaven, offering endless opportunities for exploration. The boy became, and would remain, an avid hunter and angler throughout his life.

Bill Yawkey, an affluent businessman and one-time owner of the Detroit Tigers, had legally adopted Tom after the boy's parents died, and passed along to his son a love of baseball and the outdoors. He also left him very wealthy. When Bill Yawkey died in 1919, the sixteen-year-old Tom inherited a considerable fortune, including the South Island plantation, one of several large properties along the South Carolina coast acquired in the early decades of the twentieth century by wealthy northern sportsmen. Much of the conservation land in the region today stems from those former plantations, which were used seasonally as hunting retreats.

In 1933, just after Tom Yawkey turned thirty and came into full control of the financial resources left to him, he purchased the Boston Red Sox. Over the next forty-three years Yawkey spent prodigiously to make the team a winner, coming close several times, but never achieving a World Series championship. Sometimes on the way back from spring training in Florida, the team would stop over at South Island. Various baseball greats, including Ty Cobb, who had played for Yawkey's uncle Bill, came there for hunting vacations with Tom.

Yawkey gradually expanded his holdings until he owned roughly twenty thousand acres on South, Cat, and North islands, which bracket the entrance to Winyah Bay. He typically spent winters there and paid close attention to the comings and goings of the wildlife, especially birds. He kept records, for instance, of when he saw the first white-throated sparrow or prothonotary warbler of the season.

Yawkey's deepening conservation ethic and concern over declining waterfowl populations were likely influenced by his friendship with Jack Miner, a pioneering conservationist who established a bird sanctuary just across the Canadian border from Detroit and was one of the first individuals to use bird banding to study migration routes. As duck populations along the Atlantic Flyway declined, Yawkey discontinued waterfowl hunting and began manipulating coastal marsh areas on his property to produce maximum quantities of native waterfowl foods like wigeongrass. Yawkey's experiments were successful, and the land continues to support large numbers of blue- and green-winged teal, black ducks, pintails, mallards, shovelers, and other duck species, and wading birds such as black-necked stilts and avocets. In the spring, up to a quarter-million birds have been documented on Yawkey ponds.

Tom and his wife, Jean, who died in 1992, had no children of their own but during their lifetimes focused much of their charitable giving on children's welfare. The two foundations established from their estate, the latter endowed from the sale of the Boston Red Sox, continue that focus, and support the ongoing conservation work at the Yawkey Wildlife Center.

"Mr. Yawkey was explicit in his will about how the area would be utilized. Principally it was dedicated as a wildlife refuge, a research area, and a resource for environmental education," says Bob Joyner, who became resident biologist at the center soon after the land was given to South Carolina Department of Natural Resources. "Those are the guiding principles we've been working with through the years." There is no generalized recreation access or hunting. "Mr. Yawkey wanted this land to be primarily a place for wildlife, not people," Joyner says. "He knew that if you were going to continue to have hunting, you had to give waterfowl some areas and time of refuge from hunting."

The Yawkey Center's work to sustain imperiled species such as red-cockaded woodpeckers, piping plovers, and loggerhead turtles is just a part, although an important part, of its larger mission to provide a sanctuary for native wildlife. Both rare and abundant species find refuge here. The 3,500 acres of longleaf pine forest on Cat Island harbor red-cockadeds as well as other woodpeckers, wild turkeys, and the occasional black bear. South Island offers exceptionally productive waterfowl habitat and a maritime forest of loblolly pine, live oak, and palmetto that is adapted to periodic episodes of severe natural disturbance from hurricanes. On North Island, the management orientation is of strict protection; Tom Yawkey directed that it would be a barrier island wilderness. North Island's maritime forest has been undisturbed by people since the Civil War, and its sand dunes are some of the tallest on the Atlantic seaboard.

Over his lifetime, Tom Yawkey enjoyed the land's diverse pleasures, and came to think of its value not merely as a personal retreat, but for what it could contribute to wildlife conservation, regionally and nationally. With his gift of property and an endowment to support its stewardship, Yawkey assured that development pressures would never compromise the land's habitat values, and that it would continue to serve the needs of nature.

The Yawkey Wildlife Center has become a kind of ark, carrying into the future a host of creatures distinctive to the region. With a consistent focus on Tom Yawkey's vision but adapting to meet evolving challenges, Bob Joyner and the other biologists who care for the land are helping to sail that ark through stormy waters, ever mindful of keeping irreplaceable members of the land community—red-cockaded woodpeckers, loggerhead turtles, and others—from sinking into the bottomless sea of extinction.

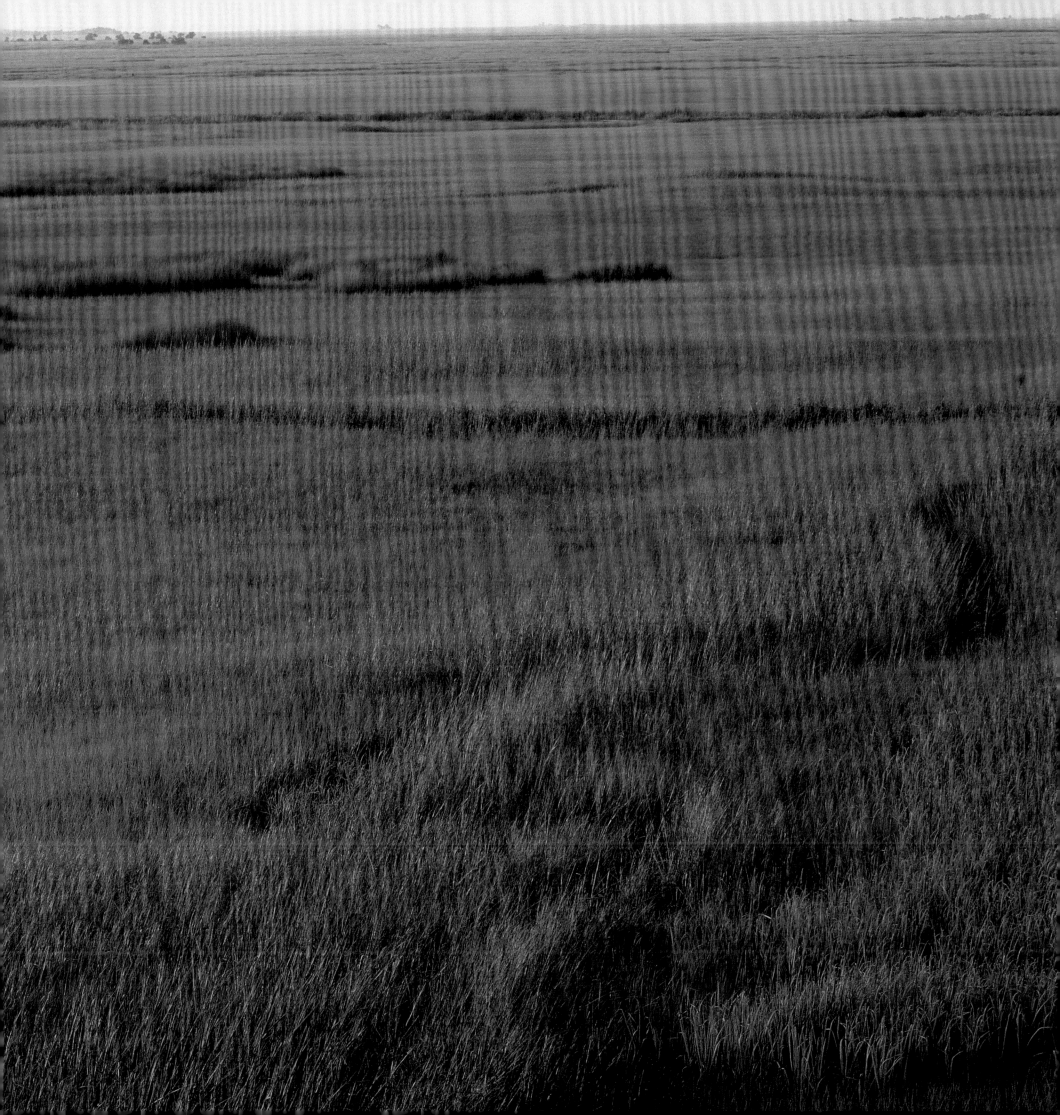

# ÁREA DE CONSERVACIÓN GUANACASTE
## Regrowing a Tropical Forest

*Daniel Janzen*          *Winnie Hallwachs*

In the dry tropical forests of northwestern Costa Rica, the fruits of the guanacaste tree often rot where they fall. The fruit, about the size of a large, flattened orange, has a tough outer husk shaped like an ear. It's an odd thing for fruits to go to waste on the forest floor, because what are fruits for? To be eaten. Plants go to great energetic effort producing tasty packages of pulp-covered seeds to attract animals, which consume and later distribute the seeds in a handy dollop of nutrient-rich dung. If the scat lands in a spot favorable to germination and survival, a tree is born.

The rotting piles of guanacaste and other fruits puzzled Dan Janzen, a professor at the University of Pennsylvania and one of the world's leading tropical biologists. Could it be that the creatures that had evolved with the trees were gone, and that none of the animals presently in the forest were well adapted to consuming the fruits? Janzen's curiosity about this question led to a classic scientific paper published in 1982, coauthored with paleoecologist Paul Martin. The two men opened a fascinating line of inquiry into physical traits and behaviors that become anachronistic when one member in a coevolved relationship goes missing.

For some trees of the Americas that produce large fruits, the missing partners are animals that went extinct around the time that people first arrived in the New World, most likely due to human hunting. "The plants not only remember the great mammals of the Pleistocene and before; they expect gomphotheres, ground sloths, toxodons, and their ilk to show up any day now," writes science writer Connie Barlow in her book *The Ghosts of Evolution*. "Thirteen thousand years is not enough time for plants to notice and genetically respond to the loss."

The guanacaste, Costa Rica's national tree and namesake of the country's northwestern province, is the victim of an ancient and invisible ecological wound. The species is now declining in areas where there are no horses or cattle to stand in for the absent Pleistocene megafauna. (Recall that the horse—a product of New World evolution—is a gift from the Pleistocene, brought back to us from its refuge in the Old World by the Spaniards.) A more pressing and recent set of injuries to the region is readily visible. For the past four hundred years, the once-continuous dry forest has been whittled away by human settlement. Like other forests throughout Central America, the land has been gradually cleared for agriculture. Farms and cattle ranches replaced an amazingly diverse biotic community with bean fields and exotic grasses. In a forest type that evolved without natural wildfires, landowners burning their pastures each year completely altered the vegetation and destroyed more and more of the surrounding forest.

Since the 1960s, when Dan Janzen began living in Costa Rica most of each year, he'd watched the forest shrink. By the mid-1980s, he and his spouse, biologist Winnie Hallwachs, realized that if a vigorous campaign to restore the forest didn't begin soon, future generations of forest ecologists would have nothing left to study, at least on the dry side of Central America. Their base of operations for research was at Parque Nacional Santa Rosa, a small protected area of twenty-seven thousand acres established in 1971. The park was suffering, one little island in an eroding archipelago of wild habitat surrounded by a sea of nonnative grassland.

The medicine for healing that ecological sickness was obvious to Janzen: "Purchase the large tracts of marginal ranch and farm land adjacent to Santa Rosa and connect it with the wetter forests to the east, stop the fires, farming, and the occasional hunting and logging, and let nature

*Anybody who wants to save tropical forests—all you have to do is put your money on the table, zero overhead, ten cents per square meter, and we add it to the conservation area.*

—Daniel Janzen

take back its original terrain." But of course, that would be impossible. The notion of restoring an entire dry forest ecosystem in Central America was, in a word, fanciful. The assumption was that once cleared, tropical forests were gone forever. Moreover, the social context presented significant obstacles. The country's national park service was young, underfunded, and its decision making heavily centralized in the capital. Although the most prosperous nation in the region, Costa Rica was very poor. "To put this in context," says Janzen, "the entire government budget of the country is equal to the budget of the University of Pennsylvania."

In 1985 Janzen and Hallwachs made a decision to step outside their comfortable sphere of academic biology and into conservation activism: "We saw that if we wanted to help make something happen, we would have to join the battle," says Janzen. "And we don't regret it one bit."

That battle continues, but by 2005 it had died down to small skirmishes over funding and management philosophy. What once seemed an impossible dream is now the Área de Conservación Guanacaste (ACG), comprising roughly 285,000 acres of terrestrial habitat and a 173,000-acre marine national park where the Peninsula Santa Elena juts into the Pacific Ocean. An expanded Santa Rosa, two other national parks, a forest reserve, two national wildlife refuges, and another forty-thousand acres of private land bought for conservation have been melded into a single legal and administrative unit, ACG, which is part of Costa Rica's national system of conservation areas. ACG has a staff of nearly a hundred people, an innovative biological education program for schoolchildren, and a multimillion-dollar endowment.

The protected area connects four major ecosystems, stretching from the Pacific's deep water and coral reefs onto sandy beaches where thousands of sea turtles arrive en masse to lay their eggs, through remnant but regenerating dry forests up to mist-shrouded volcanoes covered with cloud forest, then down to the even-wetter Atlantic rainforests. With some 235,000 identified species—more than in all of the United States and Canada—packed into a space smaller than Rhode Island, ACG is a global biodiversity hotspot, and the most promising example of tropical forest recovery on Earth.

The story of how the conservation initiative in Guanacaste took shape could fill a book, and does, actually, a good one called *Green Phoenix*. Highlights of the story include innovations in ecological restoration and fundraising. ACG benefited from Latin America's first major "debt-for-nature" swap, an arrangement by which a developing country's foreign debt is lessened in exchange for in-country conservation actions. There was even a measure of negative political intrigue during the Reagan years, when Oliver North's Iran-Contra operation ran a clandestine airstrip in the area to supply the CIA-backed rebels fighting Nicaragua's Sandinista government. Ultimately, the Costa Rican government expropriated and paid for the forty-thousand-acre Hacienda Santa Elena with its infamous airstrip and added it to ACG as Sector Santa Elena.

Through the years, Janzen and Hallwachs abandoned most of their research to work directly on land conservation. In *Green Phoenix* Janzen is characterized as ACG's "putative intellectual godfather" and Hallwachs as the quietly effective partner who contributed to the project's "intellectual development, its implementation strategies and tactics, and its conservation spin-offs." Janzen sums up their partnership with the quip, "She thinks, I talk."

He rejects, however, any suggestion that he was the gringo savior of Guanacaste. "The hardest part to get people to understand is that this is the result of one huge amount of effort by a very large number of Costa Ricans," he says. "We are just part of the team." Which is true. The designation

of ACG and other conservation areas in the 1980s was built on a foundation laid in the 1970s by Mario Boza and Alvaro Ugalde, who were to the Costa Rican park service what Stephen Mather and Horace Albright were to America's National Park System, its early visionaries and champions. The project benefited from an active community of Costa Rican conservationists and biologists, including Rodrigo Gámez, head of INBio, the National Biodiversity Institute, and gained crucial political support from former president Oscar Arias Sánchez and then–minister of the environment Alvaro Umaña. Even so, if not for Dan Janzen's tireless cheerleading and fundraising, much more of Guanacaste Province would still be cattle pasture filled with African jaragua grass, not recovering forest where an occasional jaguar stalks peccaries for supper.

A self-described "hard-core academic field biologist," Janzen has published hundreds of scientific papers on tropical forest organisms and interactions. He has also proven an exceptional student of the money tree, and, specifically, how to shake it. By 2005, some forty U.S. and European foundations and a handful of deep-pocketed American donors had supported the Guanacaste initiative. Roughly eight thousand contributors had made small gifts. Through the debt-for-nature swap, financial wizards from Wall Street and the Costa Rican Central Bank turned a $3.5-million gift from Sweden in recognition of President Arias Sánchez's Nobel Peace Prize into $21 million for ACG. In total, approximately $48 million had been raised for land acquisition, an endowment, education programs, and park infrastructure, including biological field stations. While Janzen is not anxious to talk about it, "several million dollars" have come directly from Janzen and Hallwachs. When he received the Crafoord Prize (ecology's Nobel), a MacArthur "genius grant," the Kyoto Prize, and other honors that came with cash awards, Janzen directed all of the money toward the conservation area. And much of his salary too: "I'm wearing the same clothes I bought twenty years ago," he says. "My wife and I spend very little money, and basically everything except what we need for food and rent goes to ACG."

From the ocean to the mountains, in forests wet and dry, the Área de Concervación Guanacaste pulses with life. The sounds of wildness float in the air—a howler monkey's scream, an anteater shuffling along on its knuckles, the raucous call of parrots in the treetops. Because ACG brings every local fourth- through sixth-grader into the forest, the voices of schoolchildren may also be heard, discussing pollination, or predator-prey dynamics, or mutually beneficial associations such as trees growing fruit to feed animals and the animals returning the favor by dispersing their seeds. By integrating every nearby elementary school's biological curriculum with the conservation area, a rural population in the Costa Rican hinterlands is becoming the most ecologically literate people on the planet. That, Janzen suggests, is crucial to developing broad-based support for conservation, so that local people see protected land as an asset to their communities. This support is fundamental, Janzen believes, if tropical wildlands are to survive. "Our goal," he says, "is that the species and ecosystems in ACG will still be present a thousand years from now."

In the tropics, where land health is decreasing as rapidly as anywhere on Earth, the Guanacaste conservation area is a happy aberration. Here, people and nature are working together to regrow the forest. While the future is uncertain, the first two decades of a thousand-year recovery program can only be judged a wild success.

# FLORACLIFF

## A Sanctuary of Her Own

*Mary E. Wharton (1912–1991)*

In the late 1930s, a young graduate student at the University of Michigan took ill with pneumonia. While in the hospital, word arrived that her fiancé had been killed in a car wreck. She prayed to God to take her life, too. For several days her condition neither improved nor deteriorated. Then, on the fourth day after the terrible news, her doctor was surprised when "every aspect of the disease was suddenly and strikingly improved," she recounted in an essay a half century later. "The explanation was known only to me; that morning I had changed my prayer. Now it was, 'Lord, if you want me to live, I give myself to you . . . to go anywhere or do anything you wish me to do for your glory.'"

It seems that God had planned for Mary Eugenia Wharton a life of science and service—to teach the richness and diversity of that part of Creation called Kentucky's Inner Bluegrass region—for that is precisely what she would do after completing a doctorate in botany and returning to her girlhood home in Lexington. As a professor, writer, and conservationist, Mary Wharton would spend the rest of her life working to understand the region's natural communities and communicate their value to the public.

It was a full life. While sharing the family house with her sister, who also remained unmarried, Wharton headed the biology department at nearby Georgetown College for nearly three decades, teaching generations of students environmental science. She became an authority on local flora, and identified several plants new to science. Wharton's dewberry (*Rubus whartoniae*), a state-listed threatened species, was named for her after she discovered it in the 1940s. She coauthored several popular books, including *A Guide to Wildflowers and Ferns of Kentucky* and *Trees and Shrubs of Kentucky*. Wharton had been called to teaching by a higher power, it suited her talents, and she simply believed in natural history education: "If you know what you see as you walk along, you see more," she wrote in one of her field guides.

Wharton also became a tenacious, if soft-spoken, defender of the landscape she loved. Her friend Bob Wilson suggests that Wharton's opponents may sometimes have underestimated the petite, well-mannered scientist, who usually ended up getting her way. "She was a refined and delicate southern lady with an iron will and determination," he says.

During the 1960s and early 1970s, the state's foremost conservation battle was over a U.S. Army Corps of Engineers proposal to build a dam on the Red River in eastern Kentucky. The dam would have partially flooded the Red River Gorge area, a land of rugged ridges and valleys containing a wealth of archaeological sites and natural stone arches. Hundreds of Kentuckians worked to save the gorge, but Mary Wharton was a key player in the ultimately successful struggle to permanently protect that stretch of the Red River. Her testimony before Congress in 1968, in which she articulated the "serious biological and ecological errors" in the Army Corps' analysis, helped advance the conservationists' cause. "The scientific value of the Red River Gorge calls for its preservation," she testified. "The guardians of our natural resources would do better to sponsor guided trips to these relic communities than to allow them to be permanently inundated and have this source of knowledge forever obliterated." Kentucky senator John Sherman Cooper subsequently wrote Wharton, thanking her "for bringing this to my attention and for the presentation of proof which convinced me to change my position and led to the change of position by the Corps of Engineers and by the House and Senate."

Later Wharton founded a citizen-led conservation group, the Land and Nature Trust of the Bluegrass. She waged a lengthy and mostly successful battle against a highway expansion along

*I devoted my professional life toward promoting knowledge, understanding, and appreciation of our natural world, and invested financial resources for the preservation for posterity of a natural area with great beauty and geological, biological, and ecological significance. It is my hope that all those who in the future will manage my bequests will do so with a similar dedication.*

—Mary E. Wharton

Paris Pike, a picturesque lane that meanders through horse farm country outside Lexington, which state highway engineers had proposed to upgrade into something more akin to an interstate highway than a rural byway. The Paris Pike controversy, the loss of central Kentucky farmland to rural sprawl, and other indignities to the land she witnessed were clearly foremost in her mind while working on her final book. In *Bluegrass Land and Life*, coauthored with naturalist Roger Barbour, Wharton highlighted the threats to the region's natural and cultural character.

Through the years of spirited public advocacy as well as teaching and writing about Kentucky's natural heritage, Mary Wharton was also, in her private life, building a sanctuary of her own. From 1958 to 1989, in at least fifteen separate transactions, she purchased land along the Elk Lick Creek in southern Fayette County, much of which was reverting to woodlands after having been cleared for agriculture in previous decades. Over time she assembled the multiple parcels into a 278-acre preserve, called Floracliff, and founded a nonprofit organization to oversee its stewardship. When she died on Thanksgiving Day in 1991, Wharton left an estate of nearly $800,000 to endow the sanctuary. Bob Wilson, the longtime Floracliff board president, recalls that Wharton was fiercely protective of the area. While the property was still in her name, she allowed little access and didn't even want flagging on the trees to delineate trails.

"Mary's primary goals were education and preservation," Wilson says. "She used the site for teaching classes, and she hoped that visitors to Floracliff would find some spiritual enlightenment from their contact with nature there." Floracliff was a place "where the human spirit may find refreshment and a place conducive to large thoughts," Wharton once wrote. Paraphrasing John Muir, she noted, "We need beauty as well as bread."

In a tactical maneuver that would have made Mary Wharton proud, Bob Wilson helped Floracliff achieve another layer of protection in 1996, when it was named an official Kentucky state nature preserve. That designation outflanked an adjacent landowner, the local water company, whose lawyers were threatening to use eminent domain to seize sanctuary lands and build a road to a pumping station on the Kentucky River.

Nature preserve status neutralized the eminent domain threat for good. It also formally recognized the site's natural attributes, including plant diversity (more than four hundred species) and an extraordinary geological formation called a tufa, one of the best examples in eastern North America. The sixty-one-foot-high tower of travertine rock looms from the base of Elk Lick Falls, and was built over eons as the falling waters precipitated the mineral calcium carbonate. The precipitate gradually accreted into the present spire, now standing like a sentinel over Mary Wharton's beloved sanctuary.

At Wharton's direction, Floracliff is generally closed to public use, but preserve manager Carey Ruff organizes regular events that allow visitors an opportunity to experience the land. Mary Wharton traced her interest in natural history to early childhood, when her grandmother taught her about flowers and birds, and Floracliff's mission includes programming that fosters an appreciation for the region's distinctive ecology. Wildflower walks and volunteer work days to help control exotic species also help build a constituency that knows the land and supports the organization dedicated to its ongoing care.

In the spring, visitors to Floracliff are treated to a riot of wildflowers, an ephemeral exhibit of floral beauty that Mary Wharton especially cherished. Famous for its rolling topography and fleet horses, the Bluegrass region of central Kentucky offers some of the richest soils in the world due to the underlying limestone. From that good dirt sprout carpets of Virginia bluebells, false rue anemone, larkspur, and many other blooming plants—splashes of color dotting the forest floor as if God had used a paintbrush to liven up the drab postwinter woods. Mary Wharton knew them, both as scientist and protector. They gave her pleasure, a gift she was happy to pass on: "The enjoyment that you get from acquaintanceship with [plants] is not exclusively the privilege of botanists," she wrote.

Where Wharton once led outings of budding scientists, Carey Ruff today leads nature lovers through the forest, making introductions. She points out the limestone pavements in the creek, raccoon tracks in the mud, a comely little butterfly called the Zabulon skipper, and the American bladdernut, an understory tree whose papery seed pods can be dried and shaken like a rattle. When a visitor goes to pick up a fluorescent green caterpillar with a spot on its back that looks like a tiny saddle, she quickly issues a warning: The saddleback caterpillar's handsome appearance belies a prickly demeanor; tiny hollow spines lead to poison glands under its skin. The naive critter that tries one for a snack, or person who touches one, will receive a ferocious sting. Stopping by a patch of fire-pink, a wildflower whose brilliant red, star-shaped blossoms stand out among the various hues of green in the forest, Ruff wonders aloud, "How can you not be moved by this beauty?"

Surely this is the legacy of commitment to the land that Mary Wharton had hoped for. Thanks to her, this oasis of quiet and birdsong on the edge of Lexington's metropolitan sprawl will persist. The pawpaws, blue ashes, and chinquapin oaks may grow toward the sky at their own pace. In the green shadows, an occasional river otter may be seen splashing in the Elk Lick Creek, which pools and drops on its way to the Kentucky River.

1994

# EL REFUGIO HUANCHACA
## Ecological Terra Incognita

*Alan Weeden*

The maned wolf, which looks like a red fox on stilts, has especially long legs, the better for seeing over tall grass. The marsh deer, South America's largest deer species, is able to splay its hooves to gain additional surface area, the better for walking in saturated soils. These are but two of the many ways in which creatures of northeastern Bolivia's seasonally flooded grasslands have adapted to life in an area that, depending on the time of year, may be savanna or shallow wetlands. Slight variations in topography create small, tree-covered islands in the knee-deep waters, offering tiny sanctuaries of terra firma.

For a newcomer to the scene, the landscape may seem surreal. Tropical birds in ostentatious plumage chatter in the treetops. The roar of howler monkeys booms through the forest. There are even giants here: giant anteaters, with their comical protruding proboscises, shuffle between termite mounds, and giant otters frolic in the Paragua River. El Refugio Huanchaca may be a wonderland, but it's not a fictional place. It's a 125,000-acre preserve and biological field station where three major natural communities—tree-speckled grassland or "pampa," wet Amazonian forest along the river, and drier semideciduous forest—meet and intermingle. The resulting diversity of life is spectacular.

Almost untouched by the modern world, the area retains populations of endangered species, such as the giant otter and maned wolf, that have been displaced from much of their original range. About two-thirds of El Refugio is an inholding within Noel Kempff Mercado National Park, which is one of the largest protected areas in South America. Visible from El Refugio is the property's namesake, the Huanchaca Plateau, rising some 1,800 feet above the surrounding jungle and draped in cascading waterfalls. A huge sandstone escarpment discovered by British explorer Percy Fawcett (who later disappeared in the Amazon jungle), the 120-mile-long plateau along Bolivia's border with Brazil was the inspiration for Sir Arthur Conan Doyle's dinosaur stronghold in *The Lost World*.

A century later, the area's wild nature is still much a mystery; only a few major groups of organisms have been surveyed at El Refugio, and researchers find new species with each visit. Tropical ecologist Louise Emmons describes the small-mammal diversity in the refuge's grasslands as "really rich." But so far, she says, "hardly anyone has set foot in the forest" because of the challenging access. In the wet season, crossing flooded pampa to get to the forest is nigh on impossible, and during the dry season, there is no water there to support a field camp. "Much of it is pretty well unexplored," says Emmons.

But if the ecology of El Refugio remains largely an intellectual terra incognita, the place itself is no longer a lost world, protected simply by its remoteness. As throughout the Amazon basin, government-granted logging concessions and encroaching settlement nibble away at the wilderness. Without El Refugio's small staff as a deterrent, poachers and timber thieves would freely use the Paragua River to access and exploit the park, a common concern in nominally "protected" areas throughout the developing world. Thus the refuge serves as a crucial bulwark securing Noel Kempff's southern boundary.

This conservation success was made possible by three generations of the Weeden family and their New York–based family foundation. A small investment to acquire and operate El Refugio has returned conservation dividends far out of proportion to the cost. A happy outcome, but perhaps not surprising, given that the Weedens are accustomed to making smart investments.

*It's wild and unspoiled, with jaguars and pumas and all the smaller creatures scurrying about the forest floor. And you've got harpy eagles, southern screamers, jabiru storks . . . probably six hundred bird species just in Noel Kempff National Park.*

—Alan Weeden

Alan Weeden loves birds—familiar ones, like the eastern bluebirds outside his home in Connecticut, and exotic ones, like the flashy jabiru storks that frequent El Refugio's marshlands. From the Australian outback to the plains of Africa, Weeden has traveled the globe to see them. His interest in natural history stretches back to childhood in the San Francisco Bay Area, when there was still plenty of open country for the four Weeden boys to explore. "We grew up at a time when the population was six million in the entire state," he recalls. "We'd ramble around, go out to the mudflats . . . it was a paradise growing up in California in those days." A trip with his grandparents to Yosemite around 1930, when Alan was six or seven, helped foster a lifelong love for nature.

After serving in World War II, Alan migrated east and, along with his brothers, Jack and Don, helped run the New York operation of the securities firm their father, Frank Weeden, had cofounded in San Francisco in the 1920s. Weeden & Company flourished. Don became a Wall Street maverick, fighting the New York Stock Exchange to deregulate fixed commissions, and was later honored as the "father of electronic trading." Alan headed the bond department, and Jack ran operations for the company. All three were active in political and environmental issues, but Alan especially helped steer the Weeden Foundation, established by his father in the 1960s, to the intertwined issues of preserving biodiversity and reversing human population growth.

Since retiring in 1980, Alan has devoted himself to conservation, working quietly but with considerable influence. He's helped numerous environmental groups and causes. He served on the founding board of directors of Conservation International and helped launch the American Bird Conservancy. ABC president George Fenwick calls him a "bird conservation hero," whose wisdom and wealth of experience was invaluable during the group's formative years. "Every new conservation organization should have its own Alan Weeden," he says.

As president of the Weeden Foundation for twenty-one years, Alan directed its grantmaking to smaller, progressive groups. "Environmental organizations are very much like high-tech start-up firms in that so much depends upon the leadership," he says. "When you invest in small, rather than large, organizations, it is much easier to assess whether that leadership is doing a good job." And at a time when such giving was unusual for a family foundation, particularly one that also funded scrappy wilderness advocates, the Weeden Foundation began supporting land acquisition, often in the biodiversity-rich tropics.

Beginning in the mid-1980s, the foundation funded projects in Ecuador, Costa Rica, Belize, Chile, Namibia, and Peru. "I think probably a third of our grants have been made overseas to acquire, protect, or secure land," Weeden says. With his background in finance, Alan Weeden was among the first conservationists to recognize the potential of "debt-for-nature" swaps, in which a developing country's foreign debt is lessened in exchange for in-country conservation actions such as creating new parks. As part of a 1987 deal brokered by Conservation International, the foundation's $100,000 gift purchased $650,000 of Bolivian commercial bank debt and helped leverage pro-tection for the 3.7-million-acre Beni Reserve in Bolivia. It was the first transaction of its kind, and stimulated similar debt-for-nature exchanges elsewhere in the developing world. It also got Alan Weeden interested in preserving Bolivia's extraordinary, and increasingly imperiled, natural heritage.

Until the early 1990s, most of the foundation's giving toward land deals was through established organizations such as the World Wildlife Fund and the Nature Conservancy. With El Refugio, the Weeden Foundation invested directly to save the land and to create a field station where American and Bolivian biologists might collaborate on research projects. When approached by the land's owner, a prominent Bolivian businessman who had briefly considered developing a cattle ranch there but whose financial situation had dimmed, Alan Weeden jumped into a three-way partnership with the gentleman and a European investor. "We just wanted to save it," he says. "It's a remarkable piece of property."

By 2000, the foundation had bought out the Bolivian partner's interest and been given the European partner's stake in El Refugio. The cost to acquire 125,000 acres of Bolivian wilderness, with globally significant biodiversity? Approximately $400,000, less than a one-bedroom apartment in Soho. (And unlike El Refugio, where the jaguars hunt marsh deer in the pampa, in Manhattan they lounge around garages, racking up parking fees.)

The Weeden Foundation leadership has since formally skipped to the next generation. Alan Weeden's nephew Norman Weeden, a professor and researcher in plant genetics, currently serves as president; Alan's son Don is the executive director. And there is every indication that the family's investments in innovative conservation projects will continue the tradition established by Alan Weeden.

An active octogenarian, Alan continues to visit Bolivia every year or two, where he admires the red-shouldered macaws that awaken visitors to El Refugio at dawn. Unlike many people in his position, Weeden doesn't collect things ("I don't want to have to build a warehouse to keep the stuff I can't get into my house"), but he has spent a lifetime collecting experiences in wild country, particularly memories of the birds he sees there. He remains enthusiastic about birding and bird conservation, but is as modest about his ornithological knowledge as about the successes he's helped make possible through decades of environmental activism. "I'm not a very good birder," he says, "and my eyes aren't as good as they used to be—I just enjoy it." But when pressed about his life list, he admits to having seen just shy of four thousand species, and hopes to reach that milestone before hanging up his binoculars. To put that number in perspective, four thousand is roughly five times the total number of bird species that can be seen in North America, and more than 40 percent of the total number of bird species globally.

While El Refugio Huanchaca exists first and foremost as a sanctuary for the region's wild residents—from anacondas to tapirs—an adjunct benefit from its conservation is the opportunity for scientists and occasional visitors to experience life's diversity in one of the wildest places left on Earth. For Alan Weeden, the best way to do that is by watching the winged creatures in the passing nature show. "A few friends went down with me to El Refugio," he says, "and we saw about 225 species in two and a half days." He can't help but smile. "It was pretty good birding."

B lazing sunshine and grazing cattle. Arid grasslands that stretch to the horizon. A person traveling in northern Namibia might almost mistake this landscape for parts of the American West. Except for the elephants. And the lions. And pretty much the whole array of charismatic megafauna associated with the African savanna: rhinos, leopards, giraffes, buffalo, antelope, hyenas . . . All are present in this young, sparsely populated nation on the southwestern coast of Africa, a country the size of Texas and Oklahoma combined, but with fewer people than Houston. Besides occupying similar landscapes a world apart, it seems that many U.S. and Namibian livestock producers also share a deep hostility toward wild predators, which they perceive as threatening to their economic interests. In America the ire may be directed at mountain lions, in Namibia toward cheetahs, but the result is often the same. Dead cats.

# CHEETAH CONSERVATION FUND RESERVE
## Racing Extinction

The cheetah's explosive speed—from zero to sixty miles an hour in three seconds—is an extraordinary spectacle. It seems strange that such a powerful animal could be so vulnerable, but human antipathy in an implacable force. No cat can outrace bullets, and when people destroy its habitat, a creature's speed is irrelevant. There will be nowhere to run, no prey to pursue. Beyond these direct assaults on health and home, a severe population contraction ten thousand years ago means modern cheetahs have descended from relatively few ancestors, leaving them with little genetic diversity and making the species potentially more vulnerable to reproductive problems and disease.

Moreover, one tried-and-true conservation tool—establishing protected areas—is by itself not certain to sustain cheetahs, which are good hunters but poor fighters. In parks where cheetahs compete with other large carnivores for food, their kills are frequently stolen, fueling pressure for them to disperse outside reserves into agricultural lands. When they do, they are often shot or poisoned.

*Cathryn Hilker*       *Carl Hilker*       *Laurie Marker*

Now among the most imperiled cats on Earth, cheetahs once ranged across four continents, including North America, but currently survive only in Africa and Asia. As recently as a century ago, one hundred thousand cheetahs roamed the sub-Saharan grasslands, while today only a tenth that number survive worldwide. Namibia's estimated three thousand cheetahs are the most in any single nation, but that population has declined dramatically in the past two decades.

The heart of Namibian cattle country, then, in the Waterberg Plateau region, was a logical spot for American biologist Laurie Marker to launch the nonprofit Cheetah Conservation Fund (CCF). Since its founding in the early 1990s, she has grown CCF into the world's leading cheetah research and conservation organization.

Laurie Marker is a dynamo, and her vision is a key reason for the group's success. But so, too, is the cheetah's ability to capture hearts and minds. By introducing these spotted speedsters to people, by communicating their plight, and by developing conservation initiatives that emphasize both biological and social goals, the Cheetah Conservation Fund has achieved notable progress. Nonlethal predator control methods have been successfully adopted by many local farmers. (What would be called "ranches" in America are "farms" in Namibia.) With CCF as a key partner, the Waterberg Conservancy, a regional coalition of landowners committed to sustainable use of the landscape, has greatly expanded the protected area where wildlife may range

*The heart of the story is that the Hilkers, the Grahams, and other key supporters who helped create the sanctuary, simply love cheetahs. Beyond that, they understand the big picture—that carnivores are vital to healthy ecosystems.*

—Laurie Marker

freely without persecution. CCF's education programs are teaching Namibian schoolchildren ecological principles and instilling respect for native wildlife, and the organization has gained strong political support.

Perhaps most remarkably, a small group of donors has helped the Cheetah Conservation Fund assemble a one-hundred-thousand-acre wildlife preserve around its headquarters. Who would have guessed that an Ohio couple, a family from Texas, a New Jersey woman, and an Atlanta businessman would become vital actors in the cheetah's struggle to survive on the plains of Africa? But they, and other CCF supporters large and small, have catalyzed this series of minor miracles—which offers hope that humanity may yet choose a future with space enough for cheetahs.

Most people, when they say they have a kitten in the house, don't mean a cheetah. At Cathryn and Carl Hilker's rural home in Ohio, one never knows. Taking the cat out for exercise might mean a tawny feline blur racing down the driveway at highway speeds. Cathryn has hand-raised several cheetahs, following in a tradition that stretches back four thousand years. From ancient Sumeria to medieval Europe, it was fashionable among royalty to maintain cheetah companions as symbols of power and prestige. Hilker's intent, of course, was conservation, not self-glorification. The captive cheetahs and mountain lions she has trained have become emissaries in the Cincinnati Zoo's Cat Ambassador program, which she founded.

Cathryn and her husband, Carl, a semiretired aviation executive, have maintained a longtime love affair with Africa. After college in the 1950s, Cathryn lived there for a time, working with anthropologist Louis Leakey (she turned down his offer to study chimps, a project that was to make Jane Goodall world-famous). Kindred spirits in their devotion to wild cats, the Hilkers became friends with Laurie Marker and were early supporters and board members of CCF. They offered to buy property in Namibia for use as the group's headquarters.

For the first few years after Marker moved to the Waterberg Plateau region in 1991, funding for the new conservation initiative was thin, and local landowners were generally hostile to an American woman who wanted them to stop killing wild cats. She was told precisely where she and her damned cheetahs could go. But through persistence, and a consistently nonconfrontational approach, she gained their respect, particularly as the guard dogs that CCF gave away eliminated livestock losses from predation. "The best record of success," says Carl Hilker, "is when one farmer tells another, 'Well, ever since I got a guard dog from those crazy Americans, I've never lost an animal.' That says more than all the preaching in the world."

In 1994, when Laurie Marker called from Namibia with news about an eighteen-thousand-acre parcel for sale, Carl Hilker visited his banker and got on a plane with a down payment. He contributed most of the purchase price. A $150,000 loan from the Weeden Foundation, an environmental grantmaker based in New York City, covered the balance, and the land and first year's operating costs for the new headquarters were secured for $560,000. The loan was subsequently repaid with the help of Atlanta businessman Phil Osborne, and the Hilkers donated the land to the California-based WILD Foundation, which held title and acted as CCF's fiscal agent in the United States for more than a decade. Vance Martin, who heads the WILD Foundation, has also been a crucial player in the Cheetah Conservation Fund's success, serving as CCF president since its inception.

In 1996, two years after the initial land purchase, an adjacent farm went on the market, and because its access road bisected the new cheetah conservation area, it was imperative to secure the property. The land had been managed as a hunting reserve and, atypically for the region, had not been badly overgrazed by livestock. It was extraordinary wildlife habitat, connected on one side to Waterberg National Park, and included towering cliffs where the Waterberg Plateau rises six hundred feet from the surrounding plain. The Hilkers again rushed into the breach, and bought the land.

Five more contiguous properties have been purchased since, "always through some happy accident," says Carl. Each time an opportunity arose to expand the protected area, he says, "somebody would step forward with a checkbook." In three instances, the land protectors were CCF USA board chair Annie Graham and her husband, Bob, a Texas couple with a deep interest in carnivore conservation. Another purchase was funded by Susan and Art Babson, long-standing and very generous CCF supporters from New Jersey. All the donors were people who had come into Laurie Marker's orbit, been captivated by the cheetah, and committed their resources to help the species survive.

"Now we have seven Namibian farms that were all directly provided by U.S. donors and U.S. dollars," says Carl. Current Namibian law prevents foreigners from owning land, so six of the seven properties are held by a Namibian charitable trust, and one is a privately held corporation; they are managed jointly as the Cheetah Conservation Fund headquarters. The bulk of the reserve is strictly protected for wildlife, and part is used as a model farm to demonstrate ecologically sound livestock management.

Cathryn Hilker will tell you that the decision to devote her life's work to saving cheetahs was not her own. It was made by Angel, a cheetah kitten Cathryn picked to help raise funds in 1981 for a new carnivore house at the Cincinnati Zoo. Subsequently Cathryn was asked to bring Angel to a local public school. That visit was so popular that an ongoing education program was launched. One day, when Cathryn and Angel were to give a presentation, a moment of intense, nonverbal communication between them led Cathryn to an epiphany: "She was totally imprinted on me," Cathryn recalls. "She was giving me her life. I knew that I could do no less." Perhaps the group of philanthropists who helped create this sanctuary for African cheetahs were similarly chosen, called to give something of their life's energy in a great cause, preventing extinction for the fastest creature that roams the earth.

On the second Namibian property the Hilkers purchased, Carl found a multitrunked leadwood tree twenty-nine feet in circumference. The tree is massive, and likely ancient, for individual leadwoods may live for two thousand years. Cathryn and Carl find it a comfort to know that the arboreal elder will continue to be a witness to wildness, as it has for centuries—watching the parched landscape grow green after seasonal rains, seeing the steenbok and kudu wander by looking for the sweetest grass, ever ready to flee from a blur of spotted fur. "You can't save anything unless you save the wilderness—the habitat—first," Carl says.

Laurie Marker is fond of saying, "Save the cheetah, change the world," to encapsulate her vision of an ecologically robust and socially just society in Namibia and beyond. Is she optimistic about the cat's prospects? "Only if we can awaken people to realize that there won't be any cheetahs left in twenty-five years unless we change," she says. "I'm always hopeful," she continues, "and will be until my dying day, but I most hope that the necessary changes that will allow wild predators to flourish come a bit more rapidly."

Changing the world, and saving a place in it for large carnivores, is a formidable prospect. But each cheetah that stalks supper under the Hilkers' leadwood tree, that can lead its one wild life in freedom, represents conservationists' tangible progress toward that noble end.

# BLANTON FOREST
## The Rediscovered Wilderness

*Marc Evans*

Most boys growing up in the Chicago area in the late 1950s wanted to be Ernie Banks, slugging home runs at Wrigley Field. Marc Evans dreamed of being Daniel Boone, exploring the wilderness. He loved rambling about in the patch of woods at the end of his street, climbing trees, getting dirty. It was his own terra incognita, the dark Kentucky woods of his imagination. "Most of our free time was spent in those woods," he recalls. "Then one day we started seeing surveyor stakes." Evans and his buddies pulled the stakes, but it was a token gesture. How could a few kids stop the march of progress? The bulldozers arrived. The forest disappeared. In its place stood a typical suburban housing development with a few old oaks left as lawn trees.

Now in his fifties, Marc Evans is still working to save wild forests, and, despite the gray hair in his beard, he's still playing Daniel Boone, albeit in a fashion suited to our times. As the ecology program manager for the Kentucky State Nature Preserves Commission, Evans conducts natural area inventories for the state's 120 counties. It's a big job, just right for a person like him who has both a supersized love for nature and a childlike enthusiasm for bushwhacking through rhododendron thickets (he ranks them for difficulty the way kayakers rate white water) in search of Kentucky's natural wonders. He does it for science, and for sheer love of the land. "It's probably been a good day if I come home very dirty, covered with scratches," he says.

Being a state agency biologist is not the most lucrative occupation, but Evans likes his job: "They give me 25 million acres as my backyard, I've got a helicopter at my disposal, and I get to explore." Evans has used his sleuthing skills to good effect; he is responsible for finding more than half of the natural areas now represented in the state's nature preserves system. The capstone of this career in conservation was helping to preserve Blanton Forest, a biological gem in the heart of eastern Kentucky's coal mining country. Evans was astounded to discover a large stand of never-logged forest, roughly 2,300 acres, while doing inventory work in Harlan County in 1992. His energy level, which is perpetually on high, went into overdrive. Evans spent years courting the land's owners and cofounded a new nonprofit, the Kentucky Natural Lands Trust, to buy the property when they were ready to sell. He helped raise money for the forest's purchase and worked to shepherd the area through its formal dedication as a state nature preserve.

The campaign to save Blanton Forest was ultimately a collective victory. Hundreds of Kentuckians made donations of time and energy to see it permanently protected, but if not for Marc Evans, the land on Pine Mountain that Grover Blanton purchased in the 1920s, and which his daughters still owned in the 1990s, almost certainly would have been sold to loggers. The ancient oaks and hemlocks would have been skimmed off, and the state's largest tract of primeval forest—incomparable for ecological research and enjoyment—would have fallen, as virtually all of Kentucky's original forests did after Daniel Boone and his followers blazed the wilderness road and established Boonesborough in 1775.

Blanton Forest is a land of superlatives: It has magnificent cliffs and rock shelters, and jumbled boulders dripping with moss. It has hundreds of species of plants and four major forest types. It has big trees, some up to four feet in diameter and more than three hundred years old. It has a bewildering array of ferns, lichens, and wildflowers. It has the blackside dace, a small, imperiled fish with race-car-style red and black stripes. (The dace's sporty good looks didn't keep it from swimming onto the federal endangered species list as Appalachia's formerly clear mountain streams grew murky from coal mining and careless logging.) Blanton Forest has mountain bogs at

*I couldn't believe an old-growth forest of this size still existed in Kentucky.*
*I felt like I'd died and gone to botanist heaven.*
—Marc Evans

the headwaters of its streams, the most pristine example of these rare wetland communities known in the state. It even has cliff-jumping snakes.

Once, when Marc Evans emerged from the woods onto the appropriately named Knobby Rock, he noticed some two dozen black ratsnakes and black racers sunning themselves on the stone promontory. The snakes reacted to his presence by slithering to the cliff's edge and hurling themselves off the precipice, presumably landing safely in the tree branches below.

More prosaic than snakes with the chutzpah to leap into the void to escape an approaching botanist (one wonders if they would be similarly shy of a herpetologist), Blanton Forest also has ground-nesting wasps. During the fundraising campaign to buy Blanton Forest, Marc Evans regularly led walks for potential donors. One such walk occurred in the autumn, when wasps are still active. Someone near the front of the group stepped on a nest, kicking up a frenzy of stinging insects defending their homeland. Evans turned around to see a fundraiser's worst nightmare: "It was chaos," he says. "People were screaming and running through the forest, ripping off their clothes." Eventually the wasps retreated and the group reassembled to finish the hike, but Evans went home feeling depressed. "I was certain the day had been a disaster," he recalls.

Here was a magical place, the greatest natural area discovery in the state's recent history. Local residents, many of whom had spent time as kids at the adjacent Boy Scout camp, generally supported preserving the forest. But public and private funding for land conservation in Kentucky is relatively scarce, and this project was in deepest Appalachia, an ecological and social landscape America has pointedly ignored and which even Kentuckians often forget. Blanton Forest is far from the state's centers of power and commerce; to buy the tract and endow its perpetual stewardship, a brand new land trust was attempting to raise $2.5 million in private donations that would be augmented with $1 million of state funding. Like the trail to Knobby Rock, it was an uphill climb, and the wasps didn't help.

Fortunately, two young girls on the hike had a decidedly different view of that day's adventure in the autumn woods. Afterward, they visited their grandmother and told her that strolling among the towering trees with leaves ablaze in color "was like walking through a rainbow." Could she please help save the forest? She could. Due to age, the girls' grandmother would never hike the trails through Blanton Forest herself, but she would help make sure that its tapestry of life stayed unfrayed. She made an anonymous gift of $500,000 toward the Blanton Forest campaign. The James Graham Brown Foundation of Louisville contributed an equal amount. Several other donors made large gifts, hundreds of people made smaller donations, and an adjacent landowner gave property worth $400,000 to expand the sanctuary. The fundraising drive was off and running like the thoroughbreds at Kentucky's Churchill Downs the first Saturday in May.

Launched in reaction to crisis or opportunity, most of the United States' 1,500 land trusts have a creation story similar to that of the Kentucky Natural Lands Trust (KNLT): a local treasure will be lost if people do not collectively rise to its defense. The narrative may vary in details—whether the property is large or small, pristine or in need of restoration, agricultural or wild—but when the outcome is successful, the confidence built within a community of conservationists continues to grow. The victory, rather than an end, is a beginning.

With KNLT, that continuing story is multipronged. The trust owns the 3,090-acre Blanton Forest State Nature Preserve and oversees its use with a full-time sanctuary manager. Scientists have developed a design for enlarging the preserve to roughly 6,700 acres to more fully protect the area's ecological attributes. And as neighboring landowners consider conservation, the land trust and its partners will work with willing sellers to fill out the sanctuary.

The success of the Blanton Forest campaign also emboldened the Kentucky Natural Lands Trust to launch an ambitious effort to protect ecological integrity along the whole of Pine Mountain, the 120-mile-long ridge upon which Blanton Forest sits. That landscape-scale project, to be accomplished over decades, will enlist communities, private landowners, governments, and the forest products industry to develop a system of conserved lands on Pine Mountain—some nature preserves, some managed timberlands—that will keep wildlife habitat intact.

Should that happy end come to pass, people will likely look back at the Blanton Forest campaign as a watershed moment for conservation in Kentucky, but even today the state's environmental leaders recognize it as a landmark. Hugh Archer, a founding board member of KNLT who was also central to the Blanton Forest success, says, "In twenty-five years of working on natural area projects, this is the high point." And Archer's opinion carries considerable authority; he was the long-time commissioner of the state's Department of Natural Resources and now serves as KNLT's executive director. "The old-growth forest here is awe-inspiring," he says. "It had to be saved."

Could there be another pocket of primeval forest out there somewhere, hidden among the hills and hollows, just waiting to be found and preserved by conservationists? Walking in Blanton Forest one spring day with his friend Hugh Archer and some visitors, Marc Evans hedges: "Prior to discovering this, I would have bet a million dollars that we didn't have a 2,300-acre tract of old-growth forest in Kentucky. We're too good at cutting trees down. Now I wouldn't make that bet."

As a kid, Marc Evans couldn't save his backyard wilderness from being destroyed. As a grown man, the Daniel Boone of Kentucky botanists keeps poring over maps, flying over forests, and, at the slightest provocation, crawling through the gnarliest rhododendron thickets to find nature's last strongholds. Along with his colleagues in the Kentucky conservation community, he's working to make certain those places need never fear the bulldozer's arrival.

# HIGHLANDS NATURE SANCTUARY

## Building the Arc of Appalachia

*Larry Henry and
Nancy Stranahan*

The song of a chuck-will's-widow, larger cousin to the whip-poor-will, drifts through the dark. Cricket frogs sing from a nearby pond. It's past midnight and Nancy Stranahan is crouched before an orchid. The entourage of apprentice naturalists accompanying her would have missed the yellow lady's slipper had it not been ringed in a halo of light from her flashlight. The director of the Highlands Nature Sanctuary, Nancy arranged to meet the property owner this evening to sign a purchase agreement, after which her group stayed on to explore this rare prairie remnant in a typically forested region of south-central Ohio.

Named Ka-ma-ma Prairie after the Cherokee word for butterfly, the seventy-eight-acre cedar barrens will become the latest addition to the Highlands Nature Sanctuary's portfolio of conserved lands. With some five hundred identified species of vascular plants (over forty of which are state-recognized rarities), more than sixty kinds of butterflies, and scores of birds, amphibians, and small mammals, Ka-ma-ma is perhaps the finest example of alkaline shortgrass prairie in the state. Preserving it is just one highlight in a string of successes orchestrated by sanctuary cofounders Nancy Stranahan and Larry Henry, whose ultimate goal is to see interconnected conservation lands across a region they call the Arc of Appalachia, a ninety-mile-long fertile crescent stretching from Chillicothe south to the Ohio River. It would seem the most unlikely of dreams to come true, but Highlands Nature Sanctuary supporters are helping restore wilderness in this long-settled corner of the American heartland.

Helping visitors understand the ground they stand on is central to the sanctuary's mission. "We teach woodlands literacy," says Nancy, pulling out a map that shows the temperate broadleaf forest's historic range. "We want urban people in Columbus to say, 'I live in what was once an immense forest that covered the eastern third of our continent. It's cut down, but that's what's supposed to grow here.'" Larry Henry and other experts teach numerous groups each year about the area's trees, wildflowers, butterflies, freshwater mussels, and other wildlife. "The Arc of Appalachia is where three ecoregions converge," he says, referring to where midwestern glacial plains, the Kentucky Bluegrass region, and the western Appalachian foothills meet. The convergence leads to exceptional species richness. The expression of that richness aboveground reflects the land's deep-time history—whether, for instance, glaciers scraped and freshened the soil on their last southward trek—and its bedrock geology.

"If you were to walk northeast to Pennsylvania," says Larry, "you'd see plants adapted to the old acidic soils of Appalachia all the way. But here you've got not only sandstone and shale, as in the Appalachian foothills, but also limestone and dolomite bedrocks. This gives you caves and springs, and the result of all that is phenomenal diversity." Describing the state's southernmost bulge, which is bounded by the Ohio River, Larry concludes, "We're in one of eastern America's botanical hotspots."

Nancy and Larry acknowledge a common reaction to the sanctuary's mission: "Wilderness? In Ohio? Are these people crazy?" To most people, wilderness means Alaska. Ohio is farmland and rust belt cities. Even locals don't often stop to remember that the Buckeye State was once covered with buckeyes and black gums, oaks and hickories, and dozens of other tree species. The eastern deciduous forest that greeted European settlers, and which they promptly set about clearing, was one of the great natural wonders of the world. And could be again.

*Even as most science is still working on microcosms, we're trying to draw connections.*
*We're thinking with the heart, and thinking big.*
—Nancy Stranahan

Stranahan and Henry are Ohio natives, she from Cleveland, he a coal miner's son whose dialect reflects his hill country roots. Larry worked his way up from emptying park trash cans to the top civil service job in Ohio State Parks. Nancy, who had become hooked on nature as a teenager, finished college and later became chief naturalist for the state parks system. Burned out on bureaucracy, they left their government jobs in the early 1980s to run a small business. They bought a piece of degraded farmland outside Columbus and nursed it back to health, operated a market garden, and became vendors at the city's historic North Market. Their retail business morphed into a successful bakery and café called Benevolence. They were comfortable financially, but something was missing. "By midlife, the goal of questing after the American dream was fading fast," recalls Nancy. "There was a hunger in us for wildness, and to serve something other than ourselves."

A trip to Central America offered an opportunity for intense personal reflection: "I realized I had always been hungry for life," Nancy says. "In the rainforests of Costa Rica, I was finally filled . . . completely surrounded by life in a density and diversity I had never known before." They thought of staying in Costa Rica, living the life of hip American expatriates, but the high of experiencing pristine nature on their first trip to the tropics soon burst. On their second sojourn south, Nancy recalls garbage befouling a coastal reef and plastic milk jugs covering the surface of a river bay. On a third trip, to Brazil, the forests were afire from slash-and-burn agriculture.

"An illusion was broken," says Nancy, "the illusion that there is somewhere left to go." As a teenager she had written an essay about moving north to Canada with a hawk on her arm. "You think you leave those childish fantasies behind—that you are going to escape to the wilderness—but I hadn't," she says. "And now I knew that there was nowhere I could go to escape the pain of seeing the natural world wounded. If you care, you are going to have to suffer."

Back home they realized that what they truly desired, says Larry, was "to buy and save land." And they wanted to do it in Ohio. "We had seen more beautiful places," Nancy adds, "but who cares about this place? We discovered, to our shock, that we cared really, really deeply." Originally they intended to simply donate an ecologically valuable property to the state nature preserves system, but once they rediscovered Highland County (Nancy had been a seasonal naturalist at a nearby state park just after high school), they fell in love with the area. Despite relatively dense human settlement elsewhere in the state, there was wildness aplenty left to protect in the southern Appalachian foothills. Land conservation opportunities arose so quickly that they formally launched the Highlands Nature Sanctuary in 1995.

For nine years, they juggled management responsibilities for their business in Columbus and for the sanctuary sixty miles south in Highland County. The two entities shared interns, and the bakery/café produced profits, all of which were recycled into land purchases. Ultimately the bifurcated life grew tiresome, and they sold Benevolence in 2004 to focus on conservation. Through its early years, the sanctuary's growth largely resulted from Nancy and Larry's commitment and energy. But in organizations, as on the land, natural succession happens. After a decade, some thirty-eight separate properties totaling roughly 1,600 acres had been secured in the Rocky Fork Creek watershed. By 2007, the group had raised roughly $9 million for land protection and had preserved nearly 3,000 acres. This expanding ribbon of green reflects not just the sanctuary founders' charisma but an engaged board of directors and a growing community of people dedicated to protecting wildlife and wild habitat. "On any

given day," says Nancy, "the sanctuary is a beehive of volunteer activity. It is really magical, and I am in a constant state of amazement and appreciation."

Unlike most nonprofits, the Highlands Nature Sanctuary eschews standard membership-building strategies. Supporters receive just one fundraising appeal annually and may choose to receive a sanctuary newsletter via e-mail. No telemarketing, no tote bags, no deluge of direct mail. "We hate all that," Nancy says. "We're just not going to do it." Yet the organization is thriving without it, which is almost as miraculous as the wildflowers that carpet the forest floor here in April.

Also atypical is the group's approach to land protection, which is based not merely on saving the last best scraps of nature but on rewilding the landscape. In much of North America, natural areas are few; reconnecting fragmented lands into whole and healthy ecosystems is the only means of achieving landscape-scale conservation. Many of the properties the sanctuary has preserved had structures on them. "Most nature preserves and land trusts don't know what to do about houses, so they either avoid them, or even more deadly, they cut them out of the preserve and resell them," explains Nancy. "We ask ourselves, 'In fifty years will we regret not buying the land beneath this house when we had the opportunity?' And then we buy them."

Work parties tear down older buildings, useful materials are recycled, and the sites begin to recover. If houses have considerable value or a mortgage to retire, they are rented to sympathetic tenants or remodeled as visitor lodging, thereby generating income and often attracting new supporters who come to hike or bird-watch at the sanctuary. When the mortgages are paid off and the sanctuary boundaries expand, these structures will be demolished, too. "We see houses as temporary stories on the land," says Nancy.

It's a bold dream to imagine an ancient forest again covering much of the East, particularly when most Americans' conception of wild nature is Yellowstone or Yosemite. But the Rocky Fork Gorge, which anchors the Highlands Nature Sanctuary, is as impressive in its way as any purple mountains' majesty. The creek, among the most pristine waters in Ohio, supports seventeen species of freshwater mollusks. It has been polishing and cutting through the rock for millennia. The walls of the gorge are draped in ferns. On a late winter's day, snow trilliums burst forth, to be followed by successive waves of wildflowers until the leaves bud out. In the summer, the forest canopy shades the creek, keeping the water cool and the fish happy.

It's hard to imagine any visitor here not feeling awed by the massive sycamores, charmed by the Blackburnian warblers singing overhead, healed, at least for moment, by the Rocky Fork's rushing waters. To be fully present here is to be open to acts of communion. The power of the place is genuine—it comes from the land and the people, and the growing connection between them.

# SHAWANGUNK RIDGE GREENWAY
## Room to Roam

*Robert Anderberg*

On the wall of Bob Anderberg's house in upstate New York is a framed photograph. The image shows a small figure on a massive rock wall. The climber is a younger iteration of Anderberg, ascending a route that in climbing lingo would be deemed "highly exposed." What lies outside the frame is unseen but easily imagined: sheer emptiness.

There are many places to fall in love with the natural world, but perhaps none better than alpine wilderness, which demands from those who enter it a high level of fortitude, commitment, and skill. Certainly many eco-luminaries came from the ranks of mountaineers. John Muir and David Brower, the most prominent evangelists for wild nature of the nineteenth and twentieth centuries, respectively, were first called to conservation by their love of mountains.

Bob Anderberg continues in that tradition. Vice president and general counsel for the Open Space Institute (OSI), a leading regional land trust, he has been exploring both vertical and horizontal surfaces of upstate New York's Shawangunk Ridge for decades. Before he was old enough to drive, he and a buddy hitchhiked to New Paltz, walked up onto the ridge, and threw down their sleeping bags. He was smitten. "For a kid from Long Island," Anderberg recalls, "it was the wilderness."

A young man seeking the freedom of the hills was perfectly in step with the region's history. As early as the 1820s, nature-loving pilgrims from downcountry began vacationing in the Hudson River valley. The Shawangunks' ascendance as a resort area began in 1870, when brothers Albert and Alfred Smiley opened their Mohonk Mountain House adjacent to one of the ridge's skytop lakes. The elegant hotel is still in operation, now surrounded by the 6,600-acre Mohonk Preserve. Ladies strolling woodland paths and gentlemen rowing wooden boats later gave way to more adventurous pursuits.

Since the 1930s, when Fritz Wiessner began putting up first ascents on the local cliffs, "the Gunks" have been a climber's mecca. The ridge's eastern face presents long, fractured cliffs of bitterly hard Shawangunk conglomerate, laid down over softer Martinsburg shale some four hundred million years ago. That luscious rock is cream-colored, mottled with shades of gray and red and flecked with dark green lichen. Bob Anderberg longed to be close to it. He landed a seasonal job as a climbing ranger in the Gunks during the 1970s and, excepting law school and professional obligations that temporarily pulled him away, has essentially never left.

Anderberg is ambitious in his vision for the Shawangunks, which are the New York portion of a 245-mile-long mountain range stretching across multiple states. (In New Jersey the range is called the Kittatinnies, and in Pennsylvania it's known as the Blue Mountains.) "The Open Space Institute has defined a mission here, and we're pursuing it vigorously," Anderberg says. That mission is to keep the northern part of the ridge ecologically intact, a laudable, if problematic, goal for an area within marginally commutable and definitely weekend range of New York City. Intense development pressure in the area has grown since the terrorist attacks of 2001 caused many urban dwellers to consider country life.

Just as a fallen climber might dangle from a safety rope, the wild places that conservationists work so hard to save are generally threatened with obliteration, hanging by a thin line of hope that spirited people will rally to their defense. Local groups of activists, including Friends of the Shawangunks, have done just that, fending off several large-scale development projects that would have scarred the ridge. This kind of reactive environmentalism, and the opportunistic land conservation along the ridge since the Smiley brothers' era, have been crucial to saving some exceptional places but did not fully protect the ridge's ecology. A more systematic, proactive approach was needed to safeguard the Shawangunks' natural communities and preserve habitat connectivity for wildlife. The Open Space Institute stepped into the breach. In collaboration with other nonprofits and state and local governments, OSI is helping to build the Shawangunk Ridge Greenway. "I envision a continuous swath of protected parkland stretching forty-eight miles along the ridge, from Wurtsboro to New Paltz," Anderberg says.

A good bit of this vision has already been achieved since OSI became active in the Gunks in the mid-1980s. "Thus far we've purchased roughly nineteen thousand acres on or adjacent to the ridge, helping to expanded the network of public and privately held conservation lands to over forty-three thousand acres," says Anderberg. "We're far from done, but we've saved for all time some of the most magnificent landmarks of this remarkable little mountain range."

Most properties bought by the Open Space Institute have subsequently been conveyed to public ownership. Bob Anderberg has been central to this success, negotiating and closing dozens of land deals. His work in the Gunks, however, is in addition to supervising all the organization's legal business, mostly from a Manhattan office. "Bob has very little field time built into his job," says Joe Martens, president of OSI. "He's doing these deals on the weekend. He just lives and breathes conservation."

Not unlike the black bears who live along the Shawangunk Ridge, Bob Anderberg likes to ramble. Since giving up technical rock climbing, he has channeled his energies into exploring the ridge's wildest nooks on foot, and sometimes on his belly. "I've always thought that if you really want to get to know the Gunks, you have to crawl on your stomach through the pitch pine," he says. (Adopting a snake's-eye vantage point is, fortunately, not the only way to see eastern timber rattlesnakes, one of the area's notable wildlife attractions.) The country continues to surprise him. "After hiking here for more than three decades, I still see something new every weekend," says Anderberg. "This is an extraordinarily varied landscape, with windswept cliffs, talus fields, secluded glens, ice caves . . . it's fabulous habitat and also exceptionally beautiful."

Among the Shawangunks' exceptional natural areas is Sam's Point Preserve. In 1997, the Open Space Institute bought 4,700 ridgetop acres from the village of Ellenville. The Ellenville tract, now expanded to 5,500 acres and renamed Sam's Point, had been owned by the town for over a century and was subject to various extractive uses, from commercial berry picking to tourist trap. "If you were on your way to the museum of the world's largest ball of twine, this was your next stop," Anderberg says of the formerly commercialized ice caves on the preserve, which are actually deep ridgefront crevasses that hold snow long into the summer. The Nature Conservancy now manages Sam's Point under a long-term lease, and the bulk of it has been added to the Minnewaska State Park Preserve.

Like Anderberg's favored style of hiking, the conservation success here came only after a long bushwhack through a political thicket. He worked on the Sam's Point acquisition for nine years, gradually building support for a deal whereby the Open Space Institute purchased the land, which secured for the village of Ellenville a cash windfall and future revenue. (Once the land is in public ownership, the state makes payments in lieu of property taxes to local governments.) "He just doesn't give up," says Annie O'Neill, a longtime board member of the local conservation group Friends of the Shawangunks. "Bob is amazing—he was tireless in his pursuit of this, and the preserve would not have been created without him."

A June day at Sam's Point: The mountain laurel's bright pink blossoms are in full bloom. Clouds hang low in the valleys, and the land rolls away into mist like a giant otter's back. The dwarf pitch pine barrens natural community covering the ridgetop is both unusually attractive—a gnarled forest in miniature—and globally rare. The ice caves, now stripped of tacky tourist accoutrements, are notable, too, and not just for the respite from the heat they offer to human visitors. The year-round cool, damp microclimate supports an ice cave talus natural community, with plants such as black spruce and creeping snowberry that are more typical of Canada than the Hudson River valley.

Sam's Point Preserve, Witch's Hole Conservation Area, and the Vernooy Kill and Shawangunk Ridge state forests—these and other lands along the ridge might not have been protected if not for Bob Anderberg. His passion for the Gunks, the leadership demonstrated by OSI's trustees, and a broad coalition of groups dedicated to the region are crucial factors in the Shawangunk Ridge Greenway's incremental protection. But so, too, is another kind of green. By 2005 the Open Space Institute had invested roughly $17 million in the Shawangunks, virtually all of it from Lila and DeWitt Wallace, cofounders of *Reader's Digest*.

As a young married couple in 1922, they launched the magazine out of their Greenwich Village apartment. *Reader's Digest* reached more than a million subscribers by 1935, and at the time of Lila and DeWitt Wallace's deaths in the 1980s was the most widely read periodical in the world, anchoring a global publishing empire. The couple, who had no heirs, were active philanthropists during their lifetime, and left to charity an estate valued at more than $3 billion. The bulk went to cultural and medical institutions, but the Lila Acheson and DeWitt Wallace Fund for the Hudson Highlands was created to support two conservation groups, Scenic Hudson and the Open Space Institute, and helped underwrite land protection in the Shawangunks and throughout the Hudson River valley during the 1980s. The assets were legally split between the two groups in 1991, with each receiving roughly $130 million to support future land preservation work.

It would be hard to overestimate how important this bequest has been in maintaining the region's traditional character. "Lila Wallace was deeply committed to the history and beauty of the Hudson Highlands, and during her life preserved historic landscapes, farms, and natural areas," says Kim Elliman, chief executive officer of the Open Space Institute. "Her philanthropy continues through the dedicated fund held by OSI that conserves her treasured landscapes of the Hudson River valley."

Bob Anderberg never met the Wallaces, but through their gift his dream for saving the Gunks is coming true. More than a hundred years ago, Anderberg's great-grandfather helped assemble the lands that would become Algonquin Provincial Park in Ontario, one of eastern North America's premier wild areas. Today Anderberg is also attempting to save an enduring resource of wilderness, and one can envision the completed Shawangunk Ridge Greenway as a destination for ramblers and climbers and others seeking wild beauty a century hence. Moreover, future generations of black bears—the descendents of the bruins enjoying this year's feast of huckleberries at Sam's Point Preserve—will still have room to roam.

# FRESH TRACKS NATURE PRESERVE
## New West Meets Old

*Lauren McCain*          *Nicole Rosmarino*

Consider prairie dogs—those handsome rodents whose colonies, called "towns," once covered millions of acres of the American West. Ecologists, particularly of the new school, tend to view prairie dogs as "keystone species," indispensable players in a rich web of life associated with prairie dog burrows. Ranchers, particularly of the old school, tend to see them as vermin who eat grass that should profitably feed livestock. "Varmint" hunters, particularly of the subculture that congregates for prairie dog shooting sprees, enjoy using high-powered rifles to make the little creatures explode in a fine red mist. Animal rights activists, particularly of the confrontational variety, dutifully interrupt or shut down those killing jamborees whenever they can.

Now imagine you are in the latter camp. You are an activist in Boulder, Colorado. You're bright, idealistic, righteously contemptuous of injustice. You have a passionate commitment to the underdog—in this case, prairie dogs, which have suffered more than a century of relentless persecution on both public and private land. All that shooting, poisoning, and habitat destruction has resulted in current prairie dog numbers that are more than 98 percent reduced from historic population levels. Development along the Front Range from Colorado Springs to Fort Collins is exploding. Every week, acres of grassland, often with active prairie dog towns, are scraped away to make room for more houses, roads, and mini-marts. Despite the best efforts of conservationists to raise the profile of prairie dogs and their imperiled habitats, there are few regulatory impediments to anyone's firing up the bulldozer and obliterating a prairie dog colony, or using these ecologically valuable and highly social animals for target practice.

More precisely, you are Lauren McCain and Nicole Rosmarino, friends and fellow grad students pursuing PhDs in political science at the University of Colorado. You and your fellow activists have just been arrested for disrupting a prairie dog shoot by sneaking onto a prairie dog town and linking yourselves together with chains and bike locks, halting the massacre until the sheriff can haul you off.

That is how McCain, Rosmarino, and other arrested activists associated with Rocky Mountain Animal Defense found themselves spending the long Fourth of July weekend in 1997, not outdoors watching fireworks or camping in the mountains, but sitting inside the Kit Carson County jail. Jail food is notoriously bad, but the group didn't have to worry about it. Employing standard civil disobedience techniques to make their incarceration annoying to the system, they were on a hunger strike. As it did for civil dissent trailblazers Henry David Thoreau and Martin Luther King Jr., a little jail time gives a person time to think. *How can I more effectively resist the injustice I am fighting?*

Among the small band of animal defenders, ideas were percolating. Out of jail, the group convened a meeting to formulate their next move. The activists were frustrated. They wanted legal safeguards for prairie dogs (and would later achieve an incremental victory when most competitive prairie dog shoots were banned in Colorado), but felt that new tactics were needed. "We felt we weren't making any progress," Rosmarino recalls. "We realized that we wanted to buy land where we could assure protection for prairie dogs and other wildlife." They began hunting for a chunk of prairie.

*One night I had gone out to the preserve to watch a lunar eclipse. Burrowing owls were fluttering through the air, I was sitting in the dark listening to the grasses rustle in the wind, and just as the Earth's shadow hit the moon, coyotes burst into song.*

—Nicole Rosmarino

Baca County sits in the far southeastern corner of Colorado, abutting Oklahoma and New Mexico. The county's population peaked at 10,570 in 1930 and has been declining ever since. As farms were abandoned after the Dust Bowl era, the federal government began buying land, and today the Comanche National Grassland occupies much of the county. At the turn of the millennium, Baca County had just 4,517 residents, about 2 per square mile. It's arid here, a tough place for ranching.

Like the native plants and animals that flourished despite the shortgrass prairie's hot summers, cold winters, and sparse rainfall, the indigenous cultures that inhabited the Great Plains when Europeans arrived—Arapaho, Kiowa, Comanche, and others—were well adapted to the land. The new settlers had little appreciation for those adaptations, which were tuned to the land's ecology and tied to spiritual practices believed to maintain reciprocity between humans and the other animal nations. European-Americans generally viewed the grasslands either with contempt—as a wasteland—or with the rose-colored glasses of agricultural boosters. Many pioneers crossed the ocean of grass on their way to somewhere else, and those who stopped to homestead had a utilitarian view of the land. They got their living from it, as best they could, by taming it.

Then and now, the sky above the prairie seems almost impossibly big. For Easterners who had spent a lifetime wrapped in the comforting bosom of hills and trees, the landscape sometimes induced psychological distress. In one English visitor it produced disdain. Charles Dickens, seeing America in 1842, commented on the prairie's "very flatness and extent, which left nothing to the imagination, tamed it down and cramped its interest. . . . It was lonely and wild, but oppressive in its barren monotony. I felt that in traversing the Prairies, I could never abandon myself to the scene . . . but should often glance towards the distant and frequently-receding line of the horizon, and wish it gained and passed."

Too often, newcomers to the prairie mistake vastness for emptiness. The landscape that stretched before the pioneers was anything but empty—it teemed with life. Pronghorn antelope, North America's fastest animals, raced across the prairie, teasing the wolves that hoped to catch them. Ferruginous hawks and golden eagles soared overhead. Great herds of bison moved across the land like shadows from a passing thunderstorm. That prairie landscape is now greatly diminished, fenced in, plowed under, its wild bison and wolves a distant memory. But some people dream of the land as it might be again—unfettered, wild, and untamed under an azure sky.

In the fall of 1998, Lauren McCain, Nicole Rosmarino, and several other such dreamers launched the Southern Plains Land Trust. Robert Ukeiley, the attorney who had defended them during their prosecution for disrupting the prairie dog shoot, did the legal work and also became a founding board member. Within a few months, a likely property near the Comanche National Grassland had been identified—1,280 acres of worked-over ranchland in Baca County, near the town of Pritchett. By urban Colorado standards the land was cheap, just $192,000, but for the nascent land trust, that was a big sum to round up. An anonymous donor gave $20,000, nearly half the down payment; prairie dog champions Neil and Kathy Boucher contributed $10,000; board members all made personal donations and solicited gifts from their friends; and the Southern Plains Land Trust took title. Fresh Tracks Nature Preserve was born, the name inspired by a set of circling prints left by a coyote as it hunted prairie dogs on the sanctuary.

Then came the political backlash. Local ranchers spread rumors about the hippie liberal environ-mentalist radicals from Boulder who wanted to import truckloads of plague-infested vermin to Baca County. The local state senator quickly helped pass legislation that outlawed relocating prairie dogs from one Colorado county to another unless the receiving county's commissioners voted approval, effectively eliminating one potential tactic for saving animals in the path of development. But the new land trust was undeterred. Members held work parties and tore out the bottom two wires of fencing that had kept livestock in but impeded wildlife movement. After seventy-five years of being grazed by cattle, the land was free to follow its own course, to recover its wildness.

Nicole Rosmarino moved to Pritchett for three years to be the Fresh Tracks Preserve caretaker while writing her doctoral dissertation and following up on her formal petition to list the black-tailed prairie dog under the Endangered Species Act. She watched the land begin to heal, a process accelerated when a fire, likely set by an arsonist, burned over several hundred acres. Land trust members were delighted. They'd been thinking about how to return fire, a crucial natural agent in the prairie's cycle of life, to the land. Native plants, including blue grama, buffalo grass, western wheatgrass, needle-and-thread grass, and yucca thrived; invasives like snakeweed were knocked back by the fire. Pronghorn, mule deer, badgers, swift foxes, skunks, coyotes, pocket gophers, and a bobcat were seen on the sanctuary. The bird diversity was incredible. But one creature fared less well—the prairie dogs whose plight had initiated the preserve's founding.

When the Southern Plains Land Trust purchased Fresh Tracks, a few prairie dogs were present, part of a large colony centered on the adjacent ranch. Rosmarino and others had been monitoring that prairie dog town, which was growing, and the land trust had inquired about purchasing the area. Instead, the rancher hired someone to poison the animals. "I don't know when I've ever felt more rage," says McCain. "I'm convinced that the landowner poisoned the colony to spite us."

The conservationists' experience in Baca County is not unusual. Sometimes land preservation is popular. Sometimes it's not, particularly when the goal is to protect the full array of wildlife, including species perceived to be a threat to economic interests. The land trust has enjoyed increasing local support through the years, however, and has attracted several conservation buyers to purchase ranchlands in the area. Those properties are now managed for native species, including bison. And despite the initially unfulfilled task of prairie dog restoration, the preserve is sustaining many kinds of wildlife.

Like similar groups across the continent, the Southern Plains Land Trust was conceived of necessity and born into poverty. It was, and is, a grassroots, low-budget affair. McCain and Rosmarino ran up credit card debt, strong-armed family members for donations, even used personal loans to help make the annual mortgage payment for Fresh Tracks in the early years. Of course the preserve is small relative to the need for protected areas in the region, but it embodies a dream as big as the prairie sky. The founders and supporters of Fresh Tracks are saying, with their actions: Look at this thousand acres of grassland and multiply its story a thousandfold. Imagine formerly abused land regaining vigor from horizon to horizon, offering safe haven to wild creatures great and small.

# FOREST LODGE
## Portrait of Natural Beauty

*Mary Griggs Burke*

Mary Griggs Burke is a student of beauty. She's had many teachers, from Georgia O'Keeffe to Walter Gropius to Kaikei, the twelfth-century Japanese sculptor, but perhaps none so important as a place: the woods and waters of northern Wisconsin's Lake Namakagon. It was here at Forest Lodge, her family's northwoods retreat, where she collected childhood memories beginning in the 1920s . . . swimming, exploring, canoeing to Champaign Island for a picnic among the pines. At Forest Lodge she developed an interest in natural history and a deep connection to nature's beauty that matured into a lifelong commitment to fostering aesthetic appreciation.

After studying painting at Sarah Lawrence College and art history at Columbia University, Burke became, through decades of scholarship and acquisitions, the foremost private collector of Japanese art outside that country. Her contributions to cross-cultural artistic understanding culminated in the Japanese government's awarding her one of its highest honors in 1987, the Order of the Sacred Treasure, Gold and Silver Star.

Forest Lodge, with its 872 acres and compound of historic log buildings, remained Mary Burke's own sacred treasure. When Burke's grandfather, Crawford Livingston, purchased the property in the 1890s, the land had been scalped. Paul Bunyan and his great ox Babe, mythical stand-ins for an army of northwoods lumberjacks, had transformed the forests of the Upper Midwest into a land of slash and stumps. The wave of logging that swept over the region after the Civil War and peaked a few decades later was remarkable both for its rapaciousness and speed. The old-growth white pines of Michigan, Wisconsin, and Minnesota—trees that often grew four feet in diameter, that stretched two hundred feet into the sky, and that had witnessed the seasons change for several centuries—had once seemed limitless. But with the arrival of loggers, the old-growth trees were quickly leveled, their massive hulks skidded over the snow in winter by teams of horses and oxen. Spring's high water sent great rafts of logs downstream to sawmills.

As the initial wave of lumbering passed over an area, and as wilderness recreation became popular in the nineteenth century, prominent families like the Livingstons often purchased inexpensive cutover forest land for their summer retreats. The same phenomenon occurred back east as wealthy New Yorkers built their "great camps" in the Catskills and Adirondacks. A log-based vernacular architecture developed, and rustic retreats sprouted on lakeshores from Maine to Minnesota. Often several tracts were assembled into a single ownership, ranging from hundreds to many thousands of acres.

And then a long, slow miracle occurred. Sometimes multiple generations of a family tended a particular place, seeking not to exploit its timber but to receive its bounty of beauty and wildness. So it was at Forest Lodge. "In 1916, Grandfather gave Forest Lodge to my mother, his oldest daughter, . . . who gave it to me in 1943," Mary Burke later wrote in a short reminiscence about her connection to Lake Namakagon. Through the decades, the land was a nexus for family life where friends and relatives would gather to reconnect with each other, and with the cycles and seasons of nature.

Mary had no siblings, and the setting provided a cast of natural characters to fill the imagination. The land also provided physical objects to reinforce a child's developing aesthetic sense. Burke's younger cousin, Eleanor Briggs, who has been visiting Forest Lodge for more than sixty years, recalls how her great aunt, Mary Burke's mother, would decorate the long dining room table: "She'd make these tiny landscapes using moss and mushrooms and little figures . . . it was

*I hope it is apparent how much I love and value Forest Lodge. I want to be sure*
*this land remains protected to show what can happen when a good-sized tract*
*of land is allowed to recover on its own from logging.*
—Mary Griggs Burke

so exciting to help her do that as a child." The adults at camp also reinforced the site's magical ambience, making a "fairy mailbox" (a foil-covered cereal box wedged into a tree) where arriving children might find small gifts left for them by woodland fairies.

Forest Lodge offered respite from worldly cares to the people who vacationed there, even as it offered physical refuge to the wild creatures in residence. Over the course of a century, nature's healing powers transformed the hillside overlooking Lake Namakagon into a stately forest, a process that Mary Burke has watched for nearly ninety years. "I have seen what happens to land that has been logged over, losing its virgin trees, and how, if untouched, it can renew itself," she wrote. "I grew up with the second growth and feel a deep love for the trees." But Burke and her late husband had no children, lakefront property in the region was highly desirable for development, and for a time the fate of Forest Lodge seemed uncertain.

"She was very worried about what would become of the land when she went," says Eleanor Briggs. "She wanted to protect and preserve it." Mary Burke began discussions with various conservation groups about Forest Lodge during the 1990s. Briggs, whose long experience in land protection includes founding New Hampshire's Harris Center for Conservation Education, consulted frequently with Burke during this process. Ultimately Burke forged a partnership with Shaun Hamilton of the Trust for Public Land, a national land conservation organization. They developed a plan that would keep the Forest Lodge property intact, and that would use the buildings to reinforce connections between people and the land, a key goal for Burke. "Mary very much liked the idea," says Briggs, "that it would become a retreat center to help perpetuate appreciation for nature in all its wildness."

When Mary Burke donated Forest Lodge to the Trust for Public Land in 1999, former Wisconsin senator Gaylord Nelson, the founder of Earth Day, hailed it as "the most magnificent private gift to the public I can recall." The property, which had been appraised at more than $6 million, but which might have brought three times as much if subdivided and fully developed, was then sold by the trust to the federal government to become part of the Chequamegon National Forest. Wisconsin's congressional delegation helped secure the appropriation, and included language in the bill that codified Burke's wish that the land never be logged.

"There will be no timber harvest, no recreational development, and vehicle traffic will be limited to existing roads," says Shaun Hamilton. "She wanted it to stay just like this." With the proceeds of the sale, the Trust for Public Land established an endowment to support the maintenance of Forest Lodge's historic structures and to develop programs there following Mary Burke's death. She retains exclusive use of the buildings and approximately one hundred acres during her lifetime. Part of the money also went to support the trust's land protection program in the region, the Northwoods Initiative. To Hamilton, the Forest Lodge story symbolizes the pressures facing wildlands across the northwoods: "Probably the premier feature on the lake is this three and a half miles of undeveloped shoreline—both sides of the water in the narrows of the lake. It's such a stark contrast to the pressure and development on all lakes in this region. There's this raw, powerful natural beauty, and at the same time there's threat all around it."

Second-home development, shoddy logging practices, invasive exotic species, motorized recreation, and global climate change present a daunting suite of threats to the land's ecological integrity, but every conservation deal completed by the Trust for Public Land, other land trusts, or public agencies is an incremental step toward a regional landscape with adequate protected areas for wildlife to flourish. With time, and enough nature lovers emulating Mary Burke, perhaps venerable, wind-sculpted pines will again watch over every lake, cradling nests where eaglets or osprey chicks squawk to be fed.

Once upon a time, long ago, Mary Burke's father taught her to ski and skate while on winter adventures to Forest Lodge. She laced on bear-paw snowshoes to navigate the deep snow. In summertime, her perfect playground was a grove of ancient hemlocks spared by loggers that seemed magical to the little girl from St. Paul. Seventy-some years later, at Burke's request, the U.S. Forest Service designated that part of Forest Lodge the Fairy Land Research Natural Area. Strolling through those woods, one may hear the hemlock branches rustling high above, stroked by a breeze off the lake. Or perhaps it is the wood fairies that Burke sought as a child, still dancing among the trees.

Burke continues to enjoy spending time at Lake Namakagon. The land offers a stream of memories and comforts to a woman in the twilight of life: the sound of water lapping against rock, loons singing in the darkness, the smell of pine needles where the sunshine slips through the forest canopy and strikes earth. Nature has painted a portrait of wildness here, and, like the Asian art Burke loves, her intent is for people to see and appreciate it. Most of the property is open to the public for skiing, hiking, and nature study, and the arrangements she has made for Forest Lodge's future assure that it will remain a sanctuary for wildlife and people.

When first light pokes through mist rising from the lake, it will never illuminate garish clearcuts or lakefront condos. From dawn to dusk and forevermore, the scene will feature ferns and flowers, rocks and moss—objects of natural beauty protected by a generous act.

# GORGES STATE PARK
## Permanent Green on the Blue Wall

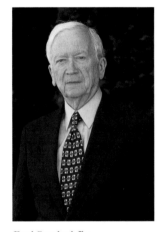

*Fred Stanback Jr.*

Mosses don't clamor for attention. They're short. Humble. Not like wildflowers, those preening showboats of Kingdom Plantae who dress to the nines in hopes of attracting pollinators. In their modest way, though, mosses are amazingly successful. Sometime around 350 million years ago they learned to live on land, the first plants to do so, and have been spreading across the globe ever since. The most primitive of plants, without roots, flowers, or fruits, mosses have evolved into a group of at least twenty-two thousand species. "They are," writes bryologist Robin Wall Kimmerer, "the undisputed masters of their chosen environment." That environment is the surface of things—rocks, trees, fallen logs—in generally shady spots. Such as, for instance, the tree-lined banks of Bear Wallow Creek in North Carolina's Gorges State Park.

Presumably one would need to ask a black bear to know whether the stream is as excellent for ursine bathing as its name implies, but the surrounding terrain, particularly the splash zones at the base of the creek's numerous waterfalls, could hardly be better habitat for mosses and their kindred bryophytes—spleenworts and liverworts. These moisture-loving plants thrive in the rocky chasms carved by Bear Wallow Creek, the Toxaway River (which also runs through Gorges State Park), and other nearby rivers that cascade off the Blue Ridge escarpment.

Where the low, rolling hills of the Piedmont meet the Blue Ridge Mountains, the elevation rises two thousand feet in just over three miles. For people approaching on foot, this looming band of cliffy, forest-clad peaks would have been a daunting barrier indeed. Viewed from afar in the hazy light characteristic of southern Appalachia, the escarpment takes on a steely bluish hue, thus its moniker, "the blue wall." Water-laden air from the Gulf of Mexico slams into the wall and lets go. The rains are heavy and frequent, dropping more than eighty inches of annual precipitation, making the area the wettest spot in the eastern United States. The resulting temperate rainforest is one of the ecologically richest areas of the country.

The geological processes that created the escarpment and its half-dozen major gorges are ancient and ongoing. All that water issuing forth from the heavens runs downhill—fast—slowly carving into rock. Along the blue wall, scenery meets biological rarity. "The escarpment gorges are a wonderful refugium because they are wet, low enough in elevation not to be too cold, and rugged enough to offer cool, sheltered areas," explains Mike Schafale, an ecologist with North Carolina's Natural Heritage Program. Scores of plant species already on, or proposed for, state and federal endangered lists are found here. Of these, nearly two dozen are mosses, including the southern dung moss (imagine the natural history details and you're probably right) and the gorge moss, a species known only from chasms in China and the Blue Ridge escarpment. The gorge moss's largest known population was destroyed when Duke Power Company built a dam just below the confluence of the Toxaway and Whitewater rivers in the early 1970s, at the base of the blue wall.

Duke Power (now Duke Energy) considered the region attractive for generating hydroelectricity and began buying land on the escarpment, in both North and South Carolina, in the 1940s. By this time, virtually all the region had been subject to logging. Much of the Duke land came from the Singer Company, which had logged its timberlands to supply lumber for sewing machine cabinets. The power company continued forestry operations through a subsidiary and generally allowed public access. In the 1990s, when Duke decided to shed most of its real estate holdings, state officials and conservation groups scrambled, fearing the land would be developed and closed off to traditional uses such as hunting, fishing, and hiking.

*Leave it to nature. Nature did pretty well managing these forests for millions of years.*
—Fred Stanback Jr.

Saving the former Duke lands was a hugely complicated task, involving multiple public agencies in two states, private groups, and individuals. When the deal was completed in 1999, it was a major conservation victory. Some 40,000 acres of Duke property in South Carolina were added to public ownership through a mix of public and private funding, including a $10 million challenge grant from the Richard King Mellon Foundation. These lands, managed as state wildlife management areas, are open to multiple recreational uses and some timber production. On the North Carolina side of the border, the Nature Conservancy helped broker a deal whereby the state acquired 10,000 acres, from which the 7,200-acre Gorges State Park was created.

Gorges State Park is managed primarily to protect its wilderness character and unusual natural communities, and is off-limits to hunting and logging. It's a permanent home for obscure mosses and green salamanders and stream-splashing black bears. It's a landscape where human visitors may find rejuvenation in a natural setting, test their hiking mettle against the area's rugged topography, or seek out the southern Oconee bells, a wildflower whose pink and white splash of color in the springtime woods can be found only along the blue wall. This small wilderness park of dramatic waterfalls, rare plants, and future old-growth forest was made possible by Duke Energy's bargain sale of the land, funding from the North Carolina state legislature, and private contributions. A $1-million lead gift, made anonymously at the time, came from Fred Stanback Jr.

It could be said that Fred Stanback is, like the Carolina star-moss of Gorges State Park, a rare and precious member of the land community. And similarly modest. His support of environmental and social causes in western North Carolina has been expressed without fanfare, usually anonymously. A concern for community and affection for the natural world is a Stanback tradition. Fred's son, Brad, remembers how his grandmother, Elizabeth Stanback, stressed the importance of individuals giving back to society, using the familiar biblical aphorism, "Of those to whom much has been given, much is expected." Elizabeth, who died in 2002 just shy of her ninety-ninth birthday, made the largest gift ever to Catawba College in Salisbury to help build its Center for the Environment. Multiple generations of Stanbacks pooled contributions to help save land threatened by development on Grandfather Mountain, the Blue Ridge Mountains' most famous peak. And the love for the land so evident in Fred's life has been passed along to his children; Brad and his spouse, Shelli, are immersed in conservation work through the Long Branch Environmental Education Center and the American Chestnut Foundation.

Born of a place and bonded to it, Fred Stanback has lived in western North Carolina all his life, excepting a few years away for graduate school at Columbia. Now retired from the family headache powder business that his father and uncle started in the 1920s, he remains an active conservationist, engaged particularly in forest protection and the problem of human population growth. "My doings are small compared to others," he says when asked about his work on these issues, and then deflects praise toward activists working to stop abusive logging practices in the South's national forests. Stanback is a gentleman, but some things make him angry: "I think clearcutting is something that enrages a lot of us, particularly on mountain slopes, where you know there's going to be terrible erosion."

The comment is telling. Stanback grew up in a small town and spent weekends and summer vacations at the family's farm in the country. As a kid in the late 1930s, he learned about soil conservation and has never stopped being concerned about the health of the land. As a longtime board member of the Nature Conservancy's state chapter, he's well versed in the scientific arguments for protecting biodiversity but acknowledges that his fundamental connection to the landscape is aesthetic: "I like big trees . . . big natural areas, particularly if it's riverfront. I recognize the value of the longleaf pine forest, but it doesn't quite stir me the way the hardwoods do."

Fred Annand of the Nature Conservancy has known Stanback for years and calls him "the most effective philanthropist for conservation in the history of western North Carolina." Stanback doesn't like to carry the entire burden for any particular project but rather "likes to use his money to leverage other resources," says Annand. "Time and again he's offered his support as a carrot to draw funds from other sources that otherwise might not be there if it wasn't for his challenge."

Besides their central role in the birth of Gorges State Park, timely gifts from Fred Stanback and his wife, Alice, have preserved scenic lands along the Blue Ridge Parkway and helped secure some twenty-seven miles of frontage along the Little Tennessee River. Their support was also instrumental in protecting eighteen thousand acres in the South Mountains, an outlier range of the Blue Ridge within an hour's drive of ever-expanding Charlotte. That project is a particular favorite of Fred's. He'd seen a newspaper story about botanist William S. Moye, a Thoreauvian field naturalist who spends long periods tramping the South Mountains, where he has documented more than one thousand species of vascular plants, including many rarities. Moye's proselytizing on behalf of the area's botanical wonders prompted Stanback to contact Fred Annand at the Nature Conservancy and, as for so many threatened places before and since, offer his help. With a major gift from Stanback to attract other financial support, the Nature Conservancy worked with a local land trust to buy the tract and transfer it to the state. In 1998 the South Mountains Game Land was established, contiguous with South Mountains State Park. With subsequent additions, roughly forty thousand acres of Bill Moye's favorite stomping grounds are now public land, forever protected from development.

The conservation success stories at Gorges State Park, the South Mountains, and numerous other sites around the region are heartening, but Brad Stanback worries that western North Carolina's population boom portends a closing window of opportunity. "I fear that in another decade all the land will either be conserved or developed," he says. One hopes that his father, Fred Stanback, has inherited genes for longevity, but even so, he probably has but a few more decades to enjoy the landscape he's helped to preserve. With every sanctuary of wild habitat secured, though, Stanback is creating a timeless legacy.

The mosses of Gorges State Park have already benefited from his concern. So too have the rare orchids of the South Mountains, and the Weller's salamanders of Grandfather Mountain. His rambles in the woods may be less strenuous than when he was a young man—"I can't do maybe what I once did, but I still enjoy being out for day hikes"—but Fred Stanback's contributions to protecting North Carolina's wild character show no sign of slowing down. If anything, his generosity seems to grow with the expanding human population and burgeoning threats facing his beloved Blue Ridge Mountains.

# LOOMIS FOREST
## Tracking Cats and Dollars

*Mark Skatrud*

*Mitch Friedman*

*Paul Allen*

A snowshoe hare peers out from his hiding place. A lodgepole pine blown down by wind has pulled several other trees with it, creating a tangle of woody debris that lies crisscrossed on the forest floor, a perfect hideout from predators. The snowy woods appear free of potential dangers, and the hare leaves its cover to seek breakfast. Bad choice. Once in the open, he sees too late the furry blur that is the lynx, which today will call him breakfast. While Tennyson may have described nature as "red in tooth and claw," that summation of life's harsher realities is probably too poetic for our bumper sticker culture. Let's just say, "Predation Happens."

Or at least it does, fortunately for the lynx, this winter morning in the largest tract of state-owned forestland in Washington. The 134,000-acre Loomis Forest abuts the federal Pasayten Wilderness Area to the west and conservation lands in British Columbia to the north, making this expanse of rugged terrain along the Canadian border some of the biggest and best remaining lynx habitat in the Lower Forty-Eight. It's one of the last places for nature's original choreography—the ancient dance of predator and prey—to continue as it has for millennia, with its cast of players largely intact.

As a species, Canada lynx are beleaguered, among the rarest wild cats in the United States, and have been formally listed on the federal endangered species list since 2000. While most forest carnivores are broadly inclusive in their diets, lynx are more discriminating. When opportunity or circumstances dictate, they may dine on small mammals, birds, or deer carrion, but snowshoe hares are the lynx's overwhelming favorite meal. The two species are so closely linked in life and death that lynx population levels may cycle in concert with the surfeit or scarcity of hares in the woods. Solitary in nature, and slightly smaller than but similar in appearance to bobcats, lynx have distinctively larger paws that help them travel in, and on, deep snow. The mottled-gray cats once hunted hares across the northern woods of the Pacific Northwest, Midwest, and New England, and in high-elevation conifer forests of the Rocky Mountains. But through trapping and habitat destruction, their range and numbers have dramatically declined.

While no human witnessed this hare's last moments, the fatal interaction that took place is readily inferred a few hours later by wildlife tracker Mark Skatrud. The tracks and blood on the snow tell the story. A longtime forest activist with a local conservation group, Friends of Loomis Forest, Skatrud and other volunteers have been monitoring wildlife populations via tracking surveys for more than a decade. They've amassed a huge database about wildlife movement, information that helps them assess, and often oppose, ecologically destructive management practices proposed by Washington's Department of Natural Resources. "We know where lynx use the landscape," he says. "We don't want these corridors, these high-use areas, to be impacted by clearcuts."

Skatrud is fiftyish and wiry, keenly intelligent, and thoroughly comfortable in the woods. When he came to the area in the late 1970s, he set up his tipi on a small private inholding in the Loomis. Soon after, he noticed cougar tracks in the snow. For a kid who'd grown up rambling the tamed woodlots near his house in North Carolina, here was big, wild country to explore, home to big, wild creatures. He was hooked. "It's just what I love to do," Skatrud says. "Being out in the woods, especially in winter, following tracks—learning what the animals do."

The wildness that Skatrud cherished, however, was under assault. The state Department of Natural Resources managed Loomis Forest to generate income for public school construction. Like millions of acres across the West, these "school trust lands" were originally granted to the states by the federal government and are typically leased to ranchers for livestock

*The success of our campaign to save the Loomis wildlands proved to me that
the people of Washington state care about our forests, and understand that trees
can be worth more standing than cut.*

—Mitch Friedman

grazing, logged for timber, or both, whatever maximizes revenue. Conservationists have long been frustrated by this archaic linkage to education funding that pits one public good, clean water and healthy forests, against another, well-funded schools. The Loomis's evergreen forests of lodgepole pine, Engelmann spruce, Douglas fir, and ponderosa pine were being punctured by clearcuts, and in the mid-1990s, the state announced plans to expand logging into the last remaining roadless strongholds.

Mark Skatrud knew the Loomis backcountry better than anyone. He and Mitch Friedman, founder of the regional conservation group Conservation Northwest (formerly the Northwest Ecosystem Alliance), had written the original petition to list the cat under the Endangered Species Act in 1991. Skatrud and Friedman understood that the habitat targeted for new roads and clearcuts—roughly thirty-five thousand roadless acres in three tracts, all contiguous with other protected lands—was crucial for lynx. Ultimately, wildlife advocates successfully preserved roughly twenty-five thousand of those roadless acres through an innovative media and fundraising campaign that put the Loomis Forest wildlands at the top of Washington State's conservation agenda.

At the time, however, prospects for blocking the logging looked grim. The state believed it had a legal obligation to manage the forest in a way that generated dollars for schools (although in the Loomis case, even maximum destruction represented only marginal net income), and there was no clear path to leverage new ecological protections for school trust lands. Along with Skatrud, who had become board president of the Northwest Ecosystem Alliance, Friedman ran through a litany of strategic options, none of them with much chance of success. It looked like the conservationists' slim hope was to sue the state over whether the new roads constituted a "taking" of an endangered species, that is, whether the habitat destruction represented an unlawful killing of grizzly bears, protected under the Endangered Species Act.

Friedman was discussing the Loomis's plight with Andy Kerr, a longtime player in Northwest conservation politics, when Kerr suggested, "Why don't you just buy it?" A very unlikely scenario, but when a protracted legal battle over bears appeared imminent, a judge ordered the parties into pretrial talks, giving Friedman a chance to discuss the idea with Department of Natural Resources commissioner Jennifer Belcher. If conservationists could raise funds equivalent to the appraised timber value from logging the Loomis roadless areas, would the state amend the land's deed language and permanently shift it from school trust status to a natural area designation? The answer was yes.

It was a novel approach. There was no precedent for it anywhere in the West. In 1998 the parties struck a deal that would protect two of the three blocks of roadless habitat. (The third was already under logging contract and has been mostly lost as lynx habitat.) The conservationists had until July 1 of 1999 to secure funding, and in hindsight, Friedman speculates that state officials and hostile legislators probably assumed the agreement was a good way to get pesky environmentalists off their back. "If they really thought we could raise the money, I doubt they would have agreed to it," he says. "But they honored their end of the bargain when we pulled it off."

Friedman decided to go where the big money was, in the bank accounts of Seattle millionaires spawned from the high-tech boom. "Stock options for wilderness!" might have been the Loomis Forest Fund's unofficial mantra. Few of the thousands of people who made donations, large and small, had visited the Loomis, but many were active outdoors people, loved the wilderness, and saw value in protecting lynx habitat. The campaign held house parties and public events, got terrific media attention, and made saving the Loomis wildlands a sexy issue. Just ten minutes shy of the deadline, however, the conservationists were still $2 million short of the appraised timber value of $13.1 million. From the lobby of the Department of Natural Resources building, Friedman phoned an anonymous angel, and the goal was met.

Then, one final boulder—a big one—was dropped in the conservationists' way. Pressure from pro-logging interests helped increase the final timber appraisal to $16.5 million. The Loomis Forest Fund was given just three additional months to find another $3.4 million. It took one week. Friedman made sure the inflated price tag made the newspapers. The next day he got a call from someone at a Seattle-based foundation asking what he planned to do. Friedman wasn't sure, but suggested that conservationists might have to sue over the new appraisal. Within days the foundation phoned back: Microsoft cofounder Paul Allen would make up the difference.

Through a suite of charitable foundations he's established, Allen is one of the nation's most generous philanthropists. Environmental grantmaking is not a primary focus, but over the course of several years the Paul G. Allen Forest Protection Foundation gave more than $41 million to conservation projects in the Northwest. While no longer making forest-related gifts, the foundation was for a time a leading institutional investor in land conservation. Paul Allen hadn't intentionally deferred making a gift to the Loomis crusade so that he might swoop in at the last moment to save the day, but it worked out that way. The man who owns Seattle's pro football and basketball teams clinched the victory for the Loomis Forest lynx.

In 2000, the Loomis Forest wildlands were designated a state-managed natural resources conservation area, with permanent deed restrictions on commercial logging and nonemergency road building. While a great victory, Mitch Friedman hopes it need never be replicated. "We should not have had to pay a ransom to keep the state from selling clearcutting contracts in the Loomis backcountry, where timber values were low and habitat values superlative," he says. "Our position all along was that we needed to save the Loomis today and fix the system tomorrow." Conservation Northwest has continued working to reform the school trust lands system in Washington, and Friedman is confident that someday public lands logging and grazing revenues will be decoupled from education funding enough to allow better management and, in special places, outright protection of the land.

The conservationists' implausible success was achieved with a diverse cast of forest heroes: Mark Skatrud, a man whose commitment to wildlife and simple living led him to the Loomis; Mitch Friedman, the astute strategist whose exuberance for protecting wild places helped open checkbooks from Seattle's high-tech crowd; and Paul Allen, the Microsoft billionaire whose foundation made a crucial gift. To be sure, the snowbelt forests where lynx hang on still face a range of threats, from gas and oil drilling to global warming. But there are creatures—lynx certainly, and fishers, wolverines, and even an occasional grizzly bear—that now have a much better chance at life, liberty, and the pursuit of prey because of people who worked to save the Loomis Forest wildlands. And succeeded.

# GREENFIRE PRESERVE
## Healing Nature

*Ann Down*

Jon Marvel is one of the most controversial, and effective, environmental activists in the West. An architect who became increasingly incensed over cow-damaged public lands, he founded the Western Watersheds Project to take on the ranchers, politicians, and government agencies who perpetuate livestock grazing as the dominant use of vast stretches of the public domain. The Idaho-based conservation group has been particularly successful in using lawsuits and the threat of legal action to make agencies enforce existing law. "Livestock production is the single largest negative impact on all land in the world," Marvel says. "Just in the western United States, three hundred million acres of public land are affected annually, and the costs—to healthy watersheds, wildlife populations, and the pocketbooks of American taxpayers—are staggering."

In a landscape where livestock are ubiquitous, and where there are few examples of what the land might look like absent grazing, what better way to advance the debate about healthy lands and waters than to offer up an example for all the world to see? Western Watersheds Project is doing just that with its Greenfire Preserve, 432 acres of sagebrush grasslands along the East Fork of the Salmon River in central Idaho.

Set in a high valley in the White Cloud Mountains, and abutting public land on three sides, the preserve owes its name to American conservation icon Aldo Leopold, author of *A Sand County Almanac*. In that book's essay "Thinking Like a Mountain," Leopold recalls an incident from when he was newly posted to Arizona's Apache National Forest in 1909. He and his fellow forest rangers were perched on rimrock eating lunch when they caught sight of a wolf fording a river below. They jumped for their rifles and pumped lead down the mountain, killing a she-wolf and her pups.

"We reached the old wolf in time to watch a fierce green fire dying in her eyes," Leopold later wrote in what became one of the best-known passages in conservation literature. "I realized then, and have known ever since, that there was something new to me in those eyes—something known only to her and to the mountain. I was young then, and full of trigger-itch; I thought that because fewer wolves meant more deer, that no wolves would mean hunters' paradise. But after seeing the green fire die, I sensed that neither the wolf nor the mountain agreed with such a view."

During an era when wolves and other predators were widely persecuted, Leopold came to understand their vital role in the land community. Without them, deer would become overabundant and decimate the vegetation, and the soil would begin to wash away. "I now suspect that just as a deer herd lives in mortal fear of its wolves, so does a mountain live in mortal fear of its deer," he wrote. Leopold went on to found the scientific discipline of wildlife management; he was a seminal thinker about ecological restoration and an early advocate for establishing federal wilderness areas, which he argued were valuable not just for recreation, but as an ecological benchmark. Wilderness areas serve as a "base datum of normality," he wrote, "a picture of how healthy land maintains itself as an organism." Which is precisely the goal for Greenfire Preserve—a place where people are helping the land heal, but where nature does most of the work. "We developed short-term objectives, including immediate removal of livestock," explains preserve manager Stew Churchwell. "But the overarching long-term goal is to retire the fifty thousand acres of federal grazing allotments attached to the property and help restore the native wildlife and habitats of the site."

With more than a mile of river frontage and six federal grazing allotments (long-term leases allowing private ranchers to graze their livestock on public lands), Jon Marvel had long been aware of the ranch's conservation potential. When the land was to be auctioned in 2000, he brought it to the attention of a key Western Watersheds Project supporter. She agreed to buy it and donate it to the organization to become a wildlife sanctuary. That conservation buyer never wanted public recognition for her generosity and for years remained anonymous. When she formally transferred title in 2001, Ann Down's gift to the Western Watershed Project was the largest in the organization's history, valued at over $1.3 million.

Ann Down is a striking woman, trim with silver hair. An avid hiker, she finds spiritual balance in wild country. "It nourishes and heals, being in nature," she says. After spending most of her life in California and raising a family in the San Francisco Bay Area, Down was drawn to the mountains and moved to Idaho in the early 1990s. "I love living in a small town, love having access to the wilderness," she says. Down's engagement in conservation issues came later in life. Now she runs a small family foundation that focuses on children's health and environmental preservation.

Down generally invests in smaller organizations, helps them develop a stable funding base, and then moves on to assist other groups. She's helped support a school for blind children and a midwife-training program in Tibet, distribution of solar cookers in Africa, and a project that brings surgeons to Bhutan for reconstructive surgery on children with cleft palates. She also likes to see in person how her grants are fostering good works in the world. "If you write a check and put it in the mail, there's not much emotional impact in that," she says. "But if you go and live the way these people live, share their experiences, then you really understand the importance of their work. I wonder why more people don't do this, because it's so gratifying. I've made friends around the world through this foundation—something I never expected."

Closer to home, Down supports a number of groups working to protect the Northern Rockies. She once flew in a small plane over the Idaho backcountry and found the Bob Marshall Wilderness and Sawtooth Mountains "spectacularly beautiful." But the bird's-eye view was a revelation: "From the air you can see the destruction created by the mines, the roads, the timber industry. A lot of it's well hidden, but when you fly over, it's apparent." For a person with her deep connection to the natural world, seeing the way human action was carving up the wilderness prompted a desire to help preserve it. After meeting Jon Marvel through a mutual friend, Ann's relationship with Western Watersheds Project was forged, eventually leading her to buy the ranch that would become Greenfire Preserve.

"It's been heartening to see the changes just in the past few years since the cattle have been off the land," she says. "It really stands out—it shows what healthy land should look like." Whether supporting a safe house for victims of domestic violence or a sanctuary for wildlife in the heart of cow country, Down believes that acts of compassion are the means to personal and planetary healing. "I feel there is an interrelatedness, an interconnectedness to all things," she says. "We need to practice reverence for the earth and respect for all living things."

The Greenfire Preserve is a tangible example, "a place where people can visit and get inspired," says Down. "Two or three times a year we have a gathering when volunteers come and we tear down fences, or do weed control, or help plant trees . . . people just get passionate about the place." It's clear that this kind of active engagement in the world is a source of great joy for her. "It has been so personally fulfilling, this direction my life has taken," says Down. "I'm sixty-eight, and when people get older, their lives often tend to get smaller, more fear-based—they travel less and are less open—and I find my world has been expanding exponentially." In a voice that betrays

good-natured bemusement, she concludes: "I never know what's coming around the corner, where I'm going next, and I like it that way. That's a nice thing to be able to say at my age."

Since Greenfire Preserve's creation, an ambitious ecological restoration program has begun on the land. Fencing that could impede wildlife movement has been removed. Former alfalfa fields have been reseeded and now grow native grasses and flowers. Riverbanks beaten down by cattle hooves now support hundreds of planted willow and cottonwood seedlings, which hold and stabilize the soil. More than thirty-eight thousand acres of public land grazing allotments where cattle had roamed for decades have been given back to wildlife. (The allotments are not permanently retired yet—there presently is no mechanism to do that—but the privilege to graze has not been exercised by Western Watersheds Project.)

Perhaps most impressive, a small island in the East Fork that had been severely eroding has been stabilized. "The sediment that the erosion was causing was definitely a problem for spawning beds downriver," says Stew Churchwell, "and the side channel that the island created was critical habitat for young salmon and steelhead." Churchwell landed a Clean Water Act–related grant to restore vegetation and save the island. "It's been tremendously successful, a model project," he says.

Beleaguered Chinook salmon, steelhead, bull trout, and other river residents are not the only creatures to find refuge at Greenfire. Mule deer, bobcats, wolves, elk, black bears, river otter, and bald eagles use the property. A pair of peregrine falcons has successfully fledged young on a nearby cliff. Mountain lions have visited, too, moving under cover of darkness but leaving their tracks in fresh snow. The abundance of wildlife using the preserve is all the more encouraging given that the site had been intensively ranched for more than a century.

Nature's resilience may be the ultimate manifestation of grace—but the miracle of Greenfire Preserve is not only how overgrazed land can heal from past abuse, but how hearts and minds can be changed. The good tidings that the preserve offers to bald eagles, beavers, and bobcats extend also to people, helping them learn how to be better members of the land community. Ann Down's gift seems to multiply over time as Greenfire offers secure habitat for wild creatures, quiet satisfaction for its benefactor, and a signpost for visitors pointing back to Aldo Leopold's land ethic, that "a thing is right when it tends to support the integrity, stability, and beauty of the biotic community. It is wrong when it tends otherwise." By this measure, the healing work being accomplished at Greenfire Preserve—primarily by nature, assisted by Ann Down, Jon Marvel, Stew Churchwell, and many Western Watersheds Project supporters—could not be more right.

# KINEO PRESERVE
## Northwoods Gem Protected

*Roxanne Quimby*

**M**ount Kineo rises dramatically from a peninsula jutting into Moosehead Lake. The mountain's hulking form and eight-hundred-foot-high cliffs loom over the cerulean waters of Maine's largest lake. It's a magnetic place. People have been drawn here for millennia, first for the flintlike gray stone called rhyolite, which makes excellent spear points, scrapers, and other stone tools, later for the region's wilderness qualities and exceptional beauty.

The ice sheet that covered and sculpted Mount Kineo's profile melted roughly twelve thousand years ago. With warming temperatures, the forest returned, recolonizing a barren land, and with the trees came animals and people. Imagine a sunny fall day, say, around six thousand years ago, at the talus slope below the cliffs. Smoke rises from a campfire, kids play by the water's edge, and a crisp breeze off the lake hints of cold weather to come. Surely the people looked up occasionally from their meticulous, painstaking work chipping a knife edge in brittle stone to admire the scene—woods and waters stretching to the horizon.

Fast-forward through the centuries, and the scene is still exquisite. Today most of Mount Kineo is in public ownership, managed as a state park, and the hiking trails to the summit are among the most popular in Maine. The panorama from the top has long enchanted visitors. Henry David Thoreau, who visited the area in the 1850s, described the "glorious wild view" looking out at the broad lake, its "numerous forest-clad islands . . . and the boundless forest undulating away from its shores on every side." The area stood to become considerably less beautiful in 2001, however, when a forested seventy-seven-acre piece of private land stretching across the peninsula at the mountain's base was approved for subdivision. Up to a dozen new lakeshore homes would have fragmented wildlife habitat, tarnished a natural icon that Mainers have cherished for generations, and potentially blocked public hiking trails to the summit.

Then, like an old western, a stranger rode into town to save the day. This hero wasn't shod in cowboy boots and riding a white steed, but wore Birkenstocks and drove a Civic Hybrid. Armed not with a six-gun, the newcomer merely brandished a checkbook, bought out the developer, and declared the land safe. Public access on the hiking trails would continue, and the property would be preserved as wildlife habitat. The townspeople cheered! Well, no, they didn't. Grumbled, mostly. Folks were happy enough to know they wouldn't be seeing rustic mansions sprouting at the base of Mount Kineo, but few would offer a word of thanks to the person who bought the land and established the Kineo Preserve—Roxanne Quimby—Maine's most controversial private landowner, and a fearless conservationist.

Quimby is the cofounder and longtime CEO of Burt's Bees, a company that sells personal care products made with natural ingredients. In a story line right out of the movies, she finished art school in San Francisco in the 1970s, joined the back-to-the-land movement, and ended up in rural Maine, where she chopped wood, lived in a cabin without electricity or running water, and started a family. After her marriage broke up and with kids to support, she was waitressing and barely scraping by when she met beekeeper Burt Shavitz in 1984. A marketing natural, Quimby counseled Shavitz that it would be more profitable to sell his honey in small jars with attractive labels at craft fairs than in big tubs. She also wondered if the large quantities of beeswax he kept in an old shed might have some use. Before long she was selling beeswax candles and mixing up various creams and potions in an old one-room schoolhouse in the sticks. By 1992 the company was selling half a million beeswax candles a year and truckloads of lip balm. Quimby later bought out Shavitz and in 2003 sold an 80 percent stake in Burt's Bees to an investor group for a reported $180 million.

*I'm an artist. I'm a beauty junkie. I just want the most beautiful thing in the world*
*to be around me, and that's nature.*
—Roxanne Quimby

Quimby's business savvy made her a player in a burgeoning industry, but her ecological worldview has made her a lightning rod for criticism in the Maine woods. Indeed, one anticonservationist darkly warned fellow property rights activists not to underestimate her, because "she's smart, she's green, and she's rich."

Why do some people find an ex-hippie entrepreneur so threatening? Two reasons: First, because Roxanne Quimby has been buying land. Not just the small tract at the base of Mount Kineo, but big pieces of cutover timberland. By 2006 she had spent roughly $33 million to purchase seventy thousand acres. While nothing to sneeze at, that figure is paltry compared to the area of Maine controlled by paper companies and timber investor groups. A handful of corporations own the bulk of the state's unorganized townships, a vast unpopulated area the size of Connecticut, Rhode Island, and Massachusetts combined. More than seven million acres of industrial timberland in the state have changed hands since 1998. While alarming to conservationists, these sales have incited little populist backlash, even as liquidation logging increased, timber companies shed assets, and paper mills, long an economic mainstay in the region, were shuttered.

Instead of directing their ire at large timberland owners for business practices that undercut the health of Maine's human and natural communities, many local people found in Roxanne Quimby a convenient villain, ironically, because she doesn't perpetuate those practices. She doesn't want to log the forest. She's not building a private hunting estate. Racing through a winter wonderland astride a buzzing snowmobile is not her cup of tea. Rather, she'd like the heavily logged timberlands that she's purchased—"working forests," in the local vernacular—to get a vacation for a while, maybe enjoy some peace and quiet punctuated only by birdsong. No chain saws and skidders, no airplanes spraying clearcuts with herbicide to kill the birch and maple trees because spruce and fir make better pulpwood for the paper mills. Much of northern Maine has been managed for over a century as a paper plantation controlled by absentee corporations. An outspoken advocate for wild nature like Roxanne Quimby who will challenge that status quo is deeply threatening.

The second reason Quimby has some people rattled is that she's been a prominent supporter of a new Maine Woods National Park, an idea proposed in the 1990s by the conservation group RESTORE: The North Woods, and embraced by a growing number of individuals and organizations. It's a bold idea for a 3.2-million-acre national park and preserve centered around the existing Baxter State Park, New England's largest wilderness area, with the Moosehead Lake region as a gateway community. Some polls suggest that a majority of Mainers support the national park idea, but for years, vocal opposition kept Maine's congressional delegation from asking the National Park Service to conduct a feasibility study of the proposed park.

"That's how I knew it was a good idea," says Quimby, "because everybody was so upset about it. Somebody asked me, 'Why does it create so much opposition?' and I think it's because it's so simple . . . a national park is something everybody understands." For now, Quimby's lands are held by a private foundation dedicated to land conservation, but she has indicated a willingness to donate them to the public at some point in the future—exactly what former Maine governor Percival Baxter did to create Baxter State Park, and what George Dorr and John D. Rockefeller Jr. did to help create Acadia National Park. These are historical precedents for private conservation philanthropy that Maine Woods National Park proponents, and opponents, know well.

Say "New England," and most people imagine bucolic scenes of dairy cows, autumn foliage, and clapboard-covered village architecture. Say "Maine," and most people think of lobsters and lighthouses. They may be surprised to hear that a huge expanse of forestland, long subject to logging but virtually undeveloped and unpeopled otherwise, still exists in the northeastern United States. But it's true, and there is no other place in the Lower Forty-Eight with more potential for creating a big new wilderness park. Roxanne Quimby knows it, and has the pocketbook to help make it happen.

As economic globalization continues to propel a transition in the forest products industry, the northwoods will continue to be the backdrop for a struggle between defenders of the status quo and visionaries who recognize the landscape's wilderness potential. Quimby has thrown her lot in with those who see a future Maine Woods National Park as a key tool for diversifying the regional economy and healing a wounded land. The self-described "beauty junkie" looks at the cutover woodlands and visualizes a brighter future there: "It has the potential to be beautiful again—some places already are that they haven't managed to destroy. But another fifty or seventy-five years, if we make it that long, particularly if we encourage it, then the beauty will be restored," she says.

After replacing herself as Burt's Bees CEO in 2004, Roxanne Quimby has more time for her painting, quilting, and conservation activism. She's in her fifties, has loads of energy, and has hinted that she may consider running for governor someday. One hopes that a future Governor Quimby might be more successful than Percival Baxter in using public office to advance conservation; he failed to persuade the state legislature to buy Mount Katahdin and so bought it himself, spending his family fortune over several decades to assemble the land that became Baxter State Park.

History will record whether Roxanne Quimby equals, or even exceeds, Percival Baxter's legacy as a wildlands philanthropist—but from her personal history, one would be wise to not underestimate her. In any case, the natural areas she has purchased and preserved around Maine are assured of regaining their beauty and ecological health in the decades to come, and the peregrine falcons nesting on Mount Kineo will not have to give their fledglings flying lessons over a new lakeside subdivision.

# YAKOBI ISLAND
## Trees of Salmon

*Richard Goldman*

Water is everywhere. In the pulsing waves that strike Yakobi Island's cobble beaches. In the tide pools and estuaries. In the rivers that flow off the land. In the chunks of glaciers that float past. In the bodies of salmon, who swim between worlds.

Water fills the air and the trees. Sitka spruce and western hemlock needles drip moisture stolen from fog. When a great tree falls, its bole may molder on the forest floor for centuries, gradually returning nutrients to the soil. Squeeze a handful of the tree's punky fibers and water pours forth as if from a sponge. No creature is unaffected by the flowing currents here, both oceanic and atmospheric, that shape life on land and sea. Indeed, the coastal rainforest of Southeast Alaska's Alexander Archipelago is the largest remaining intact temperate rainforest on Earth— a land of moss and muskeg, black-tailed deer, salmon, and bald eagles. The biotic community is shaped by climate and geography. The region is unusually mild for its latitude, the weather damp and cool year-round, with areas like Yakobi getting a hundred inches of precipitation yearly and experiencing temperatures more typical of Seattle than of Fairbanks.

The relative abundance of food provided by nature allowed indigenous peoples time to develop a rich material culture. From totem poles to tools, the Haida and Tlingit imbued the artifacts of daily life with great artistry and were able to make a living from the land for several thousand years without substantially reducing its wildness. Beginning with Russian colonization in the 1700s, though, the region's ecological and cultural integrity has been under assault. First came the Russian whalers, then fur traders who decimated seal populations, then gold miners, loggers, industrial fishing fleets, and oilmen. Both before and after America purchased Alaska from Russia in 1867, the land has been perceived by newcomers as a frontier to be exploited.

Today the ideology of industrial exploitation continues in the Tongass National Forest, which covers seventeen million acres of the Alaska Panhandle, including Yakobi Island. The Tongass has long been a battleground in the war between industry and conservationists over public lands logging. The Forest Service has allowed more than a million acres of old-growth forest in Southeast Alaska to be leveled since World War II, the timber often sold for a pittance. That figure is striking when one considers how much of the Tongass is boggy scrub—less than 5 percent of the forest has the well-drained soil needed to grow the towering spruce and cedar coveted by loggers. Most of the easily accessible stands are long gone.

The big pulp mills in Ketchikan and Sitka that ran on public timber are shuttered now, and the timber economy is in decline, although conservationists have not yet won protection for all remaining roadless areas in the Tongass. If the future of this national forest is unknown, its recent past is clear to anyone flying into Juneau: the clearcuts, both on the public land and on Native corporation land, are breathtaking. For a newcomer to the country, the garish sight—as if some alien spaceship sucked up whole sections of forest with its cosmic industrial vac—is fascinating in a horrific way. Looking down on Prince of Wales Island calls to mind being a kid leafing through a medical textbook, ogling photos of the really awful things that sometimes befall a human body. It is repellent, yet one is compelled to look.

But wait—this is a happy story, a tale of wilderness preserved. Memories of clearcuts recede as one sits on Yakobi Island's northern tip, looking over Cross Sound toward Glacier Bay National Park. The waves lap against land, and the pleasing sound washes away the image of forest giants, a few exceeding seven hundred years old, reduced to bleeding stumps and slash. Here stands a vibrant, primeval forest that will live on, unmolested. On this wild island, sea lions will be free to

*When we can help with a project, and see it go through to its conclusion,*
*and it's a positive one, the sense of satisfaction is almost overwhelming.*
—Richard Goldman

haul out on the beaches, brown bears will fatten up during the salmon runs, and passing kayakers will find a safe harbor, thanks to San Francisco businessman Richard Goldman.

While Congress designated much of Yakobi a federal wilderness area in 1980, parts of the island remained unprotected. The University of Alaska owned an 836-acre parcel on the northern tip of Yakobi extending from several miles west of Cape Bingham to just east of Soapstone Point. The tract included twelve miles of coastline, thirty small islets along the Yakobi shoreline, and several lakes and streams. The property was just one tiny part of the university's statewide landholdings, which, like "school trust" lands across the West, are managed to generate revenue for education, typically from oil and gas production, logging, or other resource extraction. "They have the right to make as much money as they can out of university trust property," says Buck Lindekugel, an attorney with the Southeast Alaska Conservation Council. "They can log it, subdivide it, or sell to a cruise line." The Cape Bingham land didn't offer enormous timber value, but it had the realtor's trifecta of values: location, location, location. "You could have a hotel or resort right across from the mouth of Glacier Bay, right in the midst of this incredible scenery, surrounded by an incredible coastal marine ecosystem," says Lindekugel. "That could have happened, and we were afraid it would."

The University of Alaska's role in promoting development is long-standing, with one of the most outrageous examples being Operation Chariot, a scheme hatched in the late 1950s by Edward Teller, the father of the hydrogen bomb. With support of the Atomic Energy Commission, which at the time was marketing the "peaceful atom," Teller proposed to detonate several nuclear bombs at a point on the northwest Alaskan coast, thirty miles south of the Inuit village of Point Hope. The blast supposedly would form a new deepwater port where coal mined inland could be loaded for shipment to Japan.

The university president at the time helped secure large grants from the Atomic Energy Commission to conduct studies, and showed the door to a couple of pesky biology professors who questioned the wisdom of nuke-based "geographical engineering" in the Alaskan Arctic. Operation Chariot later collapsed of its own absurdity and thanks to skillful opposition by conservationists and the Inuit community at Point Hope, but frontier-style economic boosterism lives on in Alaska.

In the 1980s, the state of Alaska gave the university logging rights on some coastal state-owned lands, and the Southeast Alaska Conservation Council sued to stop the massive logging project. In the litigation settlement, the university relinquished cutting rights on some of the most sensitive areas, and gave the Forest Service a ten-year option to purchase its Cape Bingham tract on Yakobi Island. But the Forest Service never found the money.

With time running out, the Conservation Fund, a national land conservancy, began negotiations to save the land. In 2001, the fund bought the parcel for $1.5 million, then donated it to the Forest Service for addition to the West Chichagof–Yakobi Wilderness Area. A lead gift of $1.2 million, which made the deal possible, came from the Richard and Rhoda Goldman Fund. It was just part of a multiyear, $5-million grant to underwrite Alaska land conservation projects. That grant also helped the Conservation Fund add nine thousand acres to a national wildlife refuge on the Alaska Peninsula, purchase private inholdings in Wood-Tikchik State Park and Lake Clark National Park and Preserve, and secure an addition to the Chilkat Bald Eagle Preserve, where the world's largest concentration of bald eagles gathers each year. Several other land deals brokered by the Conservation Fund and the Nature Conservancy also were completed using the Goldman gift. It was, relative to the foundation's assets, a small investment—but one that reaped tremendous dividends for wilderness and wildlife in Alaska.

Now in his eighties, Richard Goldman, the founder of Goldman Insurance Services, is a longtime conservation donor. In 1951, he and his late wife, Rhoda, an heir to the Levi Strauss clothing company fortune, launched their foundation, through which they have given more than a half-billion dollars to environmental, educational, cultural, and Jewish causes. Richard is better known outside the Bay Area for the Goldman Prize, given annually to six grassroots environmental activists from around the world. A large cash award and extensive media coverage make it the Nobel Prize of environmentalism.

Beyond his support of environmental initiatives around the world, Richard Goldman has also been outspoken within the philanthropic community, advocating that charitable foundations spend their assets more aggressively to fight social and ecological problems. Goldman is making annual grants exceeding 10 percent of the foundation's endowment, and prods fellow philanthropists to ramp up their giving: "These are not times to conserve," he has said. "These are times to stretch."

On Yakobi Island, the hemlocks lining Soapstone Creek stretch high into a foggy sky. A man from California who has never seen these trees has accorded them the primary wish of all living things—to live and die a natural death.

When salmon come up the creek in spring (they are anadromous fish, spending most of their life in the ocean but returning to their natal streams to spawn and die), the bears are there to greet and eat them. The bears gorge themselves and amble off. Their piles of fishy dung fertilize the forest. The trees and other plants grow up, holding the soil together during endless rainy days. The riparian vegetation filters runoff and keeps stream banks stable so that eroding sediments don't cover the gravel stream bottoms salmon need to lay their eggs. When a tree falls in the forest, it becomes the home and food of countless invertebrates. In the creek's clear rushing waters, stoneflies, mayflies, and other insects grow from eggs to adulthood, providing food for juvenile salmon before the fish head out to sea. In the elegant summation of Alaska naturalist Richard Carstensen: "Trees are made of salmon. Salmon are made of insect-processed trees."

Ecologists have lately become adept at quantifying this kind of energy flow through ecosystems, showing how the forest benefits from bears acting as nutrient transmission facilitators, sprinkling the salmon's final blessing across the land. Like every attempt to understand the intricacies of wild nature, such research has value. But the dry prose of scientific journals only partially illuminates the Alaskan rainforest's ecological relationships. For a witness at Soapstone Point, watching the whales go by, these matters are a mystery and a marvel. In the rhythms of this watery land, the circularity of life is manifest, its beauty ultimately irreducible to data sets, at least until scientists learn to measure grace.

# LOS AMIGOS CONSERVATION CONCESSION

## Saving the Rainforest

*Gordon Moore*

Those neon-colored amphibians of the tropical rainforest are often beautiful but deadly. The various species popularly grouped as "poison dart frogs" are named for the indigenous peoples' habit of coating their arrowheads with the animals' natural toxins. Through an age-old arms race with predators, the frogs have evolved internal chemical weapons ranging from unpalatable to lethal. Their attention-getting looks are what biologists call aposematic, or warning, coloration, the opposite of camouflage. Poison dart frogs *want* to be noticed, are advertising to whoever who might consider them for lunch, "You know who I am—mess with me and you'll regret it." For these Amazonian amphibians, as for certain rap singers and politicians, it seems that personal toxicity combined with marketing prowess is a winning combination.

Along with jaguars and parrots, the showy little frogs grace innumerable "Save the Rainforest" T-shirts. Campaigns built around these wildlife celebrities have made "tropical rainforest" synonymous with nature under siege. Most American schoolkids know something of the Amazon basin's ecology. Many could speak knowledgeably about slash-and-burn agriculture, deforestation rates, "paper" parks (designated reserves without on-the-ground protection), and the loss of indigenous cultures. Most everyone, young and old, is familiar with the metaphor of the Amazon rainforest as the lungs of the planet. It is remarkable, really, how quickly that image has supplanted an earlier notion of a dark and steamy jungle peopled by savages.

Clearly, environmentalists have done a good job communicating both the value of, and threats to, Amazonia, a landscape of superlatives. While under increasing assault, it remains the planet's greatest wilderness—a forest so vast, and emitting so much water vapor, that it helps create its own weather. The region's namesake river carries more freshwater than any other in the world; the Amazon and its more than one thousand tributaries collectively drain an area roughly the size of the contiguous United States.

That watershed is the globe's richest in species diversity, and eastern Peru is perhaps the most exceptionally fecund part of Amazonia because its soils are enriched by nutrients washing down off the Andes. The area around Manu National Park, including the Los Amigos River watershed to its east, is a natural focus for conservation. Only a day's boat ride upriver from Puerto Maldonado, a bustling frontier town of twenty-five thousand, the forest here is threatened by illegal logging and poaching, and thus represents the generic social and political challenges facing the Amazon basin.

Wet season or dry, in the Los Amigos watershed there is always something blooming. Something fruiting. Something rotting. The forest smells moist and earthy, perhaps a little rank from decay, like a fruit market at the end of a hot day. Counterintuitively in a landscape of such abundance, the soils are thin. Leaf litter and other material that drops onto the forest floor are decomposed and appropriated so quickly that deep organic soils never develop. In contrast to a temperate forest, most of the minerals in the system are held in the living material aboveground. A landscape more filled with life would be difficult to imagine. Creatures are everywhere—insects and bats and wild cats (including not just jaguars, but pumas, ocelots, and margays, too), filling every niche, from below the surface of the soil to high in the forest canopy.

*Just seeing the rate at which the natural world was disappearing—I began to think we might be the last generation that would have wild places left on Earth.*

—Gordon Moore

It was notable, then, when the Amazon Conservation Association, a U.S.-based nonprofit with affiliates in Peru and Bolivia, signed an agreement with the Peruvian government in 2000 to protect Los Amigos. Throughout the developing world (and the United States and Canada), governments regularly award logging concessions to timber companies to cut trees on federal lands, but Peru is the first country to implement a parallel program for nonextractive uses, and Los Amigos was the first conservation concession granted.

"We have a forty-year perpetually renewable lease to manage the area for biodiversity conservation," says ecologist Adrian Forsyth, president of the Amazon Conservation Association. The group makes no direct payment for the concession but took on significant and costly obligations, including developing a scientific field station, offering fellowships to Peruvian scientists, and launching sustainable development projects with local communities. The first order of business was stopping timber theft. "At the time, there was a mahogany rush on, and there were many loggers in the watershed illegally," says Forsyth. "We had to work very delicately to get them out, so it's now 100 percent logger-free."

The brainchild of Forsyth and Peruvian conservationist Enrique Ortiz, the Los Amigos Conservation Concession pioneers a hopeful new tool for saving nature that is already being emulated elsewhere. More immediately, it assures that these four hundred thousand acres will stay forever wild, but the positive effects are felt throughout the region. The purchase of a former mining company inholding and placement of the research station at the confluence of the Los Amigos and Madre de Dios rivers allows field staff to monitor all traffic into the watershed, crucial to securing not only the area covered by the concession, but also an adjacent reserve established for indigenous peoples, and the eastern edge of Manu National Park. This success was built on creative vision, cooperation with the Peruvian government, and private conservation dollars. Many American donors helped, but the core support of $5 million to secure the concession, purchase private land where the field station sits, and develop related infrastructure came from Gordon Moore.

Gordon Moore is a septuagenarian who earned a PhD in chemistry and physics before entering the nascent field of semiconductors in the 1950s. He cofounded the silicon chip maker Intel in 1968 and helped direct its phenomenal growth, becoming a high-tech titan, and billionaire, in the process.

When Moore was born in the San Francisco Bay Area in 1929, there were fewer than six million people in all of California. By 2005, the state's population was nearly thirty-seven million. It doesn't take an advanced degree to understand the practical realities of that growth curve. Many of the wild places where a kid could ramble about during the 1930s and 1940s are long since under concrete. Growing up in the small Bay Area town of Pescadero, Moore remembers having access to "lots of open space," learning to hunt deer with his dad, and fishing after school with an older cousin. "We had a good-sized stream that ran right behind the house," he says. "I could literally sit on the end of our porch and fish for steelhead trout."

Moore has maintained the angler's obsession ("trying to outwit a fish is something I can focus on completely," he says) even while building one of the world's leading technology companies. He and his wife, Betty, he notes, "ended up spending almost all our vacations running off to increasingly remote locations" for fishing trips. In the early 1960s they explored the Baja Peninsula, then, as that area became developed, moved on to Costa Rica and Panama. "When we first went

to Costa Rica," he says, "I think there was only one tiny little resort for fishing, with a half-dozen cabins set up on the Pacific Coast—now it's darn near end-to-end resorts."

Time and again, Moore saw how once-pristine areas subsequently became high-rise hotels and golf courses, prompting in him a growing desire to help save wildlife. That interest has grown during his association with Conservation International. A longtime board member, in 1999 he gave that organization $35 million to launch the Center for Applied Biodiversity Studies. In 2000 he and Betty launched a foundation to support conservation, scientific research, and a variety of projects in the San Francisco Bay Area. Endowed originally with a multibillion-dollar gift of Intel stock, the Gordon and Betty Moore Foundation immediately became one of the top ten U.S. grantmakers.

A year later, the Moore Foundation made the biggest donation ever to a conservation group, pledging $261 million in grants to Conservation International to help protect "biodiversity hotspots" around the globe. This approach, popularized by Conservation International, maximizes efficiency by focusing on the biologically richest and most imperiled habitats. Of course, it doesn't solve every ecological problem—less species-rich regions are worthy of concern, too—but if a few dozen biodiversity hotspots identified by ecologists were preserved, totaling just 2.3 percent of Earth's land area, it would go a long way toward slowing the current global extinction crisis.

In philanthropy, as in business, Gordon Moore is first a scientist. He applies his engineer's mind to problems and seeks solutions. He wants his foundation to embrace conservation strategies that are both practically achievable and measurable. "My view is that unless you can see some way that the things you're doing have a permanent impact, they're probably not worth doing," he says. Moore Foundation initiatives include North Pacific salmon fisheries, marine microbiology, and the Amazon basin; in the latter area, the Los Amigos Conservation Concession is just one of many projects supported with Moore money. A major grant in 2001, for example, helped establish Peru's three-million-acre Cordillera Azul National Park, and the foundation is planning to invest some $300 million in Amazon conservation between 2005 and 2015.

"The only thing attractive about the biodiversity problem is that there is this bottleneck where things might get easier on the other side," says Gordon Moore, referring to estimates that project human population levels reaching ten to twelve billion later this century before stabilizing and beginning a gradual decline. Much of the growth will be in the tropics, and the pressure on natural areas from a bloated humanity will be extreme. Gordon Moore has suggested that a primary goal of his giving is to help as much of life's diversity as possible to squeeze through that bottleneck. "Maybe it's wishful thinking," he says, "but it gives you some hope at least that a finite program can have long-lasting results."

Moore will not live to see all the negative consequences of the present demographic explosion, but his grandchildren and great-grandchildren likely will. Whether they inherit a world where salmon still ascend British Columbia's wild rivers to spawn, where giant otters still flourish in the Peruvian Amazon, remains to be seen. But a world with its natural diversity and beauty intact is the one he hopes to bequeath to them.

Will future historians remember Moore primarily as a pioneer in the semiconductor industry, or as a man who helped save a living planet? Only time will tell if there are historians around to even consider the question. But if brilliantly colored frogs still live in the rainforest centuries hence, if massive ceiba trees still poke through the canopy, if tapirs and peccaries must remain ever wary to escape becoming el tigre's next meal, Gordon Moore's philanthropic legacy will likely have played a key role in their survival.

# NOKUSE PLANTATION
## The Once and Future Forest

*M. C. Davis*

Some people enjoy a good novel. M. C. Davis prefers the *Statistical Abstract of the United States*, that compendium of information about American economic and demographic trends produced annually by the Census Bureau. He trolls those data-rich waters, fishing for clues to better anticipate the future. He often finds them, for M. C. Davis has a gift, an ability to recognize patterns before others do, and with that knowledge, make money.

Davis used to buy troubled companies, fix their problems, and resell them. Before that, from his late teens into his early thirties, Davis played professional poker, using his winnings to put himself through college and law school. "I had a wife and some babies to support, and it was good money for part-time work," he says.

Today his investment company buys and sells rural timberland. By working harder than potential competitors and using his well-honed poker logic, Davis usually makes the right bets. He just has a knack for it. "Drop me in the desert flat-out broke," he says, "and I'll be back in a week with a good set of clothes, drivin' a nice car, and I may not have a million dollars in my pocket, but I'll be well on my way." Now that kind of bravado from most people would ring false, a loser's empty boast. Spend a few days with M. C. Davis, and you wouldn't wager against him.

Davis moves fast and talks slow, his southern drawl peppered with expletives. His affable demeanor isn't just good for making friends; it may distract a competitor, at least temporarily, from recognizing who the smartest person in the room is. Do the Harvard Business School types ever hear that accent and underestimate him? "Hell, yes, they do," Davis says. "But only once."

Davis's earthy, down-home talk is no act. He's a country boy who grew up poor, momma and stepdaddy and a pack of kids crammed in a trailer. An upbringing like that can lead to many places, but one wouldn't expect it to produce an innovative conservationist with a passion for saving black bears and gators and longleaf pine forests. Davis, however, is one of a kind. He's charismatic and funny. He tells great stories. People like him. Manley Fuller, president of the Florida Wildlife Federation, which named Davis the 2003 Florida Wildlife Conservationist of the Year, wryly suggests that "people like M. C. Davis could make you rethink your opposition to human cloning."

For a person who by his own estimation is "about half rich," Davis is frugal. Not a monk, but certainly not extravagant. At a socialite's Christmas party, he refuses the $800-a-glass champagne. That's waste—and he hates waste. He admires people who work, work like crazy, as he has, all his life. He is scornful, in a bemused way, of bloated bureaucracies in all forms: of how some nonprofits can raise so much money yet do so little with it; of the way government employment will "suck the creativity right out of a man"; of how his competitors require teams of accountants and lawyers and fancy office buildings while he and a staff of three "can do $150 million of business a year out of a double-wide on a dirt road." (And when the trailer floor gets soft, he just hires a man to crawl under there with some cinder blocks and prop it up.)

"I used to be to the right of Attila the Hun," Davis says, describing his politics. And that seems to amuse him, too—that a self-described redneck conservative could turn tree hugger. In Florida, where growth is god and making money the state religion, where the population has expanded by more than 600 percent in his lifetime, Davis is a proudly conservative conservationist who dares to question the dogma of unlimited growth. He grew up in the Florida Panhandle and stayed. He knows what Walton County was like before the boom. He remembers, and is hell-bent on seeing some of the area's wildness restored.

*I do not believe that we in Walton County are under any moral or economic obligation to let every rich sonuvabitch in the world come live here.*

—M. C. Davis

As an adult, M. C. Davis was busy making money and had little time to roam the pine flatwoods of his youth. Then, in the early 1990s, he attended a presentation at the local high school about imperiled Florida black bears. Something clicked. He wrote out a check to support a bear conservation program run by Defenders of Wildlife. Once he embraced the cause of conservation, he did so with gusto. As he puts it, he began to nurture his own "biophilia"—using a term coined by biologist E. O. Wilson to describe the innate human tendency to love wild things. Davis read Wilson's *The Diversity of Life*, and *Saving Nature's Legacy* by ecologists Reed Noss and Allen Cooperrider. He read John Muir and Aldo Leopold, patron saints of the American conservation movement, and generally immersed himself in ecological literature.

Soon he was well versed in the fundamentals of conservation biology—how isolated habitats lose species over time, and why the answer to biodiversity loss is to link and expand conservation lands, restore natural processes, and let nature heal. Then Davis began investing in projects and organizations that advance landscape-scale conservation and protect endangered species. Beginning in 1995, he and his friend Sam Shine partnered to buy thirty thousand acres of Mallory Swamp in Lafayette County, Florida. They funded a restoration project and environmental education programs for local school kids there, and later sold the land to the state as a wildlife management area.

With his awareness of the escalating threats to nature, Davis's dreams got bigger. It doesn't take a person of his intellectual firepower to foresee the Florida's Panhandle's future: more roads, more traffic, more shopping centers. It does take a visionary to see a broad swath of wild habitat reconnecting the landscape from the Blackwater River State Forest across Eglin Air Force Base and east to the Apalachicola National Forest. Existing public and military lands in this part of the Panhandle already make up nearly one million acres off-limits to development. By conserving another million or so acres in strategic spots, a wildlife corridor of several million acres could be created. Davis is a key player in that initiative, the Northwest Florida Greenway, which has support from the Nature Conservancy, other conservation groups, local politicians, and the military.

At 463,000 acres, Eglin is America's largest air force base and a dominant player in the regional economy. It's also an oasis for wildlife, with the most expansive tract of old-growth longleaf pine forest left in the world. Those old pines are among the last, best habitat for the federally endangered red-cockaded woodpecker, whose numbers have crashed as the mature longleaf pines they need for nesting have been eliminated from the South.

While bird lovers praise the woodpecker recovery program at Eglin, politicians, from county commissioners to the governor, understand that a corridor of undeveloped land in north Florida is necessary if the flight paths used by the air force are to remain viable. Golf course condos and low-level training flights don't mix; retirees setting up for their next putt don't much appreciate being buzzed by jets. Military readiness and habitat connectivity are thus complementary arguments for establishing the Northwest Florida Greenway.

A key section in the potential wildlife corridor was secured in 2002 when M. C. Davis assembled several tracts of former industrial timberland into a private nature preserve he calls Nokuse Plantation. Nokuse, pronounced "no-Go-see" after the Creek Indian word for black bear, comprises about fifty-three thousand acres in two large units contiguous with Eglin. Davis has invested more than $50 million in Nokuse (conservationist Sam Shine has purchased one small contiguous tract as well) and has launched an ambitious program to restore native longleaf pine forests to the property.

"The longleaf pine–wiregrass natural community once covered more than eighty million acres—it was the dominant forest type across the entire gulf coastal plain," says conservation biologist Reed Noss, who has consulted on the Nokuse Plantation and Mallory Swamp projects. "Now it's more than 98 percent gone. By incrementally removing the off-site pines [loblolly and slash pine, planted for commercial logging and not native to the site], restoring natural processes, including periodic fire, and controlling invasive exotic species, M. C. Davis is attempting to reknit the pieces of a functioning ecosystem."

Can it be done? "Sure it can," says Davis. "It'll take a lot of work and some money, but it's achievable." Years of human labor are ahead, and decades, even centuries, of natural recovery before ancient pines again tower over parklike grasslands. In typical frugal fashion, Davis aims for maximum efficiency. He's assembled a team of scientific advisors but insists he will not "spend a pile of money trying to know the unknowable before we do anything." He understands that ecological restoration on a landscape scale is necessary but believes it must be cost-effective. "Nature has to do 98 percent of the work here for us," he says.

The way some men in his tax bracket might show off their yachts or private jets, Davis is tickled to show visitors around Nokuse, pointing out its natural attributes: A steephead ravine where underground springs seep from a sandy bank, giving life to a tangled jumble of flowering plants, shrubs, and trees. Beaver ponds where the water shimmers in the late afternoon light. The blackwater slough where Davis once found dozens of lounging young alligators. Unlike a passing fancy, M. C. Davis's love affair with Nokuse Plantation seems destined to last. He is enthralled by its biodiversity. He loves it as it is, and as it will be.

And that is the ultimate paradox for M. C. Davis, or anyone like him who seeks to preserve some significant part of the landscape for posterity: Much of the world has been badly damaged. The remnants of pristine nature in the contiguous United States are mostly small islands of wildness amid a sea of destruction. A conservation philanthropist committed to restoring wounded lands must expect most of the returns on his or her investment to come long into the future.

Nokuse Plantation is a vibrant place today, but its beauty and ecological vitality, if Davis succeeds, will be far greater a hundred years hence. Davis has lived to see his part of the South get discovered by the world, hordes of people descend on its Gulf Coast beaches, golf courses sprout like mushrooms after a rain. Now he's using his entrepreneurial skills to chart a different course.

He imagines Nokuse Plantation embedded in a network of conservation lands stretching across the Florida Panhandle, offering safe passage for wildlife. He sees Nokuse's wild future—black bears meandering through regal stands of longleaf pine, red-cockaded woodpeckers raising chicks, snakes in the cypress swamps—maybe even, someday, Florida panthers and red wolves stalking deer through the wiregrass.

# IZEMBEK NATIONAL WILDLIFE REFUGE COMPLEX

## Gift of the Great Land

*Richard King Mellon (1899–1970)
and Constance Prosser Mellon
(1910–1980)*

Could there be a more dramatic sight than the Alaska Peninsula—where fire meets ice, and land touches sea? Where snow-clad peaks, some venting steam from fires deep within the Earth's crust, loom from the Pacific? Where the mountains, and occasional human visitors, witness a wildlife pageant that is remarkable even for Alaska?

Far less known than the Arctic National Wildlife Refuge or Denali National Park, the Izembek National Wildlife Refuge Complex, an administrative grouping of multiple federal refuges that covers 2.9 million acres of the peninsula's southern tip, can compete with any spot in North America for grandeur. "It's a primeval landscape, one of the wildest, least-visited parts of Alaska," says Brad Meiklejohn, Alaska representative for the Conservation Fund, a national land conservancy.

Picture caribou kept wary by wolf packs and the occasional wolverine, that embodiment of northern wilderness, largest and fiercest member of the weasel clan. Think of streams running thick with salmon, and alder thickets teeming with brown bears coming in to feast. Imagine the Izembek Lagoon coated with shorebirds, seasonal concentrations that almost defy enumeration—hundreds of thousands of Pacific black brants, Steller's eiders, and tundra swans foraging in the eelgrass.

"The volume of life is staggering," says Meiklejohn, who suggests that the wildlife spectacle is produced by the "strong confluence of marine and terrestrial components" of the ecosystem: "You've got big herds of walrus and sea lions and seals, as well as caribou, salmon, and bears." Brad Meiklejohn is a former backcountry ranger and avid birder, the type of person who uses his time off from saving wilderness to explore it, often flying off to birding hotspots to pad his life list. "The entire world population of emperor geese gathers at Izembek twice each year during migration," he says. "It's quite spectacular to see swirling clouds of shorebirds like smoke over the water."

Izembek presents a picture of wildness, the kind of image that helped reshape American attitudes toward Alaska. When Secretary of State William Henry Seward negotiated the territory's purchase from Russia for $7.2 million dollars in 1867, ratification of the treaty barely passed the U.S. Senate, and initial reaction was scornful. One Missouri congressman ridiculed the deal to acquire "an inhospitable and barren waste" that would "never add a dollar to the wealth of our country." (Ironically, congressmen 140 years later would use similar rhetoric about the Arctic National Wildlife Refuge's being a frozen wasteland to argue for oil drilling there.) But attitudes toward "Seward's Folly" began changing as economic boosters saw dollar signs in Alaska's scenery, and were entirely overturned by the Alaska gold rush of the 1890s. Writing in *National Geographic* in 1901, U.S. Geological Survey director Henry Gannett stated: "The Alaska coast is to become the showplace of the Earth."

Some highlights of that showplace are the string of national parks and wildlife refuges on the five-hundred-mile-long Alaska Peninsula. Much of the conserved land here dates to passage of the Alaska National Interest Lands Conservation Act (ANILCA) in 1980, a landmark law in U.S. conservation history. In the stroke of President Jimmy Carter's pen, ANILCA formally protected 104.3 million acres of federal land in Alaska, doubling the National Park and National Wildlife Refuge systems, and tripling the acreage in the National Wilderness Preservation System. One of the new wilderness designations permanently protected 300,000 acres at the Izembek National

Wildlife Refuge Complex. Despite its extraordinary achievements, ANILCA represented a compromise among conservationists, pro-development state politicians, and Native tribes. Vast expanses of Alaska wilderness were preserved for future generations, including several million acres along the peninsula, but many areas of outstanding wildlife habitat remained unprotected. Especially vulnerable to development were private property, state lands (when Alaska became a state it had been allowed to choose more than 100 million acres of the unreserved federal domain for its own purposes), and lands managed by Native corporations.

As part of the 1971 Alaska Native Claims Settlement Act, a cash payment of $962 million and forty-four million acres of federal land were given to regional and village corporations associated with indigenous people. In exchange, the Native corporations renounced future land claims. In the ideal scenario, a village corporation selected the tribe's traditional territory, but due to conflicting claims, this was not always possible. Some village corporations ended up with land assets far from their community, areas that perhaps had never been used by the tribe for hunting and fishing. In such cases, there might be even greater pressure for shareholders to allow development that maximized revenue to the corporation.

On the Alaska Peninsula, the Sanak Corporation of the Sanak Island band of Aleut people came to own a large tract contiguous with existing refuge lands. In the late 1990s, the corporation approached the Conservation Fund with an offer to sell more than thirty-seven thousand acres, including forty miles of wild coastline southwest of Cold Bay, for addition to the Izembek Refuge complex. Brad Meiklejohn went looking for the money. The benefactor that stepped forward was the Richard King Mellon Foundation of Pittsburgh, one of the best-endowed private charitable foundations in the United States. With the Mellon Foundation underwriting the purchase, the Conservation Fund brokered a transaction in which the Sanak Corporation lands were acquired in two stages for roughly $3.3 million, then donated to the U.S. Fish and Wildlife Service. The Native residents retained subsistence use rights to hunt and fish on the land.

The caribou never saw the press release, but a new standard had been set for privately funded habitat preservation in Alaska—it was the largest single conservation gift, in acres and dollars, in state history.

If the Richard King Mellon Foundation had secured only the Izembek lands, it would have made a lasting contribution to America's natural heritage. But that deal, consummated in 2002, was merely one project, albeit a spectacular one, funded through the foundation's American Land Conservation Program. Working in partnership with the Conservation Fund, from 1988 to 2002 the foundation invested approximately $400 million in conserving 190 different parcels at eighty-one sites, including two other imperiled Alaskan properties. The Izembek gift is especially noteworthy because it put the foundation over the one-million-acre mark of lands protected through its grantmaking, with at least one project in every state.

Heir to a banking and industrial fortune, Richard King Mellon (1899–1970) became a prominent civic leader and businessman instrumental in Pittsburgh's mid-twentieth-century renaissance. His wife, Constance Prosser Mellon, served as chair of the foundation from its creation in 1947 until her death in 1980. The Mellons were active outdoors people and conservationists, and their sons, Richard P. Mellon and Seward Mellon, continue to direct the foundation's giving to reflect the family's interest in protecting wildlife habitat. In *From Sea to*

*Shining Sea*, a book-length report on the American Land Conservation Program, Richard and Seward Mellon challenge private citizens to help "preserve the land we all share." They write of their hope "that other families and individuals will enjoy and benefit from the outdoors as our family has. We believe the private sector has an obligation to augment the conservation work of state and federal agencies."

That familial commitment to conservation is now written on the land in ways large and small—in a tiny strip of Florida beachfront that is a critical nesting site for marine turtles, in several hundred acres added to Antietam National Battlefield, and in some 374,000 acres of Nevada's Sheldon National Wildlife Refuge, where the foundation helped purchase and retire livestock grazing permits, freeing up the land for wildlife and outdoor recreation. Timely gifts from the foundation added key tracts to Rocky Mountain, Redwood, and Mammoth Cave national parks. Many public agencies and nonprofits have received support, but the National Wildlife Refuge System has benefited particularly, with numerous expansions to existing units, and two new refuges created—Louisiana's Big Branch Marsh and North Carolina's Pocosin Lakes—thanks to the Richard King Mellon Foundation's largesse.

From the writings of Henry David Thoreau to those of Terry Tempest Williams, a body of American literature has celebrated the recreational, scenic, and ecological benefits of wilderness areas. Perhaps no one has written more eloquently than Wallace Stegner about how the wilderness idea has helped forge our national character and history, how it is an intangible resource, yet vital to our spiritual health. So, too, is the idea of Alaska valuable, apart from the place itself, and even for people who will never visit the state whose name comes from the Aleut word "Alyeska," meaning "the great land."

A landscape so large and chockablock with life offers a gift that modern humanity, with its Alaska-sized hubris, desperately needs: humility. On a personal level, wild country like Izembek teaches a sense of scale most directly. The storms may be fierce. If you read the weather wrong, your kayak may be swamped by the swells. The brown bears are large. If you do not show respect, you may be lunch. And if Vulcan is of a mind to let off steam, Mount Veniaminof or one of the other active volcanoes along the Alaska Peninsula may erupt, showing how little geological forces care about the hopes and dreams of human beings. On a collective level, Alaska, the place and the idea, beckons us to explore the wild without and within—it challenges us to adopt an American land ethic worthy of the American landscape.

Mere words on paper will never adequately describe even this small part of Alaska, the great land, made greater still by the Richard King Mellon Foundation's gift to posterity. No language spoken by people can fully capture the wolverine's demeanor, reflect the salmon's shimmering colors, or communicate the salty taste of the air when wind drives waves onto cobble beaches at Morzhovoi Bay. Whether or not human visitors are present to experience these natural riches, the wilderness of the Alaska Peninsula is priceless simply because it is. Wildly perfect in its own right.

# MONTE LEÓN NATIONAL PARK
## Patagonia Wild

*Kristine McDivitt Tompkins*

"This day I shot a condor. It measured from tip to tip of the wings, eight and a half feet," wrote a young Charles Darwin on April 27, 1834. Darwin was on the multiyear expedition chronicled in *The Voyage of the Beagle*, collecting specimens and impressions that would launch an intellectual revolution. Following the convention of the day, he had killed the gigantic Andean condor, product of a giant land, in the name of science. Surveying the vast expanse of Argentine Patagonia, he wrote: "Everything in this southern continent has been effected on a grand scale."

At the mouth of the Santa Cruz River, the Beagle anchored, and Captain Robert Fitzroy led an exploratory party upriver, passing by lands that many decades after would be settled as a private ranch, the Estancia Monte León. But during Darwin's visit, the semiarid Patagonian steppe was home only to wildlife and the indigenous peoples who lived from the land. Darwin thought the country "extremely uninteresting," seeing everywhere "the same stunted and dwarf plants" covering "level plains." The wildlife was more remarkable—herds of guanacos, the wild camelids from which llamas were domesticated, and pumas, whose tracks "were to be seen almost everywhere on the banks of the river."

Farther north, Darwin had observed the common rhea, a large, flightless bird native to the region, which he called an ostrich. In southern Patagonia, he sought out the smaller, rarer species of rhea called avestruz petise ("petite ostrich") in Spanish. He saw several bands of the "excessively wary" fowl, and in an uncharacteristic lapse, even ate one when a colleague shot what Darwin initially thought was a juvenile bird of the common sort. "It was cooked and eaten before my memory returned," he wrote. He quickly collected the remains and reported, "From these a very nearly perfect specimen has been put together, and is now exhibited in the museum of the Zoological Society." Back in England, ornithologist John Gould named the species Rhea darwinii after Darwin.

Similar in appearance and habit to African ostriches, rheas have been proposed as an example of parallel, or "convergent," evolution, in which similar physical traits arise independently in response to comparable environmental pressures. Whether rheas and ostriches are truly unrelated remains a subject of taxonomic debate (the fossil evidence is spotty, and genetic analysis suggests a common ancestor), but the notion of parallel evolution is a handy metaphor for considering the striking similarities between Patagonia and the American West.

A newcomer to this country is struck by how much the Patagonian steppe resembles Wyoming—open prairie covered by bunchgrasses and low shrubs, canyons carved by wind and water, jagged mountains capped with snow. Beyond a comparable geography and climate, the recent human history of the two regions has strong parallels. European immigrants settled a harsh frontier, eliminated the local peoples through introduced disease and systematic violence, developed a pastoral economy based on sheep and cattle, and fostered a cult of nostalgia around the horse-borne men who tended the livestock. The North American cowboy and South American gaucho became cultural icons. To make way for domestic livestock, great populations of wild grazing animals—bison and guanacos, respectively—were eliminated. Native carnivores were persecuted. Overgrazing wore out the land.

Perhaps these similar histories are unsurprising given that Europeans settled the Wild West and the wild south during roughly the same era, and in both regions perceived the landscape as underutilized. The worldview of the newcomers begat land use practices that greatly diminished ecological health; in the United States the resulting destruction also spawned a countercurrent, a movement to conserve wildlife, soil, forests, and unmarred scenery. The national park idea was soon exported, and the foundation of Argentina's national parks system was laid early in the twentieth century, even as the young parks movement in the United States was gaining strength.

Argentine parks showcase some of the planet's most spectacular alpine terrain, but until recently, the Patagonian steppe ecosystem was barely represented in the national park system, and no protected area captured the singular beauty where the Patagonian grasslands reach the Atlantic Ocean. That changed in 2002, when Monte León, the country's first Patagonian coastal national park, was designated. The new park, encompassing 155,000 acres and twenty-five miles of shoreline, resulted from a collaboration between North and South American conservationists, and the generosity of the woman who once ran a clothing company named for this wind-scoured region at the bottom of the Earth.

Kristine McDivitt grew up in a much warmer landscape, but one that also offered grasslands and mountains, a rocky coast, and skies where condors formerly soared. She was raised on a family ranch in southern California. An adventurous spirit, Kristine went off to Idaho in the 1960s to a college picked more for its proximity to good skiing than for academic excellence, then returned to her home state, where she fell in with a freethinking band of outdoor enthusiasts. One of them, mountaineering legend Yvon Chouinard, was then making hardware for technical climbing, and in the early 1970s, Kristine helped him launch a new business selling apparel for backcountry sports. As one of Patagonia, Inc.'s first employees, and later as its longtime CEO, she helped the company grow into a retail powerhouse whose outerwear is popular not just with people who surf and climb and ski, but with people who want to look like they surf and climb and ski. (Which is, even in California, a much larger market.)

Burned out on business, Kristine retired from the company in the early 1990s, married Doug Tompkins, who, like Chouinard, had been a climber-turned-fashion-entrepreneur, and moved to Chile. In South America, Doug and Kris Tompkins began doing conservation work full-time, helping create several new protected areas, including a 740,000-acre wilderness park in Chile called Pumalín. In the late 1990s, Kris Tompkins decided to sell her stock in Patagonia the company and reinvest the money in Patagonia the place. Along with her old friend Yvon Chouinard and a few associates, she founded a nonprofit land trust, Conservacion Patagonica, that would help expand conservation lands in the region. That decision happened to coincide with an economic crisis in Argentina and a sustained decline in the rural economy. A century of overgrazing and a collapse in the global wool market had left the large sheep estancias generally unprofitable.

"We had heard about this property on the coast that the park service had been trying to buy for years," says Tompkins. For various reasons, the deal had never been consummated, so she asked the head of a leading Argentine environmental group to negotiate with the owners about purchasing the land. An agreement was struck in 2001, and the organization, the Fundación Vida Silvestre Argentina, bought the Estancia Monte León for $1.7 million provided by Conservacion Patagonica, all of the funding provided by Kris Tompkins from the sale of her Patagonia stock. Over the next eighteen months a master plan for the future park was developed, and the following year the land was formally transferred to the Argentine parks administration. A new national park was born.

But no birth is easy. Here was an extraordinary place that the park service wanted to save. It was private property with a willing seller—one of Patagonia's most influential families, whose roots stretched back to the 1890s, when siblings Mauricio and Sara Braun began building a sheep ranching empire in the region. A nonprofit organization stood ready to take title and then donate the estancia to the government. Best of all, a private conservationist was offering to foot the bill. It should have been simple. It wasn't, due to opposition from some provincial politicians and ranchers.

As in rural parts of the American West, antifederal sentiment in Patagonia can run strong. "We had a very tough go getting the jurisdiction passed from the province to the national parks because the provinces don't like to cede land back to the federal government," says Tompkins. To do so required a unanimous vote of the provincial legislature. For a former corporate executive accustomed to making things happen quickly, it surprised Tompkins that conservation could be so tough: "I was new to this and had no idea how contentious it would be," she says. "Land use issues hit at the heart of human beings and can cause irrational behavior. I was pretty down about that until a friend told me how long it took to create Grand Teton National Park" (more than fifty years). "Of course, now that Monte León is a national park, it was all their idea and our role is mostly forgotten. Which is fine," she concludes. "Saving the land is what matters."

When Charles Darwin wrote, "The plains of Patagonia are boundless," the country was unexplored by Europeans, and his imagination was free to drift across the land unfettered. Soon after his visit, however, the wilderness Darwin saw would begin to be bound up in the minds and legal documents of men. More than 170 years later, at Monte León, that tradition of conquest and containment is being reversed as the land is unshackled from human dominion to follow its own course.

Where the salty spray meets land, Monte León's beaches are a busy place. Male sea lions roar and tussle, defending their harems. Fabulous numbers of Magellanic penguins crowd the shoreline; their colonies, comprised of tens of thousands of individuals, emit an overpowering fishy aroma. When Kris Tompkins first visited Monte León, she was astounded at the scene: "It's an unbelievable coastline. We had been concerned about protecting the sea lions and penguin rookeries, but the physical nature of the place is so extraordinary. It is truly national park caliber."

While it will take time for the vegetation to heal from past livestock grazing, wildlife populations already seem to be rebounding. The land now belongs to Darwin's rheas, armadillos, and eagles. And it seems fitting that a park named for a mountain shaped like a lion should be a safe haven for pumas, who roam the grasslands in search of the occasional unwary guanaco. Southern right whales cruise by offshore, elephant seals haul out on the rocks, and shorebirds wade in the surf. Most of the plants and animals Darwin recorded on his visit to the area are still present. One exception is the Andean condor, and there is talk about reintroducing the species to Monte León, which would be a proper capstone to the park's creation story. For Kris Tompkins and Conservacion Patagonica, however, the successful conservation project here is merely an opening chapter in the land trust's work to help preserve habitat for penguins and rheas—and all other wild creatures at home in the remote reaches of Patagonia.

# NORTON'S ISLAND
## Under the Influence of Earth and Sea

*Abigail, Emily, and Annie Faulkner*

In the coastal waters of Maine, writer Rachel Carson experienced a world of wonders. Before *Silent Spring* made her an environmental prophet, Carson was a career employee of the U.S. Fish and Wildlife Service who wrote magazine articles and books about marine biology. Trained as a scientist but with the soul of a poet, Carson celebrated the wildness she saw in the margins between ocean and land. Calling tide pools "seas in miniature," she communicated the grand dramas that play out in these petite ecosystems—the timeless battle between predator and prey, the daily struggles for creatures inhabiting a world that is sometimes submerged, sometimes high and dry. In *The Sense of Wonder*, a short book about reinforcing a child's innate love of nature, Carson wrote, "The lasting pleasures of contact with the natural world are not reserved for scientists but are available to anyone who will place himself under the influence of earth, sea, and sky, and their amazing life."

As young children, Annie, Abigail, and Emily Faulkner came under these influences at Norton Island ("Norton's," in the local vernacular), which their father had purchased in the 1960s. Week-long camping trips to the undeveloped forty-four-acre coastal island off Spruce Head, Maine, became a highlight of summer vacation for the three sisters: "We dug clay from the clam beds, made pots, and 'fired' them in a campfire set in the rocks by the beach," Annie remembers. "We made campsite furniture out of driftwood and old lobster crates. We collected beach peas and rose hips and lots of sea glass, and took home pounds of beautiful round stones."

The expeditions often included extended family—aunts, uncles, and cousins assembled to commune in the salt air but without the accoutrements of typical beach house life. Improvements on the island consisted only of an old pit privy and a hand-dug well. "We got eaten alive by mosquitoes," recalls Annie, "and spent nights in downpours that woke us up drenched in our tents and sleeping bags."

A dense conifer forest tangled with deadfall covers most of the island. Getting temporarily lost while bushwhacking through those dark woods must have delighted the Faulkner girls. What better place could a kid imagine for playing explorer or desert island castaway? Certainly the island provided an exciting setting for childhood games, but it also augmented the girls' interest in natural history. Annie later studied geology and geography, and developed a passion for saving wilderness. Abigail and Emily pursued different academic interests, but as adults the Faulkner sisters retain a deep attraction to unspoiled landscapes. Abigail lives in Vermont with her family and chickens, and has developed an environmental education program for her children's public school. Emily raises sheep and teaches French at a Waldorf school in rural Idaho.

Beyond building fond memories and a deeper land ethic within the Faulkner family, Norton's Island was also providing a reverse image of the land use change in Downeast Maine. As waterfront houses sprouted on the mainland and nearby islands, Norton's Island continued to sprout mushrooms and wildflowers. Once, but no longer, farmed, its natural habitat did not become fragmented or disappear under concrete. Rather, under the Faulkners' ownership, the land regained wildness.

At low tide, strolling on the seaweed-covered cobbles of Norton's Island is tricky, for the footing is exceptionally slippery. That squishy feeling underfoot is a thick mat of brown and yellow rockweed, which provides security and food for a variety of creatures. Tiny air bladders keep the plants vertical when underwater, but they collapse when the tide goes out. Barnacles coat the rocks just above the rockweed zone. Higher still is a splash zone supporting creatures that thrive despite less frequent dousing. These subregions of the intertidal zone, grading from wet to dry, span just a few feet but harbor a universe of life—sea palms, kelp, sea urchins, whelks, limpets, barnacles, clams, periwinkles, crabs, and many others.

Just beyond the reach of ocean spray, the dark woods begin, where spruce trees watch over a carpet of moss and lichen. During occasional nor'easters, when snow blankets Norton's Island, its uninterrupted forest canopy provides shelter for the deer who swim between the mainland and nearby islands.

This is the community of life that the Faulkner sisters intended to preserve when they donated a conservation easement covering Norton's Island to the Maine Coast Heritage Trust in 2003. As adults, they had been given title to the island by their parents, and as they began taking their own children there for adventures in sand and seaweed, the sisters began to think about permanent conservation options. They decided to protect the island's wild character with a conservation easement—a legal agreement negotiated between a landowner and a nonprofit land trust or government agency allowing property to remain in private ownership while constraining specific land uses. The deed restrictions run with the land title, applying to all future owners. In the case of Norton's Island, the Faulkner sisters legally extinguished the right to log the property or to allow future residential or commercial development. As the holder of the conservation easement, the Maine Coast Heritage Trust is responsible for ensuring that the agreement's provisions are upheld.

Tax advantages are often available to private individuals who give conservation easements to a qualifying land trust (or, in some instances, sell land or a conservation easement on land at below-market rates), but the Faulkner sisters admit that they gulped hard when they saw the property's appraised value. The island had become very valuable, and its worth, in strictly monetary terms, would be greatly diminished with an easement that extinguished all development rights. For Annie, Abigail, and Emily, all with young families of their own, it was a substantial gift. They mulled over various scenarios, including selling the island and using the windfall to preserve a larger tract of forest elsewhere in Maine.

In the end though, Abigail explains, they chose to protect the island "partly out of nostalgia, but also because in the midst of so much intense development, its character will really stand out and perhaps provide an important wild experience for folks in the future, who might in turn become more protective of natural areas."

Preserving a coastal island would be an exceptional act for most families, but for the Faulkners, saving Norton's Island was just one chapter in a long family history of land stewardship. The sisters' grandparents, Jim and Mary Faulkner, began purchasing worn-out southern New Hampshire timberlands in the 1930s and over time assembled the 11,500-acre Andorra Forest, which has been managed for sustainable forestry and a family retreat for well over half a century. Andorra Forest passed to the next generation of Faulkners in the 1980s, and in 1990 they donated a conservation easement on the property to a New Hampshire conservation group, at the time the largest such donation in state history. Under the terms of that easement, Andorra Forest can never

be developed, responsible timber management is assured, and a 2,600-acre private wilderness area called Wildcat Hollow was established where no logging will occur. In time, Wildcat Hollow will develop an old-growth forest typical of the landscape before settlers colonized New England. The notion of creating a wilderness area on Andorra Forest was introduced by the girls' aunt, the late Emily Faulkner Stevens, an ardent conservationist who also helped protect natural areas in Wyoming and Arizona.

Annie Faulkner clearly inherited the nature lover's gene. She's been a tireless environmental activist, coordinating the New England Coalition for Sustainable Population for several years; helping lead the fight against a local highway project that threatened to damage wetlands; and serving as president of the Northeast Wilderness Trust, a regional land trust that preserves forever-wild land. Her husband, Bob King, who owns several small hydropower projects that produce low-impact electricity for New England customers, is equally committed to wildlands protection. Together, Annie and Bob have helped put together forest conservation deals amounting to several thousand acres around Andorra Forest, and support numerous environmental groups with gifts of time, wisdom, and money.

Of course it's impossible to tease out the many influences and experiences that shape a person's destiny. Who knows how a landscape of fog, barnacles, and whalebones will affect a small child? In her case, Annie Faulkner charged into the crashing spray, embracing a life of action on behalf of wild places and creatures. In a family with a long-standing commitment to civic engagement, she and Bob have chosen a wilderness path.

Continuing a family tradition, the Faulkner sisters' young children will also come under the influence of earth, sea, and sky at Norton's Island. A familial legacy of concern and action on behalf of the natural world has assured that this petite island wilderness will remain the magical destination that Annie, Abigail, and Emily knew as kids. Through the daily cycles of high and low tides, through seasonal and annual cycles, the island will be a perpetual exporter of beauty, provider of wildlife habitat, and source of wonder for future generations of Faulkners and other visitors who stroll its rocky shores.

# ESPÍRITU SANTO ISLAND
## Rising from Blue Water

*Tim Means*

While it may sound like a trendy spa treatment for the Beverly Hills set, "San Lucan xeric scrub" is neither mud bath nor rubdown by a buff Hispanic masseur. Rather, it is the type of habitat that covers the Baja Peninsula's southeastern tip and the nearby Gulf of California islands. For persons unaccustomed to the insular lingo of ecologists, though, we might say it's a desert, with creatures adapted to life in a parched land. All manner of prickly vegetation thrives here, including the cardón, the world's biggest cactus, which appears to the casual observer like a supersized saguaro.

Baja, the finger-shaped peninsula stretching 750 miles south into the Pacific Ocean from California's southern border, used to be part of the mainland. It broke off from what we presently call Mexico and has been wandering west at the rate of an inch per year. After the breach, the sea rushed in to form the Gulf of California, which today averages sixty miles across. One can do the math, or simply conclude that all this geological excitement happened a good long while ago.

In the United States, the gulf is generally called the Sea of Cortez, after the brilliantly ruthless Spaniard who conquered the Aztecs. Near its mouth, just north of La Paz and five miles offshore, lies a mountainous twenty-three-thousand-acre island that "stands high and sheer from the blue water," as John Steinbeck described it in *The Log from the Sea of Cortez*, the account of his 1940 trip through the region with marine biologist Ed Ricketts. Four centuries prior, ever on the lookout for exploitable riches when he sailed by in 1535, Hernando Cortez observed indigenous people diving for oysters and dubbed it Isla de Las Perlas ("island of the pearls"). During the Spanish Mission era in the 1600s, the island was rechristened Isla Espíritu Santo ("island of the Holy Spirit"), and that name stuck. Unfortunately, the Pericu Indians didn't, thanks to smallpox and other diseases introduced by the Spanish. The Pericu were mostly extinct by the 1880s, when a Dutch anthropologist and an American naturalist went looking for the last full-blooded member of the tribe, an elderly woman. They found her, but she would not consent to be photographed. Her visage, and her people's culture and customs, are lost to us, known only through a few historical accounts and the red-painted bones found in funerary caves.

Recent archaeological surveys have identified more than 120 sites used by the Pericu and their Paleo-Indian predecessors on the island, who, despite the sea's bounty, must have found it a tough place to get a living. The climate can be hot, despite the ocean breezes. It's certainly dry. Espíritu Santo is the proverbial uninhabited desert island—there are no permanent residents and practically no freshwater. The vegetation is sparse; save for the diminutive mangroves lining some of the bays, no tree offers shade from a blazing sun. So it is all the more remarkable that people apparently lived here for millennia. Some evidence suggests a human presence on the island stretching back forty thousand years, a time frame for human habitation in the New World that is controversial among experts who wrangle over how and when people first came to the Americas.

Chiseled by wind and water, Espíritu Santo has a sinuous form. On its eastern shore, cliffs jut from the water, their banded striations suggesting the rock's volcanic origin as alternating layers of ash and lava. Where the ocean meets softer rock, it has hollowed out sea-level amphitheaters where a passing kayaker may find shade and a natural echo chamber. A beach dominates the island's southern tip, its white sand comprised of finely polished bits of coral. Seen from above, the western shore has deep, fjordlike bays interspersed with peninsulas, forming protected coves. The water is spectacularly multihued, sometimes shimmering emerald green, sometimes turquoise, sometimes deep indigo. It is almost as if the colors, in their variety, are reflecting the treasure trove of life below.

Blessed with one of the planet's richest concentrations of marine life, the gulf is home to sea turtles, sharks, sea lions, and coral reefs that support more than seven hundred species of fish. Hundreds of bird species are residents or passing visitors. Various kinds of porpoises and dolphins roam these waters, including the diminutive vaquita porpoise, whose rapidly declining population makes it among Earth's most endangered sea mammals. Blue, fin, and pilot whales and more than a dozen other whale species use the Gulf of California during part of the year.

While the islands dotting the gulf may not be lush with greenery, they, too, harbor ecological wonders. Speciation, the evolutionary process by which new life-forms arise, requires time and isolation. Islands are ideal for providing the latter. When a species is native to a particular place, it is said to be endemic. If the natural range of the organism is small, it is called narrowly endemic. Which is why islands, both coastal and oceanic, often produce biological rarities—why, for example, Madagascar is home to lemurs and other wildlife found nowhere else. Similarly, a lucky visitor to Espíritu Santo may be fortunate enough to see several plants and animals unique to the island, including the Espíritu Santo Island sandsnake and the Espíritu Santo chuckwalla, a hefty lizard that suns itself among the rocks.

The story of how Espíritu Santo's rare endemics and common creatures came to have their habitat preserved has as many twists and turns as there are species of microalgae inhabiting the Gulf of California. The cast of players includes the American owner of an ecotourism company, a prominent Mexican businessman, various Mexican conservation groups, the government agency responsible for administering Mexico's national parks and other conservation lands, the Nature Conservancy, the World Wildlife Fund, several American foundations, private conservation donors, and the few dozen families who for a time collectively owned the island.

If the ancient challenges of living on Espíritu Santo Island can only be surmised, the modern threats to its wild character have become painfully obvious in recent decades. Overfishing has taken a toll on the surrounding ocean. Hordes of sea-kayaking and scuba-diving vacationers have discovered Baja, and tourism-related development has become a primary threat to the region generally, and to Espíritu Santo specifically. These threats came to a head in the 1990s.

The island's ecological value had long been known to conservationists. The Mexican government named Espíritu Santo a Flora and Fauna Protection Area in the 1970s, but that federal designation had little practical effect because the island was owned by an *ejido*—an association of rural landowners who hold property communally. The ejido system was created as part of a land reform movement after the Mexican Revolution of 1910. Traditionally, such lands could not be sold, but a 1992 constitutional change now allows ejido members to dispense property after completing a bureaucratic process to gain formal land title. At Espíritu Santo, some individuals did just that, and began subdividing and selling building lots on the ironically named Bonanza Beach. In 1997 they erected several cabins there, which were subsequently deemed contrary to the Mexican park service's authority and demolished. About this time, a real estate developer bought land and proposed a resort casino for the island. The situation was legally confusing, and a court battle could have set a dangerous precedent undermining conservation efforts elsewhere in Mexico.

To head off the casino threat, private conservationists stepped forward. Tim Means, an American who had founded the ecotourism company Baja Expeditions, purchased two beach lots himself, began agitating for Espíritu Santo Island's protection, and recruited businessman Manuel Arango to the cause. Arango, Mexico's leading conservation philanthropist and president of an environmental foundation, helped buy out the developer and all but one of the remaining properties for sale on Bonanza Beach, which were later donated to the federal government. These actions bought time for a group of conservationists to put together a deal covering the rest of the island.

That agreement, completed in 2003, compensated the ejido $3.3 million for the island. Roughly one-third of the cost came from Manuel Arango and other Mexican sources; one-third came from American donors through the Nature Conservancy; and the rest came in the form of a $1-million gift from an anonymous American family foundation, donated through the World Wildlife Fund. To help with the island's ongoing stewardship and management, the California-based David and Lucile Packard Foundation contributed $1.5 million to an endowment fund. It was the first time Mexican and American philanthropists had cooperated to buy and donate land for a federally protected area in Mexico, a fact that President Vicente Fox stressed when came to Baja to celebrate Espíritu Santo Island's purchase.

Today Espíritu Santo Island is open to public use and is forever protected from private development. Individual kayakers may secure a camping permit in La Paz before paddling out to explore the island's unmarred shoreline. In the same way that concessionaires provide services in American national parks, several ecotourism companies operating with permission from the Mexican government also bring visitors to the island for guided expeditions. They help limit use and are a key adjunct to park wardens for safeguarding the island's natural heritage. Local fishermen, too, sometimes camp on Espíritu Santo, continuing an ancient tradition. As much as the modern world encroaches on the Gulf of California, thanks to years of committed work by a transborder partnership of conservationists, the island should remain much the same as when the Pericu Indians gathered cactus fruit and harvested shellfish from the sea. A rock rising from blue waters, the island of the Holy Spirit will remain a sanctuary for wild things, and wild people, forevermore.

# KARUKINKA
Uttermost Part of the Earth

*Hank and Wendy Paulson*

The world was a large place when a person traveling from England to Tierra del Fuego faced many weeks of sailing on tempest-prone seas. The planet seems smaller now. In the whisp of a keystroke, great powers and principalities affect events around the globe. But even in the era when economic globalization depended on trade winds rather than streams of digital information, distant commercial, political, and religious forces could alter ecosystems. Even a seemingly inconsequential act of charity—in the form of a preowned tennis shoe—might affect a remote wilderness.

After lawn tennis was invented in Great Britain in the nineteenth century, Victorian ladies and gentlemen began swatting tennis balls about their grassy estates. Some of these sporting types gave their used clothing and footwear to the Patagonian Missionary Society, which in the 1870s established the first permanent outpost among the indigenous people at the far tip of South America. Thomas Bridges, the British clergyman who headed the effort to bring Christianity to the residents of Tierra del Fuego, at one point noticed that turfgrass typical of the English countryside was spreading around the native wigwams at his mission outpost. Unlike the rabbits, sheep, and cattle that he and subsequent European settlers purposely introduced, the grass was an accidental import. Bridges surmised that its seed had traversed the Atlantic on the soles of donated tennis shoes.

The grass was a relatively innocuous invader compared to others that followed. Introduced beaver, mink, and gray foxes would disrupt the region's natural communities in the decades to come. For the indigenous people, too, the arrival of modernity augured momentous change. Chile and Argentina, whose jurisdictions split Tierra del Fuego, granted land titles to a few settlers, who carved vast sheep and cattle ranches, estancias, from the wilderness. Domestic livestock began to displace the guanaco, the wild camelid that served as the basis for the Selk´nam peoples' nomadic hunting culture. As prey became scarce and native people began to appropriate sheep or cattle from the estancias, some large landowners hired mercenaries to hunt down and kill natives they believed had stolen livestock.

The key factor in the indigenous peoples' demise, however, was their immunological naïveté. Epidemics of measles and other foreign diseases caused mass mortality, and within a century after European settlement, the native tribes of Tierra del Fuego were extinct.

No power on Earth can undo this history, but one may take some comfort in the fact that attitudes toward wilderness, wildlife, and indigenous people today are more enlightened than when Europeans first colonized the Americas. And while distant powers continue to affect Patagonia for good and ill, a remarkable example of benevolent influence is the 2004 creation of a huge nature sanctuary called Karukinka (from a Selk´nam word meaning "our land"), thanks to the Goldman Sachs Group. Through an associated nonprofit foundation, the Goldman Sachs Charitable Fund, the New York–based investment bank gave the Wildlife Conservation Society 680,000 acres on the Chilean side of Tierra del Fuego to preserve as a natural area, as well as a multimillion-dollar cash gift for the land's ongoing stewardship. In terms of acreage, it was likely the largest donation ever by an American corporation for conservation purposes.

Through a fortuitous series of events, Goldman Sachs had come to control this Yosemite-sized tract of wild country in Patagonia. Although the site was an ecological prize, containing the biggest expanse of unlogged lenga, or southern beech, forest on Earth, no environmental group was in a position to save it.

"A critical thing to understand," says Henry "Hank" Paulson Jr., former chief executive officer of Goldman Sachs, "is that this project was market driven; it came out of the basic business we were doing." The firm hadn't set out one day to do a good deed and then looked around the globe for some pristine forest to protect. Goldman Sachs was in the business of generating wealth, something it has done spectacularly well since its founding in 1869. Fortunately for the land, however, Goldman Sachs had an organizational culture that emphasized philanthropy, the institutional skills to complete a complex transaction with multiple players on two continents, and a leader with a strong conservation ethic.

Hank Paulson's passion for big, wild places stretches back to childhood. He grew up on an Illinois farm with parents who encouraged their son's interest in nature. As a youngster he visited the Everglades, went on numerous wilderness canoe trips along the Minnesota-Canada border with his father, and became an Eagle Scout. But Paulson credits his wife, Wendy, for deepening his thinking about biodiversity conservation as an adult: "I had the innate interest—she really took it and drove it. She's a very good birder, very involved in environmental education. The vacations we took with our family were always to natural areas," he says, recalling wildlife-watching trips in Africa, Australia, and Latin America.

In his professional life, Paulson was a Wall Street luminary, the personification of an aggressive but principled capitalist, a career Goldman Sachs overachiever who helped take the firm public in 1999. Partners at the firm then, and shareholders during Paulson's tenure as chairman, made a great deal of money. (Paulson left Goldman Sachs in 2006 to become the U.S. secretary of the treasury.) Highly competitive, Paulson was a legendary hard worker, but something of an anomaly on Wall Street. He didn't drink, play golf, or socialize much with other captains of industry. He was plenty comfortable in the halls of power, but equally at home in some obscure rainforest watching birds with Wendy.

In 2002, some Goldman Sachs traders who were considering bidding on a bundle of distressed debt determined that one of the nonperforming notes was secured by forestland in Tierra del Fuego. They briefed Paulson, and he gave the green light for Goldman Sachs to get in the game. Coincidentally, he already knew something about the region. At different times Wendy and Hank had served on the Nature Conservancy's board of directors, and he had recently seen a conservancy scientist give a presentation that highlighted the rarity of far-southern-latitude forests.

The last, best example of these subantarctic forests is in Tierra del Fuego, where the Washington-based Trillium Corporation had planned to log its vast timberlands. Conservationists fought the project for years, litigating Trillium's environmental analysis up to Chile's Supreme Court. The logging opponents ultimately won. The reality was that cutting old-growth forests in such a cold, remote place, far from global markets, never made ecological or economic sense. The project went bust, Trillium defaulted on its commercial debt, and Goldman Sachs picked up the collateral assets at a fire-sale price.

Hank Paulson asked Larry Linden, an experienced conservationist and former Goldman Sachs executive, to come out of retirement and manage the firm's various financial and charitable interests regarding the former Trillium lands. After a consultant confirmed their ecological value, Goldman Sachs committed to conserving the property. Linden oversaw innumerable transactional details—negotiations with the defaulting principals, litigation to secure clear land title, and so forth. Another consultant was engaged to advise Goldman Sachs's board on the potential nonprofit partners capable of accepting a land gift of such magnitude and establishing a scientific and conservation program to maintain it. The New York–based Wildlife Conservation Society (WCS) emerged as the logical choice.

"WCS already had a very active program in Argentina and wanted to expand in Chile," says Linden. "They have great science expertise, and most of their top management is well versed in Latin American conservation work. It was just a really good fit." Linden consulted with political and business leaders in Chile about Goldman Sachs's intentions in Tierra del Fuego and found a warm reception; along with Wildlife Conservation Society president Steven Sanderson, he personally briefed then–Chilean president Ricardo Lagos. Linden also received widespread support from within Goldman Sachs. "The positive feeling about this project was overwhelming" he says.

Along with the land, which was valued at more than $26 million, came a $12.6 million pledge to the Wildlife Conservation Society for Karukinka's startup costs and stewardship endowment. The bulk of the cash grant came from the firm and the Goldman Sachs Charitable Fund, but Hank and Wendy Paulson personally gave $500,000; Larry Linden also made a half-million-dollar gift; and other employees made lesser contributions. The Patagonian wilderness was a world away from Wall Street, but the idea of saving some of it for future generations clearly resonated with the people of Goldman Sachs.

Karukinka is a place that affords a big view. It calls to mind writer Nancy Newhall's line about entering wilderness, "You shall know immensity, and see continuing the primeval forces of the world." When the leaves turn, the foliage colors resemble autumnal New England, but with Labrador-scale wetlands, Montana-like grasslands, and Norway-esque coastline thrown in. And virtually no people. The landscape may feel familiar, but it is truly like nowhere else on Earth, with its mix of peat bogs, wild rivers, lenga forests, wind-scoured steppe, and snowy mountains looking down on the Straight of Magellan. The guanacos are a definitive clue that one hasn't been dropped in, say, Alaska or the Yukon.

While the land still appears incredibly wild, outside influences have inflicted wounds that Wildlife Conservation Society ecologists will attempt to heal in the decades to come. The introduced beavers, particularly, are causing significant damage to Tierra del Fuego's forest and aquatic ecosystems. "Almost 10 percent of the plants at Karukinka are invasives," explains biologist Bárbara Saavedra, who oversees Karukinka and other WCS projects in Chile. "Even in the deepest pristine forests you can find exotic plants that were transported by beavers. It's a major challenge," she says.

No matter how much economic globalization ties together the rest of the world, one hopes that Karukinka will remain hard to get to, its wild beauty intact for the ages. Perhaps, like the Selk'nam, the current human residents of Tierra del Fuego will end up being passing stories on the land, but for now, the successful establishment of the reserve means there will be expansive country where researchers and wilderness travelers may witness the continuing primeval forces of the world.

Hank Paulson had that opportunity when he and Wendy visited Karukinka in 2005. "We camped and hiked, and had one very rigorous day where we walked through the forest and climbed way up to a high lookout point," he recalls. "We were on a cliff looking down at the fjords, there were Andean condors flying overhead, and it was just a spectacular day—I felt a great sense of pride that this property was going to be saved for perpetuity."

# CORCOVADO NATIONAL PARK
## Beacon of Wildness

*Doug Tompkins and Peter Buckley*

The fish is recorded in the memories of the people present, two men and a boy, and also on film. "You have to imagine, this is Lago Trébol, up the Tic Toc River," says Peter Buckley, "a lake visited only once in a blue moon by a floatplane, and just full of these submarine-sized trout." The photograph shows Buckley's oldest son, at the time eight or nine, wearing a grin nearly as big as the fish he holds. Behind him Doug Tompkins appears less gleeful. "Doug is kind of scowling because he'd gotten skunked, while this kid had caught a dozen fish," Buckley says. "My son will never forget that experience."

The quality of the fishing was merely a bonus; the setting alone was unforgettable. Viewed from Tompkins's small plane, the world along the Chilean coast south of Puerto Montt seemed to be zoned into horizontal bands of color: deep blue along a crenulated coastline. Above it, dark green, a primeval rainforest interrupted occasionally by waterfalls. Above that, a band of white, snow-capped mountains, with a great dormant volcano, Corcovado, lording over all.

On that day, if Volcán Corcovado had revived herself, the three people camped on Lago Trébol would have been among the few humans to see it. They had the lake to themselves. They were in one of the most spectacular wilderness areas left on Earth, a vast expanse of roadless, uninhabited country. Some 420,000 acres of federal land, much under military jurisdiction, surrounded a large tract of private property. The private land—210,000 acres, including twenty-nine miles of undeveloped oceanfront and the largest remaining stand of virgin Guaitecas cypress trees left in Chile—had been purchased jointly by Buckley and the Conservation Land Trust, a private foundation endowed by Tompkins.

A few years later, in the largest ever private donation to the government, they would give it away—to become the heart of Chile's Corcovado National Park.

When Peter Buckley was a kid, he often used to sneak into a local country club to play on their trampoline. He got pretty good, and eventually won an athletic scholarship on the University of Washington's diving team. Later, in law school, a classmate mentioned a friend who was interested in learning how to bounce on the trampoline. Buckley said sure, he'd teach him. And so in 1969 Buckley began working out with Tompkins, an elite rock climber and mountaineer, and they became friends.

Buckley practiced poverty law in San Francisco for a while and then moved to Europe. To support his climbing habit, Tompkins started an outdoor equipment company called The North Face, sold it, and cofounded the fashion giant Esprit. Professional interests intersected and ultimately the two friends ended up as business partners in Esprit International. By the late 1980s Tompkins had tired of the corporate rat race and sold his stake in Esprit. Over decades of climbing trips around the globe, he'd seen how industrial humanity was everywhere gobbling up the natural world. He read widely in the literature of ecology and eco-philosophy, started a foundation dedicated to saving wild nature, and moved to South America to do conservation work.

In time Buckley returned to the Bay Area and, a few years after Tompkins had bolted the corporate scene, similarly extracted himself from business. Subsequently he immersed himself in the Pacific Ocean (learning to surf) and in progressive causes, helping found two environmental nonprofits and a Waldorf-influenced private school.

In the early 1990s, a few years prior to the fishing trip on Lago Trébol, Buckley was visiting Tompkins in Chile. One day they flew south from Reñihué, where Tompkins lived, exploring the coast. "Every time I'd say, 'Wow, that's beautiful,' Doug would say, 'It's for sale,'" Buckley recalls. Where the Corcovado River flows into the Pacific, Buckley exclaimed, "That's really beautiful," to which Tompkins made his usual reply that the land was for sale. "We go about twenty miles farther and hit Tic Toc Bay," Buckley remembers, and I say, 'Now this is really cool—I'd buy this,' and Doug says, 'OK, let's buy it. It's part of the same property. I'll look into it.'"

The parcel's legal history was convoluted. An Italian businessman living in Santiago had struck a deal with the Pinochet-era military government to receive federal land in exchange for developing it. He had plotted a subdivision and amassed logging equipment before the agreement somehow soured. The businessman ended up owning the Corcovado land, with front companies shielding him from view, but no resource extraction was done. Most of the property remained pristine. To ensure that it would remain so, the Conservation Land Trust and Buckley bought it in 1994, splitting the cost.

Almost immediately, Tompkins began thinking about how to expand the conservation area at Corcovado. At the time, the Chilean military was shedding some unneeded properties, so Tompkins visited the general in charge of the program. Yes, the man said, perhaps some land there could be sold, but might navy ships in the Bay of Corcovado be allowed to fire their big guns up onto the snowfields for target practice? Tompkins suggested that such bombardment would hardly be compatible with the objectives of a nature preserve. The general reflected on this for a moment, then smiled and conceded the point.

While that first meeting was encouraging, the idea went nowhere because of Tompkins's increasing notoriety. Doug and his wife, Kristine McDivitt Tompkins (who, before leaving the corporate world had been the longtime CEO of the outdoor clothing company Patagonia), became the focus of a smear campaign because of their work to establish Pumalín Park, another protected area farther north along the Chilean coast.

The Pumalín project took a decade and was an uphill slog. An unfriendly presidential administration and ultranationalist politicians undermined the Tompkinses' effort to create a Yosemite-sized national park entirely through private funding. The rhetoric was harsh, and rumors about the Americans' intentions were sometimes absurd, but they gained some traction because Chile has little philanthropic tradition. There was a long history of outsiders coming to exploit the country's natural riches, but the idea of American expatriates buying and protecting land for wild nature was novel, and bred suspicion. In fact, parks-oriented philanthropy both by Chileans and by foreign nationals was not entirely unprecedented. Donated properties, including a major gift in 1970, had expanded Torres del Paine, Chile's flagship national park, but this fact and the broader history of the Chilean park system were generally unknown.

While it was personally unpleasant for the couple to be the target of so much misinformation, in hindsight it was probably beneficial for the nation. With Doug Tompkins becoming a fixture in the Chilean media, there was a sustained national dialogue about conservation policy. Tompkins's hard-driving personality may not have always made the going any easier, but his mountaineer's intensity was invaluable for weathering a blizzard of verbal attacks. Time passed, a more conservation-minded administration came into power, and the tide of public opinion regarding Tompkins and Pumalín Park began to turn.

In 2002, as Pumalín Park neared completion and with President Ricardo Lagos in power, Tompkins resumed pushing his Corcovado idea. "Doug called me and said he was thinking of donating our land to the government for a national park," recalls Peter Buckley, "and I said, 'Sure,

that sounds good.'" Through an intermediary, the president was approached with a proposition. If the private lands around Corcovado were given to the people of Chile, would the government kick in the adjoining federal land?

"We reminded him that every Chilean president since 1926 had created a national park, and he didn't have one," says Tompkins. "It was already a couple of years into his administration, and these things take time to put together." (Since the restoration of democratic rule in Chile, presidents may not succeed themselves in office.) President Lagos's reaction was favorable, but would the military, still a powerful force in the country, agree? It would. The nation's top general at the time, Juan Emilio Cheyre, is a progressive figure who has tried to leave behind the dark legacy of the Pinochet era. The land was not vital to military readiness, and undoubtedly he recognized the value of military cooperation to create a grand new national park. "General Cheyre is a real patriot in my eyes, for he is looking after Chile's natural patrimony, the national territory itself," Tompkins says. The ultimate credit, however, goes to President Lagos. "The park would never have happened without his determination," concludes Tompkins.

On a summer day in January 2005, Doug Tompkins, President Lagos, General Cheyre, various ministers and provincial governors, and a phalanx of reporters were transported south by navy ship and helicopter for the dedication. "Today we are privileged witnesses to the birth of a new national park," the president began. He highlighted the cooperation of public and private sectors, and described how the nation would benefit from this "gift of nature." Corcovado National Park, at 650,000 acres Chile's fourth largest, was born. After the ceremony, Tompkins walked along the beach with the president, looking up at the mountains. "Wow, is this beautiful," Lagos remarked.

The brackish estuaries where the Corcovado and Tic Toc rivers spill into the Bay of Corcovado are exceptional wildlife habitat. Immense colonies of shorebirds coat the beaches. Penguins scamper about the rocks. A lucky visitor may catch sight of an Andean condor with its eleven-foot wingspan, soaring on the wind. Marine mammals, including seals and sea lions, thrive in the bay, which was recently discovered to be a crucial feeding nursery area for blue whales, Earth's largest animals. The bay, once the lair of pirates, is now proposed to become Chile's first marine sanctuary, assuring a continuity of protection for wildlife from ocean bottom to mountain peaks.

Dotted through the Corcovado National Park are eighty-two shimmering lakes, many ringed with ancient forests where pumas haunt the shadows. It is a wonderland—a scenic spectacle and ecological jewel. Peter Buckley's son, now grown into adulthood, may someday bring his own children to fish in Lago Trébol, an opportunity he'll share with future generations of Chilean citizens.

Once, when the park was still his private dream, Doug Tompkins climbed Volcán Corcovado. From its heights he looked down upon the surrounding wild country. This place, he thought, should forever be a beacon of freedom and wildness—not a target for artillery practice. He and Buckley have ensured that young people drawn to the mountains, as Tompkins once was, may confront on Corcovado the perils familiar to the mountaineer, but as they traverse its snowy flanks, at least they need not worry about incoming ordnance.

# CUENCA LOS OJOS
## Crossing Borders

*Valer Austin*

*Josiah Austin*

"I don't view the landscape with the eye of a painter anymore. I'm too busy staring at the ground, looking for native grasses," says Valer Austin. She's guiding some guests down Cajón Bonito ("beautiful canyon"), bushwhacking through a luxuriant streamside forest, talking about some favorite subjects—grass and water. Here in northern Sonora, just south of the Arizona line, both are precious. Rains come infrequently. Some years they hardly come at all, and the bulk of the annual precipitation typically falls during seasonal monsoons in late summer.

Valer is explaining the practices that she and her husband, Josiah Austin, use to capture what little moisture falls on the former ranchland they've assembled on the Mexican side of the border, roughly one hundred thousand acres collectively referred to as Cuenca Los Ojos, the "watershed of springs." After Spanish settlers introduced cattle and sheep to the area in the 1700s, beginning a long history of overgrazing, many of the springs, seeps, and perennial streams that were the lifeblood of this arid country dried up. Workers at Cuenca Los Ojos are helping revive them by harvesting rain. They've built hundreds of small earth and stone check dams called *trincheras* to reduce runoff after a rainfall, a practice that goes back thousands of years to the aboriginal cultures that once populated the northern Sierra Madre Occidentale. The *trincheras*, and larger rock-filled dams called gabions, slow the rushing water. Sediment fills in behind them, and over time a formerly dry gully scoured by occasional flash floods will become a trickling stream of pools and small waterfalls. Rainfall that formerly would have been lost soaks into the earth. The water table rises, more grass and vegetation follow the moisture, and wildlife populations rebound.

The crystalline waters we walk beside in Cajón Bonito benefit from the erosion control structures scattered throughout the surrounding hills. The riparian forest is a tangled mass of willows, sycamores, and cottonwoods that shade the stream and keep it cool. Just a few yards from the water's edge the land rises sharply. The vegetation morphs into desert scrub with cholla, sotol, and agave plants interspersed with native bunchgrasses. On the canyon walls above, a small ledge supports a yucca plant the size of a man.

Before Valer and Josiah Austin bought the property in the mid-1990s, the forest here didn't exist. Cows grazed right down to the water, eroding the streambanks. Seedlings were constantly trampled and eaten, preventing young trees from becoming established. Only a few big old cottonwoods lined the stream. If Valer didn't have a photograph of the canyon in that earlier condition, a visitor simply wouldn't believe it could be the same place. The change is remarkable—a resurrection. Removing livestock, harvesting rain, and giving the land a little time have allowed a miracle to occur. "When you help plant the seeds of recovery and then watch nature take over," says Valer, "it's just inspiring."

Inspiring is the right word, too, for the landscape nature has fashioned where southern Arizona and New Mexico meet northern Sonora and Chihuahua. Broad, flat valleys—the San Bernardino and the Animas—alternate with north-south-oriented mountain ranges that cross the international border. The sky seems impossibly huge, and the mountains tend to turn dusky purple at the end of day when the sun is low on the horizon.

Despite grave insults visited on the land from previous overgrazing, the transboundary region remains one of the most ecologically interesting places in North America. As one moves from valley floor to mountaintop, there is a kind of elevator effect as different natural communities stack atop each other: desert scrub gives way to grassland, which becomes oak woodland, which then transitions into pine forest atop the peaks.

Bill Radke, who manages the San Bernardino National Wildlife Refuge on the Arizona side of the border, abutting the Austins' land, explains the other key reason for the region's abundant biodiversity. "The Great Plains, the Chihuahuan and Sonoran deserts, the Rocky Mountains, and the Sierra Madre all come together right here," he says. "So you have species associated with all those environments." The border country also supports numerous endemic species that live nowhere else; they include imperiled native fishes such as the Yaqui chub, the Yaqui catfish, and a handsome little minnow called the beautiful shiner. An even rarer creature, and one still unfortunately without the formal protections offered by the Endangered Species Act, is the San Bernardino springsnail, a tiny freshwater mollusk that lives in freshwater springs and seeps. The only documented population of the species survives on the refuge, and on the Austins' latest addition to Cuenca Los Ojos, just across the border.

"They bought that property as a kind of fixer-upper, for purely unselfish reasons," Radke says. Before European settlement, the land had supported a *ciénega*, a swampy wetland feeding the San Bernardino River. Cattle grazing and farming had worn out the soil, lowered the water table, and eliminated the *ciénega*. Stream courses were dry most of the year and badly eroded. "The Austins recognized the value of the native fishes and other endemic species and saw the potential for wetlands restoration," says Radke. "To have a neighbor like that, who shares your conservation goals and wants to partner with you, is amazing—it's as if the refuge extends across the border into Mexico."

Nature, of course, does not recognize the international boundary, an arbitrary political line that ignores ecological systems and the needs of migratory wildlife. Valer and Josiah Austin are part of a coalition of groups and individuals who envision a transboundary conservation area that sustains every member of the land community, including large carnivores. Mountain lions still haunt the rugged hills of Cuenca Los Ojos, and it's likely that jaguars traveling north occasionally pass by. The Mexican environmental group Naturalia has protected a reserve southeast of the Austins' land in the area where the northernmost known population of breeding jaguars lives, and Mexican and U.S. conservationists are collaborating to preserve additional "jaguar ranches" in the region. North of the border are two national wildlife refuges, a national forest, and several permanently conserved private ranches, in total, more than a million acres that won't ever be subdivided and developed into ranchettes. And some wildlife advocates long for the day when *el lobo*, the Mexican wolf, will be welcomed home to the borderlands.

It's a great start on a bold dream—a vision of a landscape where traditional rural economies and wildlife both flourish. But vexing challenges persist, including drug trafficking, illegal immigration, and the vast inequity between communities on opposite sides of the border. While land conservation can't solve all the cultural issues, it has dramatically enhanced border security on part of Cuenca Los Ojos. Before the Austins owned the Mexican parcel contiguous with the San Bernardino National Wildlife Refuge, smugglers often passed through there. Deep, eroded arroyos that were dry except during occasional storms offered easy passage for traffickers. After a few years of restoration work with gabions and larger earthen dams, those corridors are closed—filled with birdsong, trickling water, and a dense thicket of riparian vegetation. The smugglers have gone elsewhere.

People who know Valer Austin are as likely to describe her as a force *of*, as well as *for*, nature. In her sixties and a natural athlete, she moves with the grace of a fit person decades younger. Her passion for sustaining the land's wild beauty and integrity seems limitless. She derives joy from a mountain lion track in the dust, from black grama grass recolonizing overgrazed pasture, from helping a tiny, obscure snail fend off extinction.

To see Valer bouncing down a rutted dirt track in her hefty truck or conversing in Spanish with ranch workers about the newest gabions under construction, one would guess she hails from pioneer stock. While Josiah did grow up on a Maryland farm before becoming a successful businessman and private investor, Valer's outdoor adventures during childhood were in Central Park and the urban canyons of Manhattan. Private girls' school and university training in fine arts may not have been the perfect preparation for ranch life, but she appears perfectly at home now under Sonora's big sky.

In 1981 she and Josiah had bought a ranch in Arizona's Chiricahua Mountains. Initially they planned to use it for vacations and retirement. But here comes the cliché: they fell in love with the Southwest. The story usually ends, of course, with the transplanted easterner wearing a big hat, playing cowboy. The Austins' connection with the landscape transcended the superficial affection of hobby ranchers. Like cottonwoods sending down deep roots, they dug in.

"After a while we realized that you really can make a difference on the land—you can harvest water, you can help the grasses come back, you can improve wildlife habitat," says Valer. They moved to Arizona full-time. "We started watching nature, and then implementing restorative management practices and seeing huge, positive changes." Retirement got put off. "We thought, we'll work for as long as it takes to buy more land," she says. They began cooperating with other ecologically minded ranchers, nonprofits, and government agencies. They were honored for their wildlife-friendly management practices and never slowed down. "The more land we bought for conservation and the more we learned, the more we realized that we needed to buy more land," she says. "Now Josiah makes the money, and I spend it," she laughs. "My accountant calls me 'the sponge.'"

The Austins' first acquisition in Mexico, at Cajón Bonito, came at the urging of Wendell Minckley, an eminent fisheries biologist who knew the watershed held several species of native fish and, at the time, no exotics. Their latest came more than a decade later, in 2006. In between, they bought a half-dozen or so played-out ranches to assemble the Cuenca Los Ojos lands, pulled off the livestock, and began nursing a sick landscape back to health. When no other Americans were stepping forward to protect private conservation lands south of the border, the Austins filled an open niche.

In the same way they've tackled ecological restoration—taking a long view—they are planning for conservation permanence. In 2006 Valer and Josiah established a private foundation, also called Cuenca Los Ojos, and have recruited prominent Mexican and American conservationists as trustees. By building an organizational infrastructure to carry on their work in the borderlands, they are ensuring that the land they love, the watershed of springs, will offer bountiful grass and water to wildlife long after they are gone. "I never thought I could save the world," says Josiah, "but what I hope I can do is save a little part of the world."

# AFTERWORD

## The Donors No One Knew

A visit to Joshua Tree National Park in southern California is a bit like walking into a Dr. Seuss book. Jumbled boulders cleaved with fissures form a maze of light and shadow. The land seems outsized, with a gigantic sky. Strange, shaggy forms tower over the surrounding bunchgrass and cactus. But those Joshua trees are not really trees at all—they are arborescent (treelike) yuccas, distinctive to the Mojave Desert. The slow-growing plants may live more than a thousand years and exceed forty feet in height. After a Joshua tree's first flowering, subsequent growth shoots off willy-nilly, over time producing a wildly branched form. Mature plants develop an almost comical aspect with their spiky foliage and spreading crown.

One might imagine that these Joshua trees, being from southern California, would have an interesting sex life. Sure enough, the species' reproductive habits are noteworthy, but in a way that a Puritan could endorse. The plant has evolved a monogamous relationship with the yucca moth, which collects the sticky Joshua tree pollen from several flowers and then climbs into a blossom to lay its eggs. The ovules get fertilized, causing seeds to form; they in turn provide food for the moth's larval-stage offspring. Only a small percentage of the seeds are consumed, leaving most to be dispersed by wind and birds. With luck, a few will find purchase in the sandy soil, and new Joshua trees will sprout from the desert floor. This association between Joshua trees and their yucca moth pollinators is a classic example of mutualism, a symbiotic relationship in which both partners benefit.

It's a useful metaphor, too, for the relationships that develop between natural areas and the people who strive to save them. Throughout this book we've shared stories of places that inspired conservation action—action that in many cases came to define a life's purpose. Usually we've named names, but much wildlands philanthropy is conducted anonymously, and we'd be remiss if we failed to also honor the donors no one knew.

Consider, for instance, Joshua Tree National Park, which was secured for future generations through advocacy and philanthropy, a powerful combination for conservation.

One early advocate for preserving deserts in their natural state was Minerva Hoyt, a Mississippi native who came to South Pasadena with her surgeon husband in the 1890s. She soon developed a keen interest in plants native to the California desert, and later found solace in the austere beauty of that landscape after her husband and son died. Hoyt organized a desert conservation exhibit in New York City in the 1920s and founded the International Desert Conservation League in 1930. As the group's president, she personally lobbied Franklin Roosevelt and Mexican president Pascual Ortiz Rubio to create new protected areas on both sides of the border. Hoyt's conservation advocacy resulted in President Roosevelt's designating Joshua Tree National Monument in 1936. That victory was laudable, but partial and impermanent. Minerva Hoyt's appreciation for the desert's aesthetic and ecological values was hardly a universal sentiment in her day, and the monument's boundaries were later trimmed to accommodate mining interests.

Decades later, a subsequent generation of desert lovers successfully lobbied Congress to enact the California Desert Protection Act of 1994, which expanded and upgraded Joshua Tree to national park status. Even so, extensive private land within the park made it vulnerable to real estate speculators. Ironically, the acreage in question was formerly federal land dispersed during the nineteenth century as incentive to develop rail lines. Between 1830 and 1870, more than fifty-three thousand miles of track were laid, and nearly 130 million acres, roughly 7 percent of the contiguous United States, were given over to railroad corporations. That policy resulted in public lands across the West being pockmarked with a checkerboard of private inholdings.

Beginning in the mid-1990s, the Wildlands Conservancy, a conservation group based in Oak Glen, California, worked for nearly a decade to return a huge swath of California desert to the public domain. Ultimately, the organization purchased directly, or funded the acquisition of approximately 600,000 acres scattered across the Mojave Desert from a real estate company whose assets originally came from land grants to the Santa Fe and Southern Pacific railroads. The acreage conveyed to the Interior Department included inholdings in Joshua Tree National Park, Mojave National Preserve, seventeen congressionally designated wilderness areas, and other public lands.

It was the largest addition of private property to public ownership in U.S. history, a deal made possible largely by private funding, particularly from an unnamed California philanthropist. That gentleman sought no credit for his good works, but his giving has benefited every American, whether or not they have occasion to stroll among the supersized yuccas at Joshua Tree National Park. The conservationist in question has also enriched the lives of thousands of schoolchildren who visit the Wildland Conservancy's Wind Wolves Preserve, a nearly one hundred thousand acre nature sanctuary southwest of Bakersfield. He helped the conservancy to purchase ranchland that had been slated for a massive subdivision development, and to develop environmental education programs there.

While this individual's giving reflects anonymous philanthropy on a spectacular scale, it is typical in that the donor has a deep connection to his region's wildlife and wild places, and wants future generations to have an opportunity to experience them also. Passing along the gift of wildness is what matters, not to "stencil one's own name on a benefaction," as William Kent wrote to President Theodore Roosevelt in 1908 after he donated land to become Muir Woods National Monument.

Many of the places profiled in this book—Espíritu Santo Island, Blanton Forest, Fresh Tracks Nature Preserve, and others—were protected at least in part thanks to anonymous donors. Walking in Joshua Tree National Park at sunset, with an evening breeze to scatter the day's waning heat, one may feel affection for the Joshua trees rising from the desert floor, delight at the colors gathering in the western sky, and humility at the scale of the landscape stretching away. That sense of proportion—a reminder that our species is but one member in a great community of life—may be the richest gift of time spent in wild nature.

This generation, and the generations yet to come, owe a debt of gratitude to American conservationists, known and unknown, who so loved the land that they gave of their time, energy, and wealth to see it preserved. For wildlife and for people, forevermore.

# PHOTOGRAPHER'S CREDO

## Beauty and Biodiversity

Growing up in Mexico in the 1960s, I was fortunate to explore numerous wild places. My parents regularly took our family to remote sites where we would camp out and experience moments of intimate contact with nature. In contrast, the educational system in which I was schooled prepared young minds to believe that human beings are separate from nature—that this living planet is merely a collection of resources for us to control and possess without limit.

With the passage of time, I can say that such teachings failed to take root in my innermost being, which feels a deep kinship with all of nature. I am privileged to feel a profound connection with the diversity of life in its myriad forms. This connection grew during the years I lived in India, working as a diplomat for the Mexican government. From 1977 to 1980 I traveled widely throughout Asia, visiting natural wonders.

Unfortunately, whenever I have returned to the magical places I discovered with my parents as a child, and to those I visited as a young man in Asia, I have found only devastation and misery caused by human activity. Revisiting these landscapes of memory and loss has moved me to take action, to use landscape photography as the language through which I communicate concern for the Earth's diminishing biodiversity.

Photography is a powerful tool that can be used to educate the public, and help strengthen a new conservationist awareness and ethic. When spectators contemplate natural beauty, their inner beauty and sensitivity are awakened. Through beauty, I seek to foster cultural change, for I am convinced that if we wish to preserve the continuity of life as we know it, we must create a new culture that acknowledges and respects the value of nature. The survival of future generations of humans and all other species on the planet depends on such a new culture. Nature conservation and restoration is a mission we all must pursue.

Twenty-five years ago, I took up photography as a way to share my life experiences with other people. At first, my subjects were indigenous groups, and I came to know and enjoy their daily lives, ceremonies, and rituals. Most importantly, they introduced me to a collective vision of nature as a vast family, changing my perception of the world forever. Once I had experienced this familial closeness with the wild life around me, the next logical step was my decision to devote my energies solely to photographing nature.

In 2000, I founded the organization America Natural and launched an ongoing expedition from Tierra del Fuego to Alaska to photograph the Americas' most outstanding protected natural areas. By sharing these images, I hope to help conserve this hemisphere's beauty, integrity, and biodiversity.

In this book we present the stories of American conservationists who set an example in this regard, having succeeded, through their generosity and vision, in preserving areas that otherwise would have been completely destroyed. To take the photographs included here, I traveled during a period of three years through eight different countries, although primarily in the United States. For me, the most enriching part of this project has been learning about the outstanding positive actions taken by individuals who, despite the tendencies exhibited by society, have not forgotten the intrinsic value of nature. Through their work to save wildness, they have demonstrated that the love of the Earth has the power to transform us all.

# ACKNOWLEDGMENTS

It would be impossible to comprehensively acknowledge the hundreds of people who assisted in the production of this book, but all have our sincere gratitude. In particular, we wish to thank:

Wendy de Forest, Gilles Larrain, Jorge Sandoval, Angel Sandoval, Marina Stark, Baldev Duggal, Michel Duggal, Adriana Lopez S., Margarita Johnson, Aramara Vizcaíno, Gerónimo Matias Vizcaino, M. C. Davis, Mat Aresco, Lamar Monroe, Diane Wilks, Barbara Saavedra, Ricardo Muzo, Roger Blanco, Maria Marta Chavarria, Ma. Luisa Arias, Alejandro Masis, Alan Colter, Dave Sherman, Laura Vidic, Ernesto Vazquez Morquecho, Roberto López Espinosa de los M., Rafael Carballo, Tim Means and Baja Expeditions, Valer Austin and Josiah Austin, Oscar Moctezuma, Dina Wright, Don Weeden, Alan Weeden, Nigel Pitman, Joyce Barr, Laurie Marker, Lorraine Borden, Bob Joyner, Norman Brunswig, Michel Dawson, Steve Pagano, Mary Terrier, Fred Stanback, Hugh Archer, Marc Evans, Annie Faulkner, Carey Ruff, Dave Imbrogno, Marshall Eldred, Tom Van Slyke, Eva Horn, Robert Anderberg, Lauren McCain, Nicole Rosmarino, Mitch Friedman, Daniel Janzen, Mark Skatrud, Jon Marvel, Ann Down, Cathryn and Carl Hilker, Shaun Hamilton, Richard Hendrickson, Thomas Foye, Anda Angotti, Roxanne Quimby, Bart DeWolf, Nancy Stranahan, Larry Henry, Linda Kennedy, Kimberly King Wren, Rene Robichaud, Doug Buehler, Jan Wosbbenhorst, Erick Miles, William Stelzer, Sandra Siekaniec, Ronald Epp, Peter Forbes, Dave Foreman, Jennifer Esser, Joshua Brown, John Davis, Mary Byrd Davis, June and Fred Rydholm, Jim Northup, Bryce Appleton, Phoebe Campbell Knapp, Kristine Tompkins, Douglas Tompkins, Peter Buckley, Brad Meiklejohn, Larry Linden, Henry Paulson Jr., Wendy Paulson, Kathleen Fitzgerald, Vance Martin, Patrick Noonan, and Bruce Babbitt.

For aerial photography assistance we are grateful to pilot Rodrigo Noriega of the Conservation Land Trust; Sama Blackwall and Laurie Martin of LightHawk; LightHawk pilots Everett Cassagneres, Saul Chaikin, Timothy Drager, Steven Garman, and Jerry Hoogerwerf, and Gene Steffen; Caroline Douglas of South Wings, and Southwings pilot Darwin Jones.

Current and former colleagues Sheila Masson, Lauren de Remer, Grace Jackson, Flora Krivak-Tetley, Esther Li, Fay Li, George Wuerthner, and Debbie Ryker at the Foundation for Deep Ecology contributed greatly to this project. Sharon Donovan, the foundation's former publishing manager, showed extraordinary dedication to the book; her contributions to its successful completion are numerous and invaluable.

Thanks also to Raoul Goff, Jake Gerli, and the entire team at Palace Press; Tamotsu Yagi and Naohiro Haitani at Tamotsu Yagi Design; graphic designer Kevin Cross; Mary Anne Stewart, the copy editor with the eagle eye; and Tom Brokaw, a man with a deep affection for the American landscape.

—*Tom Butler & Antonio Vizcaíno*

# SELECTED BIBLIOGRAPHY

Abbey, Edward. *Desert Solitaire: A Season in the Wilderness*. New York: Ballantine Books, 1985.

Allen, William. *Green Phoenix: Restoring the Tropical Forests of Guanacaste, Costa Rica*. Oxford University Press, 2001.

Anderson, John M. *Wildlife Sanctuaries and the Audubon Society*. Austin: University of Texas Press, 2000.

Barlow, Connie. *The Ghosts of Evolution: Nonsensical Fruit, Missing Partners, and Other Ecological Anachronisms*. New York: Basic Books, 2000.

Bernheim, Isaac W. *The Closing Chapters of a Busy Life*. Denver: Welch-Haffner, 1929.

Berry, Wendell. *The Unsettling of America: Culture and Agriculture*. San Francisco: Sierra Club Books, 1996.

Birchard, Bill. *Nature's Keepers: The Remarkable Story of How The Nature Conservancy Became the Largest Environmental Organization in the World*. San Francisco: Jossey-Bass, 2005.

Blair, William D. *The Lady Who Saved the Prairies*. Arlington, VA: The Nature Conservancy, 1989.

Bock, Carl E., and Jane H. Bock. *The View from Bald Hill: Thirty Years in an Arizona Grassland*. Berkeley and Los Angeles: University of California Press, 2000.

Bridges, E. Lucas. *Uttermost Part of the Earth*. New York: Dutton, 1949.

Brignano, Mary and Lynn, Jack. *From Sea to Shining Sea: Richard King Mellon American Land Conservation Program 1988–2002*. Pittsburgh: Richard King Mellon Foundation, 2002.

Brooks, Paul. *Rachel Carson: The Writer at Work*. San Francisco: Sierra Club Books, 1989.

Broun, Maurice. *Hawks Aloft: The Story of Hawk Mountain*. Mechanicsburg, PA: Stackpole Books, 1977.

Butler, Tom, ed. *Wild Earth: Wild Ideas for a World Out of Balance*. Minneapolis: Milkweed Editions, 2002.

Campbell, Carlos G. *Birth of a National Park in the Great Smoky Mountains*. Knoxville: University of Tennessee Press, 1960.

Carson, Rachel. *The Sense of Wonder*. New York: HarperCollins, 1998.

Cooley, Kathleen. *White Deer Lake: Life at the McCormick Camp*. Durango, CO: privately published by the author, 2004.

Dalton, Kathleen. *Theodore Roosevelt: A Strenuous Life*. New York: Knopf, 2002.

Darwin, Charles. *The Voyage of the Beagle: Charles Darwin's Journal of Researches*. New York: Penguin Books, 1989.

Dorr. George B. *The Story of Acadia National Park*. Bar Harbor, ME: Acadia Publishing, 1985.

Earley, Lawrence S. *Looking for Longleaf: The Fall and Rise of an American Forest*. Chapel Hill: University of North Carolina Press, 2004.

Engberg, Robert and Wesling, Donald, eds. *John Muir: To Yosemite and Beyond*. Salt Lake City: University of Utah Press, 1999.

Ernst, Joseph W., ed. *Worthwhile Places: Correspondence of John D. Rockefeller Jr. and Horace M. Albright*. New York: Fordham University Press, 1991.

Foreman, Dave. *Rewilding North America: A Vision for Conservation in the 21st Century*. Washington, DC: Island Press, 2004.

Forsyth, Adrian, and Ken Miyata. *Tropical Nature: Life and Death in the Rain Forests of Central and South America*. New York: Touchstone, 1987.

Fox, Stephen. *The American Conservation Movement: John Muir and His Legacy*. Madison: University of Wisconsin Press, 1981.

Frome, Michael. *Battle for the Wilderness*. Salt Lake City: University of Utah Press, 1997.

Frome, Michael. *Strangers in High Places: The Story of Great Smoky Mountains National Park*. Knoxville: University of Tennessee Press, 1966.

Glover, James B. *A Wilderness Original: The Life of Bob Marshall*. Seattle: Mountaineers Books, 1986.

Graham, Frank, Jr. *The Audubon Ark: A History of the National Audubon Society*. New York: Knopf, 1990.

Hakola, John W. *Legacy of a Lifetime: The Story of Baxter State Park*. Woolwich, ME: TBW Books. 1981.

Harris, Ann G., and Tuttle, Esther. *Geology of National Parks. 3rd ed*. Dubuque, IA: Kendall/Hunt Publishing, 1983.

Harris, Guillermo, and Macduff Everton. *Tierra del Fuego: An Approach to Wilderness Preservation*. New York: Goldman Sachs, 2005.

Hart, John. *Muir Woods: Redwood Refuge*. San Francisco: Golden Gate National Park Association, 1991.

Haupt, Lyanda Lynn. *Pilgrim on the Great Bird Continent: The Importance of Everything and Other Lessons from Darwin's Lost Notebooks*. New York: Little, Brown, 2006.

Karamanski, Theodore J. *A History of the McCormick Family's Use of White Deer Lake Camp. Report submitted to USDA Forest Service, Ottawa National Forest*. Chicago: Mid-American Research Center, Loyola University, 1982.

Kimmerer, Robin Wall. *Gathering Moss: A Natural and Cultural History of Mosses*. Corvallis: Oregon State University Press, 2003.

Leopold, Aldo. *A Sand County Almanac*. New York: Oxford University Press, 1949.

Long, Kim. *Prairie Dogs: A Wildlife Handbook*. Boulder: Johnson Books, 2002.

Martin, Paul S. *Twilight of the Mammoths: Ice Age Extinctions and the Rewilding of America*. Berkeley and Los Angeles: University of California Press, 2005.

Meine, Curt, and Richard L. Knight, eds. *The Essential Aldo Leopold: Quotations and Commentaries*. Madison: University of Wisconsin Press, 1999.

Meine, Curt. *Aldo Leopold: His Life and Work*. Madison: University of Wisconsin Press, 1991.

Moon, William Least Heat. *PrairyErth*. New York: Houghton Mifflin, 1991.

Nash, Roderick Frazier. *Wilderness and the American Mind. 4th ed*. New Haven: Yale University Press, 2001.

Newhall, Nancy. *A Contribution to the Heritage of Every American: The Conservation Activities of John D. Rockefeller Jr.* New York: Knopf, 1957.

Noss, Reed F., and Allen Y. Cooperrider. *Saving Nature's Legacy: Protecting and Restoring Biodiversity*. Washington, DC: Island Press, 1994.

Noss, Reed F., ed. *The Redwood Forest: History, Ecology, and Conservation of the Coast Redwoods*. Washington, DC: Island Press, 2000.

Nowak, Ronald M. *Walker's Mammals of the Word. 6th ed*. Baltimore: Johns Hopkins University Press, 1999.

O'Neill, Dan. *The Firecracker Boys*. New York: St. Martin's Press, 1994.

Righter, Robert W. *Crucible for Conservation: The Struggle for Grand Teton National Park*. Moose, WY: Grand Teton Natural History Association, 1982.

Runte, Alfred. *National Parks: The American Experience*. Lincoln: University of Nebraska Press, 1997.

Rydholm, C. Fred. *Superior Heartland: A Backwoods History*. Marquette, MI: Winter Cabin Books, 1989.

Samson, Fred B., and Fritz L. Knopf, eds. *Prairie Conservation: Preserving North America's Most Endangered Ecosystem*. Washington, DC: Island Press, 1996.

Sayre, Robert F., ed. *Recovering the Prairie*. Madison: University of Wisconsin Press, 1999.

Sellars, Richard West. *Preserving Nature in the National Parks: A History*. New Haven: Yale University Press, 1997.

Servid, Carolyn and Donald Snow, eds. *The Book of the Tongass*. Minneapolis: Milkweed Editions, 1999.

Steinbeck, John. *The Log from the Sea of Cortez*. New York: Penguin Books, 1995.

Thoreau, Henry David. *The Maine Woods*. New York: Penguin Books, 1988.

Tilden, Freeman. *The National Parks*. New York: Knopf, 1976.

Vuncannon, Delcie H. *Joshua Tree: The Story Behind the Scenery*. Las Vegas: KC Publications, 1996.

Wharton, Mary E., and Roger W. Barbour. *Bluegrass Land & Life*. Lexington: University of Kentucky Press, 1991.

Wilson, E. O. *The Diversity of Life*. Cambridge, MA: Harvard University Press, 1992.

Winks, Robin W. *Laurance S. Rockefeller: Catalyst for Conservation*. Washington, DC: Island Press, 1997.

Wolfe, Linne Marsh. *Son of the Wilderness: The Life of John Muir*. Madison: University of Wisconsin Press, 2003.

Wyche, Thomas, and James Kilgo. *The Blue Wall: Wilderness of the Carolinas and Georgia*. Englewood, CO: Westcliffe Publishers, 1996.

Zahniser, Howard. *Where Wilderness Preservation Began: Adirondack Writings of Howard Zahniser*. Utica, NY: North Country Books, 1992.

Zaslowsky, Dyan, and T. H. Watkins. *These American Lands: Parks, Wilderness, and the Public Lands*. Washington, DC: Island Press, 1994.

*Laws change; people die;*
*the land remains.*

—Abraham Lincoln

# LAND CONSERVATION RESOURCES

More than 1600 local and regional land trusts across America are helping private landowners and municipalities build a green infrastructure of conserved lands that will support thriving human and natural communities. The majority of these publicly supported land trusts focus on open space and agricultural lands conservation, but a significant number also engage in natural areas protection. The Land Trust Alliance, the national coordinating body and voice of the land trust community, is an invaluable resource for individuals wanting information about land conservation. Visit www.lta.org to find a land trust in your area.

Numerous local, regional, national, and international organizations are working directly to protect wildlife and wild habitat. Conservation groups and initiatives mentioned in this book include:

AMAZON CONSERVATION ASSOCIATION
www.amazonconservation.org

ÁREA DE CONSERVACIÓN GUANACASTE
www.acguanacaste.ac.cr

BERNHEIM ARBORETUM AND RESEARCH FOREST
www.bernheim.org

CHEETAH CONSERVATION FUND
www.cheetah.org

CONSERVACION PATAGONICA
www.patagonialandtrust.org

CONSERVATION INTERNATIONAL
www.conservation.org

CONSERVATION LAND TRUST
www.theconservationlandtrust.org

CONSERVATION NORTHWEST
www.conservationnw.org

CUENCA LOS OJOS
www.cuencalosojos.org

FLORACLIFF
www.floracliff.org

HAWK MOUNTAIN SANCTUARY
www.hawkmountain.org

HIGHLANDS NATURE SANCTUARY
www.highlandssanctuary.org

KENTUCKY NATURAL LANDS TRUST
www.knlt.org

MAINE COAST HERITAGE TRUST
www.mcht.org

NATIONAL AUDUBON SOCIETY
www.audubon.org

NOKUSE PLANTATION
www.nokuse.org

NORTHEAST WILDERNESS TRUST
www.newildernesstrust.org

OPEN SPACE INSTITUTE
www.osiny.org

RESTORE: THE NORTH WOODS
www.restore.org

SOUTHERN PLAINS LAND TRUST
www.southernplains.org

THE CONSERVATION FUND
www.conservationfund.org

THE NATURE CONSERVANCY
www.nature.org

THE WILDLANDS CONSERVANCY
www.wildlandsconservancy.org

TRUST FOR PUBLIC LAND
www.tpl.org

WESTERN WATERSHEDS PROJECT
www.westernwatersheds.org

WILDLIFE CONSERVATION SOCIETY
www.wcs.org

WORLD WILDLIFE FUND
www.worldwildlife.org

# PORTRAIT PHOTO CREDITS

Page 3    John Muir and William Kent, courtesy of the National Park Service.

Page 10    Joseph Battell, courtesy of the Henry Sheldon Museum of Vermont History.

Page 18    George Dorr, courtesy of the National Park Service/Acadia National Park's William Otis Sawtelle Collections and Research Center.

Page 26    Isaac Wolfe Bernheim, courtesy of HelloMetro.com.

Page 34    Percival Proctor Baxter, courtesy of the Maine State Archives.

Page 42    Rosalie Barrow Edge, courtesy Hawk Mountain Sanctuary.

Page 50    John D. Rockefeller Jr., copyright by Underwood & Underwood/CORBIS.

Page 58    John D. Rockeffer Jr., copyright by Yousuf Karsh/www.karsh.org; Horace Albright, courtesy of the National Park Service.

Page 66    Laurance S. Rockefeller, copyright by Yousuf Karsh/www.karsh.org.

Page 74    Gordon McCormick, courtesy of Fred and June Rydholm.

Page 82    Ariel Appleton, courtesy of the Appleton family.

Page 90    Norman Brunswig photo by Antonio Vizcaíno.

Page 98    Katharine Ordway, courtesy of The Nature Conservancy.

Page 106    Wallace Pratt, courtesy of the National Park Service.

Page 114    Elizabeth-Ann Campbell Knapp, courtesy of Pheobe Knapp Warren.

Page 122    Thomas Austin Yawkey, courtesy of the Leslie Jones Collection of the Boston Public Library.

Page 130    Daniel Janzen photo by Winnie Hallwachs; Winnie Hallwachs photo by Erick Greene.

Page 138    Mary Wharton, courtesy of the Mary E. Wharton Preserve at Floracliff.

Page 146    Alan Weeden photo by Antonio Vizcaíno.

Page 154    Cathryn & Carl Hilker photos by Antonio Vizcaíno; Laurie Marker photo copyright by Suzi Eszterhas.

Page 162    Marc Evans photo by Antonio Vizcaíno.

Page 170    Larry Henry & Nancy Stranahan photo by Antonio Vizcaíno.

Page 178    Robert Anderberg photo by Antonio Vizcaíno.

Page 186    Lauren McCain and Nicole Rosmarino photos copyright by Jess Alford.

Page 194    Mary Griggs Burke photo courtesy of Mary Griggs Burke.

Page 202    Fred Stanback Jr. photo by Antonio Vizcaíno.

Page 210    Mark Skatrud photo by Antonio Vizcaíno; Mitch Friedman photo by Amy Gulick; Paul Allen photo copyright by Louie Psihoyos/CORBIS.

Page 218    Ann Down photo by Antonio Vizcaíno.

Page 226    Roxanne Quimby photo copyright by Joel Page/AP Photo.

Page 234    Richard Goldman, courtesy of the Goldman Environmental Foundation.

Page 242    Gordon Moore, photo by Stacy H. Geiken/Gordon & Betty Moore Foundation.

Page 250    M. C. Davis photo by Antonio Vizcaíno.

Page 258    Richard King Mellon & Constance Prosser Mellon, photo copyright by Bettmann/CORBIS.

Page 266    Kristine Tompkins photo by Douglas Tompkins.

Page 274    Abigail, Emily, and Annie Faulkner photo by David Weir.

Page 282    Tim Means photo by Pim Schalkwijk.

Page 290    Hank & Wendy Paulson photo by Douglas Tompkins.

Page 298    Doug Tompkins & Peter Buckley photo by Hillary Hood.

Page 306    Valer Austin photo by Antonio Vizcaíno; Josiah Austin photo courtesy of Valer Austin.

# COLOPHON

*Publisher:* Raoul Goff
*Creative Director:* Iain R. Morris
*Acquiring Editor:* Jake Gerli
*Managing Editor:* Kevin Toyama
*Designer:* Dagmar Trojanek
*Production Manager:* Anna Wan

EARTH AWARE EDITIONS would also like to give a very special thank you to Sharon Donovan, Chris Maas, Barbara Genetin, Gabe Ely, Usana Das Shadday, Mikayla Butchart, Matthew Pogar, Lucy Kee, Becca Cohen, Peter Beren, Mary Teruel, and Noah Potkin.

EARTH AWARE

Earth Aware Editions
3160 Kerner Blvd., Unit 108
San Rafael, CA 94901
800.688.2218
415.526.1370
Fax: 415.526.1394
www.earthawareeditions.com

ISBN: 978-1-60109-059-1

ROOTS of PEACE    REPLANTED PAPER

Palace Press International, in association with Roots of Peace, will plant two trees for each tree used in the manufacturing of this book. Roots of Peace is an internationally renowned humanitarian organization dedicated to eradicating land mines worldwide and converting war-torn lands into productive farms and wildlife habitats. Together, we will plant two million fruit and nut trees in Afghanistan and provide farmers there with the skills and support necessary for sustainable land use.

10 9 8 7 6 5 4 3 2 1

Printed in China by Palace Press International